British Educational Psychology: The First Hundred Years

Edited by
Christopher Arnold
and Julia Hardy

Division of Educational and Child Psychology

History of Psychology Centre
Monograph No 1

British Library Cataloguing-in-Publication Data

A catalogue record for this book is available from
the British Library.

ISBN: 978-1-85433-720-7

Printed and published by
The British Psychological Society
St Andrews House
48 Princess Road East
Leicester LE1 7DR
www.bps.org.uk

Contents

About the contributors

Dr Andy Allen is an educational psychologist in private practice and Chair of the BPS Division of Educational and Child Psychology in 2013.

Dr Christopher Arnold is a senior educational psychologist in Sandwell and was Chair of the BPS Division of Educational and Child Psychology in 2012.

Professor James Boyle is director of postgraduate training in educational psychology at the School of Psychological Sciences and Health, University of Strathclyde.

Dr Sean Cameron was co-director of the continuing professional doctorate programme in educational psychology at University College London and is co-director of the Pillars of Parenting Social Enterprise.

Dr Reem Olivia Dean is an educational psychologist in Leeds.

Adrian Faupel was professional tutor for educational psychology training at the University of Southampton.

Professor Norah Frederickson is director of the Educational Psychology Group, University College London and a senior educational psychologist in Buckinghamshire.

Dr Julia Hardy is Principal Educational Psychologist in Kingston-upon-Thames Educational Psychology Service.

Vivian Hill is course director for educational psychologist training at the Institute of Education, University of London, and a senior educational psychologist in the London Borough of Wandsworth.

Dr Mike Hymans was Principal Educational Psychologist for Brent. He now works in private practice.

Alan Labram has retired from educational psychology and lives in France.

Professor Tommy MacKay is Director of Psychology Consultancy Services and is at the University of Strathclyde.

Dr Harriet Martin is Principal Educational Psychologist for Luton. She was Chair of the BPS Division of Educational and Child Psychology in 2010.

Sue Morris is Educational Psychology Programme Director at the University of Birmingham.

Chris Reeve was Principal Educational Psychologist in Walsall from 1974 to 2002. He died in 2012.

Dr Jonathan Solity is director of the psychological and educational research-based consultancy KRM.

Dr Juliet Whitehead is an educational psychologist in Coventry.

Preface

This book is offered as a celebration of the centenary of the appointment of the first educational psychologist in England. Cyril Burt took up his post in 1913 and set a course for a profession which is constantly evolving and currently thriving and fresh. Understanding the development of our profession can help keep our current practices in perspective and yet remind ourselves that issues that were alive a century ago, are still in evidence today.

The contributors have all offered their chapters as part of the centenary celebration. We hope that you enjoy the contents and reflect on how far the profession has come in its first century.

Christopher Arnold and Julia Hardy

Acknowledgements

We are deeply indebted to all the contributors who gave their services without charge; the British Psychological Society's History of Psychology Centre with the support of Peter Dillon Hooper; the staff at the BPS Leicester office who so patiently helped in the production of this book; Jo Klett, archivist at Liverpool University; the many colleagues who suffered reading early versions of the chapters, including Simon Richards and Barbara Hardy.

Chapter 1 Origins

Christopher Arnold

Introduction

When did educational psychology begin? When did psychology begin? Is it possible to identify the first educational psychologist, or even the first psychologist? For psychology as a discipline there are points in time which suggest change, such as the opening of the first university department and the arrival of the first journals using the term 'psychology' in their titles, but these events should be seen as the culmination of thinking and activities, rather than the real origins of the discipline. We will begin by considering the ideas promoted at the time of the opening of the first university department and the first journals.

Early appearances

The first university department dedicated to psychology was opened in 1879 when Wilhelm Wundt established the Institute for Experimental Psychology in Leipzig. The first English university to have a psychology department was Cambridge, with William H.R. Rivers being appointed as lecturer in physiological and experimental psychology in 1897. By 1901 he had a room, by 1903 a building and by 1912 there was a recognisable laboratory. This department might have been founded before Leipzig's, but in 1877 the university authorities in Cambridge refused this on the grounds that it 'would insult religion by putting the soul on a pair of scales'.

The first English psychology journal was published in 1904 in which Ward defined the subject thus: *'psychology will furnish … a description of normal mental processes and their development, more or less complete, no doubt, but as systematic as far as it goes.'*

The first edition pays homage to psychologists in past centuries such as Bernadino Telesio, a sixteenth-century teacher at the University of Padua who studied mathematics and philosophy. His studies were based on the work of Aristotle (384–322 BC) and aimed to understand the 'human spirit' as part of nature and subject to natural laws; this included sensory perception, memory, reasoning and a naturalistic view of moral character. Some key aspects of our current discipline are found within this brief list.

Renaissance of science

Telesio was a good choice. His life and studies were embedded in the search for the wisdom of the ancient Greeks and Romans that characterised the Renaissance. Many modernising thinkers in different disciplines flourished in northern Italy at this time: Galileo in science, Monteverdi in music, Palladio in architecture and Titian in art. Telesio was a philosopher concerned with rebuilding the discipline and basis of understanding nature. He addressed psychology in his fifth book, *On the Spirit or Natural Soul in Man*, and in subsequent books on *Sense* and *Intelligence*. It can be difficult for modern readers to grasp the huge changes that occurred around these times. Knowledge was the domain of the Church and based on biblical scripture. If an explanation conflicted with religious principles, then the explanation must be wrong. Galileo ran into difficulties when his telescope revealed spots on the sun which rotated. Furthermore, the heliocentric view of the solar system was not accepted because some passages in the Bible clearly pointed to the earth as being the centre of everything. Galileo finessed this in a letter:

> Since Scripture is in many places not only accessible to but necessarily requires expositions that differ from the apparent meanings of the words, it seems to me that in physical disputes it should

be reserved to the last place. Thus it appears that physical effects placed before our eyes by sensible experience or concluded by necessary demonstrations should not in any circumstances be called in doubt by passages in Scripture that verbally have a different appearance. Not everything in Scripture is linked to such severe obligations as is every physical effect. This being the case, and since, moreover, it is clear that two truths can never contradict each other, it is the office of wise expositors to work to find the true sense of passages in the Bible that accord with those physical conclusions of which we have first become sure and certain by manifest sense and necessary demonstrations.

Galileo, cited in Freedberg (2002)

So if the observed phenomena conflict with writings in Scripture, it must be the interpretation of the Scripture that needs to change and develop, not the other way round.

Galileo established two rules for a scientific explanation. First, the phenomena must be independent of time and, second, that they must be independent of the observer. A phenomenon that is subject to scientific study must be repeatable and different observers must see the same things. Applied to psychology, these led directly to the principles of *reliability* and *validity*. Galileo's contribution became a turning point for scientific enquiry. In England, Francis Bacon and later, Isaac Newton developed the ideas further: Bacon's writing included rules for finding 'truths' in nature. Interpreting nature led to true knowledge provided that clear methods were followed to arrive at necessary and sufficient conditions for natural phenomena to be described. A phenomenon under examination needed to be observed and then subjected to the principle of exclusion. What are the minimum conditions necessary and sufficient to determine the nature of the phenomenon? By stripping away extraneous variables, you arrive at the essence of the phenomenon. Later, when Isaac Newton famously (and perhaps apocryphally) observed the apple increasing in speed the further it fell, he deduced that the increase in velocity was as a result of gravity *continuing* to act on the body. The phenomenon was explained by a single hypothesis (gravity) rather than more complex interconnecting physical processes. It is no coincidence that the first British psychology department was actually known as the Department of *Experimental* Psychology.

Although Telesio was quite critical of Aristotle and of the universities that based their teaching on his work, both were concerned with answering the same questions. Aristotle expressed it thus:

The knowledge of the soul admittedly contributes greatly to the advance of truth in general, and above all, our understanding of Nature, for the soul is in some sense the principle of animal life. Our aim is to grasp and understand, first its essential nature, and secondly, its properties; of these some are thought to be affections proper to the soul itself, while others are considered to attach to the animal owing to the presence within it of soul.'

Aristotle, *De Anima,* cited in Smith (1973)

Telesio was also enquiring into the nature of consciousness and sensations such as pain and pleasure. His analyses conclude:

Both the sensation and the pleasure or pain arise from the fact that the spirit itself is set in motion, dilated or contracted, by the movement imposed upon the part of the body in which it lies. And all motions and changes which occur in different parts of the body are communicated, as we have seen, to the central spirit, hence its power to distinguish different sensations in different parts of the body, arising, that is in different portions of itself.

Telesio, *De Rerum Natura,* cited in McIntyre (1904)

Telesio wrote on memory, sensation and intelligence – all still active elements in contemporary psychology – but there was no reference to psychology having the potential to cause or fight disease, although this latter element was found ancient times.

Psychology and healing

Hippocrates (460–377 BC) is perhaps best remembered for the 'Hyppocratic Oath' taken by medical practitioners, but amongst his many publications on medicine are references to the role of psychology in healing. He wrote of dreams as both windows into the soul and indications of disease requiring treatment. He produced a manual analysing the contents of dreams, signalling maladies requiring intervention and a list of prescribed treatments. Some dreams indicated a physical remedy, for example:

> *If the moon is involved [in the dream], it is advisable to draw off the harmful matter internally; therefore to use an emetic following the administration of pungent, salty and soft foods. Also, prescribe brisk runs on a circular track, walks and vocal exercises. Forbid breakfast and reduce the food intake, restoring it as before. The cleansing should be done internally because the harm appeared in the hollows of the body.*

> Hippocrates, *Tradition in Medicine,* in Lloyd et al. (1986)

Other conditions required a more cerebral cure:

> *When the heavenly bodies [seen in dreams] wander in different directions, some mental disturbance as a result of anxiety is indicated. In this case, ease is beneficial. The soul should be turned to entertainments, especially amusing ones, or failing these, any that may give special pleasure, for two or three days. This may effect a cure; if not, the mental anxiety may engender disease.*

> Ibid.

Although contemporary psychotherapy may not wish to claim this as an early example of their craft, the treatment of anxiety by distraction can still be found in some settings.

The application of the scientific method to areas we now consider psychological had to wait. The rediscovered writings of the ancient Greeks set the agenda for some time. New thinkers such as René Descartes, John Locke and Gottfried Leibniz produced texts on the relationships between the mind and body. Descartes described information travelling through nerves and causing muscles to move. His writing suggests mechanical processes:

> *Now in the same measure that spirits enter the cavities of the brain they also leave and enter the pores (or conduits) in its substance, and from these conduits they proceed to the nerves. And depending on their entering (or their mere tendency to enter) some nerves rather than others, they are able to change the shapes of the muscles into which these nerves are inserted and in this way to move all the members.*

> Descartes (1650/1972)

He considered the roles of the senses, memory and imagination and located them in areas of the brain discovered by dissection.

Locke and sensation

John Locke (1632–1704) was concerned about the nature of thought and human understanding. In his work *An Essay Concerning Human Understanding* published in 1689 he asserted:

> *Idea is the object of thinking.*
> *All ideas come from reflection.*
> *Ideas come from our senses or from the perception of our own mental processes.*
> *Children develop ideas through experience, but are born without thought or ideas.*
> *Experience shapes thought and ideas.*
> *The soul begins to have ideas when it first begins to perceive.*
> *We are not always conscious of our thoughts.*

> Adapted from Locke (1689/1995)

There are many others, but of particular interest to the educational psychologist were his thoughts on memory. He pointed out the need for contemplation, observed that attention, repetition, pleasure and pain helped to 'fix' ideas. This latter point was not original. If children had witnessed wrong-doing in Anglo Saxon times in England, they were often beaten to ensure that they remembered the events they observed and so their testimonies in court were more credible. Locke stated that 'Constantly repeated ideas can scarce be lost'. Today we might use the term over-learning, but the principle is the same.

This representation of Locke as an early psychologist may not at first, appear justified. The propositions suggest a philosopher rather than an experimentalist. Yet his interest in the senses led him into some areas now claimed by experimental psychologists. In his 1689 essay he asked a question:

> *Suppose a man born blind, and now an adult, and taught by his touch to distinguish between a cube and a sphere of the same metal, and nighly of the same bigness, so as to tell, when he felt one and t'other, which is the cube, which the sphere. Suppose then the cube and sphere placed on a table, and the blind man to be made to see. Quaere,[1] whether by his sight, before he touched them, he could now distinguish, and tell, which is the globe, which is the cube.*

Ibid.

This became known as *Molyneux's Question* and has been the subject of modern experimental psychology (Morgan, 1977). The distinction between philosophy and psychology may not be as clear as some might like.

The birth of experimental psychology

Although thinkers such as Leibniz, Kant and Hume provided early insights, it is not until the nineteenth century that experiments and the application of the scientific method can genuinely be found to advance our understanding of mental processes. The name of Gustav Fechner (1801–1887) has been offered as the father of experimental psychology.

Fechner trained as a doctor in Leipzig although he never actually practised. He became interested in applying the discipline of natural sciences to the problems of human thought and experience. His admiration for the clarity brought to the field was evident by his language: 'The natural sciences employ consistently the external standpoint in their considerations, the humanities the internal' Fechner (1860).

This resonates with the propositions from Galileo cited above. He proceeds to define a new field, *psychophysics*, which he explains: '…psychophysics refers to the *physical* in the sense of physics and chemistry, to the *psychical* in the sense of experiential psychology without referring back in any way to the nature of the body or of the soul beyond the phenomenal in the metaphysical sense' (Ibid.). He carries on: '…the determination of the general principles of psychophysics will involve the handling only of *quantitative relations,* just as in physics, where qualitative depend on earlier quantitative relationships…' (Ibid., emphasis added).

Later:

> *Psychophysics, already related to psychology and physics by name, must on the one hand be based on psychology, and on the other hand promises to give psychology a* mathematical *foundation … Based on them, as we shall see, physical measurement yields a psychic measurement, on which we can base arguments that in their turn are of importance and interest.*

Ibid. (emphasis added)

---

[1] Question

He develops the concept of *stimulus* and proposed the measurement of sensation by ratios. The sensation is measured by magnitude of the stimulus and the degree of sensitivity of the subject. In other words the sensation of two stimuli, one twice the magnitude of the other, would be the same if the sensitivity of the subject was halved for the stronger stimulus. Different parts of the body have different sensitivities and these can be determined simply. Take callipers and place the ends together. Blindfold the subject and touch their skin. Then repeat the exercise having separated the point of the callipers by a small amount. When the subject can tell that there are two points, this gives a measure of sensitivity. The minimum distance required to feel the two points is in inverse proportion to the sensitivity of that part of the skin.

His interest in ratios led him to consider the most pleasing ratios for a rectangle. He experimented by inviting subjects to consider ten rectangles each having different ratios of the component sides and found that the preferred ratio was close to the *Golden Section* or *Golden Ratio*. This ratio linked to an existing theory which found its roots in classical times. The actual ratio cannot be expressed by simple numbers as it involves the square root of five. This can never be perfectly calculated, but the visualisation is simple.

Consider a rectangle:

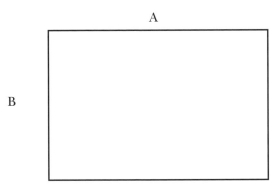

Now draw a line creating a square (C) inside the rectangle with the shorter side defining the size:

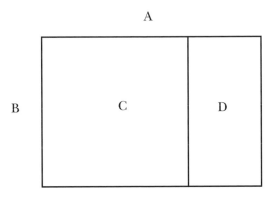

If the new rectangle (D) left over after the square has been removed has the same proportions as the original, this is the *Golden Section*. It is a shape often found in art (e.g. Da Vinci, Dali) and the ratio is used in music.

This new experimental approach to senses was a reflection of the scientific method being applied in the physical world. Helmholtz was concerned with the fundamental problems of science. What is meant by 'truth' and how does it link to reality. Natural Science seeks natural laws whereas philosophy examines our intellects and seeks to separate itself from the 'corporeal world'. There may be a divide, but both sides are relevant to the questions. As he pointed out in a lecture: 'Even the natural scientist cannot avoid these questions in the theory of sense perceptions and in the investigations on the fundamental principles of geometry, mechanics, and physics' (Helmholtz, 1878). His friend and colleague Brücke was the head of the Institute of Physiology in Vienna and they discussed problems. One of Brücke's students was to become a leading theoretician and practitioner in psychology. His name was Sigmund Freud.

Psychology and mental illness

If the emerging approaches to psychology seem far removed from helping troubled people, we must examine different influences and note the links being formed at this time.

The treatment of what we now call 'mental illness' or 'psychological disorder' has a long history. For millennia the attribution of supernatural causes was widespread. Possession by a demon, evil spirit or devil was the explanation for the behaviour of the afflicted. In prehistoric times shaman and magicians would offer treatment for differences in behaviour that were attributed to the invasion of evil forces. The brain was seen as a location for such beings and treatment could include trepanation or the drilling of a small hole in the cranium to allow the forces to escape. In Egyptian times a papyrus from 1550 BC describes recipes for herbal cures as well as advice and magic for conditions including mental retardation and epilepsy. The Greeks and Romans considered three different forms of disability: disease, blindness and insanity. This led to the development of support and treatment for people with some kind of mental (and physical) disorder. Mental disorder was considered to be a disease just like others. Hippocrates suggested cures to include rest, purposeful work and good company. Celcus used plant extracts such as hellebores which had a purgative effect by forcing the disease out of the body. However, if these methods failed, the treatment became violent with blows, whippings and chains. The use of medicines and social treatments to promoting mental health are still found now.

The Greeks and Romans worshipped Aesculapius, the god of medicine. Sufferers of mental disorder were taken to temples which were situated near springs and spas. The sufferers were led into a dark sanctum which replicated some features of the womb and recreated the security of prenatal existence. The patients would sleep and dream and on wakening, the priests would interpret their dreams (McGlashan & Reeve, 1970).

The millennium after the decline of the Roman Empire is not generally thought of as offering advances in the treatment of mental disorder. Solutions were through an ascetic lifestyle and if cures were found, they were attributed to religious miracles. In the early centuries of the first millennium AD the foundations of institutions for the mentally ill were made. In 533 AD a 50-volume text of treatments for the disabled and insane was published in Rome. This defined the afflicted and protected the state by removing certain civil rights such as the parental right to give or withhold permission for daughters to marry and enabling the parents of afflicted children to nominate alternative heirs for inheritance purposes. When the northern Europeans invaded south of the Alps, the teachings of this text were adopted across the continent.

Later, the protection of people with mental disorders was often the province of the Church for which cloistering was a positive development. In the fourth century Bishop Caesarea created an asylum for a variety of disabled people. Nicholas, Bishop of Myra, founded institutions as far away as Belgium. His name lives on as St Nicholas, often celebrated at Christmas.

Attributing the cause of mental illness to demonic possession remained commonplace for a thousand years. Calvin (1509–1564) believed that the mentally retarded were similarly possessed. Luther (1483–1546) said that they had no soul and that the Devil was the father to these children. It was quite acceptable to treat the sufferers by drowning them. The writings of two monks in the middle ages of the *Malleus Maleficarum* caused the sufferers of mental illness to be seen as witches with strange powers and practices, gained from pacts with the Devil. The burning alive of the sufferers was seen to be a purification.

The treatment of mental illness

The thirteenth century saw the creation of the mental hospital in London known as Bedlam (a contraction of Bethlehem). Incarceration was preferable to murder. The conditions leading to incarceration included 'mentally retarded, aged, deranged, albinos and epileptics', but usage extended to 'dissenters, heretics and others causing disruption of social or religious order' (in Winzer, 1993). By the 18th century the attribution of mental illness to demoniac possession was being questioned. Instead of demons, human behaviour was the cause – masturbation was blamed. Rousseau was praised for his warnings about this in *Emile* (1762), a book about the medical dangers of the practice which sold 38,000 copies before 1750. Preventative measures including cold baths, the avoidance of both boredom and excessive sleep were added to the more common prescriptions of a light diet and plenty of exercise. Treatments included ointments, medicines, 'manual restraints' and even surgery (Arnold et al., 2009).

The attribution of demonic possession and consequent confinement of sufferers was questioned by some. The eighteenth-century enlightenment allowed Phillipe Pinel (1745–1826) to experiment with different treatments. He rejected the conventional explanations of the time (the moon, liquor, the Devil, witchcraft, masturbation, etc.) and started treating the sufferers with respect and dignity. Inmates would be given attention, conversation and freedom from manacles resulting in positive outcomes including fewer killings of the wardens. This gave the methods some credibility. Sadly, Pinel got involved in politics and was accused of helping priests and émigrés during the revolution. He was also accused of having royalist sympathies and this led to him losing his job and dying destitute. However, the seeds were sewn for viewing the mentally ill as sufferers who could be treated, rather than possessed by supernatural beings. His ideas included viewing sufferers as having led disordered and distressing lives. Whilst there might be a biological predisposition to mental disorder, most sufferers were responding to the stress involved in their lives.

Advances in dissection and some understanding of the role of the brain led a German, Griesinger (1817–1868), to suggest that irritation of the brain might be the cause of disturbances of thought and emotion. He argued that there was much in common between normal and abnormal behaviour. A normal person, when intoxicated with alcohol, might behave in a similar way to an abnormal person. These ideas led to research the structure and function of the brain. Broca (1824–1880) found that people with injuries in a particular part of the brain had difficulties with speech.

Whilst physical injuries could account for some mental disorders, there were still many for which no physical cause could be found. This was a challenge to major thinkers of the time. We return to consider the role of Helmholtz. Along with Brücke he believed in materialism and determinism. The world was not the plaything of supernatural beings, but governed by rules and laws which could be discovered. The role of physics at the time was to discover the laws governing the natural world. Furthermore, the energy in the universe could be reduced to attraction and repulsion as seen in magnetism. Surely, the plight of the mentally distressed could be traced to physical causes. People with neurotic symptoms (phobias, compulsions, etc.) were sufferers of something. The fact that it was not yet discovered was a challenge.

Brücke's student rose to that challenge and Sigmund Freud started to apply Helmholtz's and Brücke's ideas to neurosis.

Healing and science

One of the principles of the physical world was that of the conservation of energy. Substantial time and experimentation was devoted to finding the mechanical equivalent of heat. Motion could be translated into heat by rubbing surfaces together and the friction generating heat. Conversely, heat could be converted into motion by machines such as steam engines. The proposition emerged that energy could not be created or destroyed, but only be changed from one form to another. Freud saw the mind as a closed energy system with a constant amount of energy at its disposal. The energy could take a range of forms and be put to a number of different uses. Like magnetism, there were two great forces, Eros (love) and Thanatos (death). Like the physical world of Helmholtz, the mental world of Freud was the result of the interplay between these great forces.

The other intellectual source for Freud was Darwin. Darwin used evidence from his own garden experiments with seeds to support the thesis of *The Origin of Species by Means of Natural Selection*. The diversity created in quite simple situations demonstrated an individual species' capacity for variation. He wrote '… I raised 233 seedling cabbages from some plants of different varieties growing near each other, and of these only 78 were true to their kind, and even some of these were not perfectly true' (Darwin, 1859/1929). Animals, too, were subject to variation and selection, but when it came to mankind the social nature of our lives created different priorities. Whilst selfishness and aggression might have been successful strategies in the primordial soup, the co-operative nature of human society needed these qualities to be bred out. Intellect and reason were the new and human way of meeting man's physiological needs. To understand man's psyche you needed to understand man's history.

Galton (1822–1911) became interested in these ideas and developed the use of question-naires as a form of collecting data. He gathered life-histories of twins in an attempt to answer questions about the influence of nature and nurture on the development of people. He hoped that the new science of eugenics would replace religion with a new universal way of developing the human race. Mankind was subject to the same processes of development that Darwin described for plants and animals. It might be the case that mankind, like flowers and animals, could advance more quickly with some selective breeding, ideas which were to find their ways into some barbaric practices nearly a century later.

Freud was interested in the workings of the psyche and helping to cure those afflicted with maladies of the mind. He was interested in the work of Anton Mesmer who seemed to induce hypnotic states during which his patients were more susceptible to suggestion. Simply by suggesting to the patients that the symptoms would disappear, they did for some time. Succes-sors to Mesmer took the methods further and in France Liebault (1823–1903) and later Bern-heim (1837–1919) were able both to cure symptoms and also induce others such as paralysis, blisters or other swellings in otherwise healthy people. Furthermore, their subjects could be persuaded to perform some unusual act (such as opening a window) after the end of the hypnotic state. The subject would not be able to explain why they did this. Charcot (1825–1895) demonstrated hysterical symptoms in men as well as women. One of Charcot's pupils, Pierre-Janet, hypnotised his patients and enabled them to tell of events that they could not remember in the waking state. Breuer found that patients who revealed these unconscious memories could be cured of their physical symptoms. Perhaps fortunately for history, the young Freud was not good at inducing the hypnotic state. He even went to a French hospital to improve his technique. It did not work and Freud was unable to hypnotise the patients he wanted to help so had to look for other methods. Breuer, however, was successful with a range of patients and agreed to publish a book of case studies with Freud about the 'talking cure'. This enabled the young Freud to develop his theories of the unconscious and the foundations of counselling were laid.

Meanwhile, others were taking the experimental method further. Ebbinghaus (1850–1909) read Fechner's *Elements of Psychophysics* and began studying memory. He was keen to apply the scientific method to his field, but wrestled with two fundamental problems:

1. The constant flux and caprice of mental events do not admit of the establishment of stable experimental conditions.
2. Psychical processes offer no means for measurement of enumeration.

Ebbinghaus (1885/1964)

His solution was to create experimental conditions which were the same for different subjects. By measuring the results taken from many different subjects he could use simple statistics to arrive at an average number. Furthermore, he produced rules which defined the distribution of results from many trials using different subjects. He used the term *probable error* to describe measures of the central tendency, so laying the foundations for the normal distribution, use of standard deviation and tests of statistical difference in psychology.

Ebbinghaus was particularly interested in memory and devised experiments to investigate the processes involved. He created a list of 2,300 syllables which were put together in random ways to create sequences of sounds which the subjects had to memorise. By using nonsense words he avoided the possible contamination of the subjects by having prior knowledge of the words or sequences. The sounds were presented in a standardised way at a rate of 150 per minute and the recall of the stimuli recorded. His use of nonsense words was heavily criticised by later researchers such as Myers and Bartlett, but even these acknowledged Ebbinghaus's contribution to the development of experimental psychology. His results did much to establish quantitative methods of analysis in psychology. Ebbinghaus's interest in memory for words led him to create a word completion task used to measure intelligence in children.

Conclusion

Towards the end of the nineteenth century these two developing areas of psychology were becoming established. There were the experimentalists and the therapists. Both drew inspiration from the application of the scientific method to problems of the mind and both believed they were making discoveries about the brain and how it functioned. Meanwhile a very different development was to establish a new field in which to work. In 1870 education became both a universal right and obligation in many countries such as the United States, the United Kingdom and France. Children would attend school until the age of 11. This provided new opportunities to apply existing ideas about the functioning of the brain to the challenges of universal education.

Vignette 1

Defining Psychology: The British Journal of Psychology
January 1904, Vol 1 No 1

VOLUME I   JANUARY, 1904   PART 1

THE BRITISH
JOURNAL OF PSYCHOLOGY

EDITORIAL.

PSYCHOLOGY which till recently was known among us chiefly as Mental Philosophy and was mainly concerned with problems of a more or less speculative and transcendental character, has now at length attained the position of a positive science; one of special interest to the philosopher, no doubt, but still independent of his control, possessing its own methods, its own specific problems and a distinct standpoint altogether its own. 'Ideas' in the philosophical sense do not fall within its scope: its inquiries are restricted entirely to 'facts.' In pursuit of these it is brought into close relations with biology, physiology, pathology and again with philology, anthropology and even literature. Its results also have important practical applications for the educationist, the jurist, the economist, quite apart from their theoretical bearing on the problems of the epistemologist and the moralist. In becoming a distinct science it has thus increased the intimacy and variety of its connexions with other sciences manifold.

As evidence of this increased importance which Psychology has now acquired, several facts may be mentioned:—First, within the last fifteen years seven serial publications have appeared in other countries—all still flourishing—devoted entirely to its affairs: this journal, the first to appear in this country, and which, it is hoped, will also flourish, adding an eighth to the number. Also there are now some forty laboratories in existence for the experimental investigation of psychological questions, most of them of quite recent date. Again, in this country half a dozen lectureships have been lately founded in different universities solely to promote the study of Psychology as a science. We have also a society of professed psychologists which meets frequently for the discussion of printed papers and the exhibition of experimental apparatus and results. And an International Congress

Journ. of Psyc. I   1

2   *Editorial*

of Psychologists held its first meeting in Paris in 1889, its second in London in 1892, and has met quadrennially in various places since. The growth of psychological literature too may be seen in the fact that the number of entries in the first Annual Bibliography published (that of the *Zeitschrift für Psychologie und Physiologie der Sinnesorgane* for the year 1890) was 1325, while the number for 1901, the latest published, amounts to 3624. Among these entries are to be found several dozen text-books of Psychology in English alone.

No wonder then that—as was stated in our preliminary circular—"the belief is widespread that the time has come for starting an English journal devoted exclusively to Psychology in all its branches," analytical, genetic, comparative, experimental, pathological, individual, ethnical, &c. Accordingly, to meet this want the publication of the present Journal has been undertaken. Within the vast range of topics just indicated it will side with no school and have no predilections. Its one aim will be to serve as the 'organ' of all alike who are working at any one of the many branches into which Psychology has now differentiated. Those which flourish most will naturally demand—and receive—the most space. Among the standards by which communications will be judged that of length will not be one. Short notes, observational, critical or historical, will be welcomed along with elaborate papers, setting forth by the aid of tables and diagrams the details of lengthy experimental investigations. But in every case, in the interests of their readers not less than in their own, the Editors are resolved stringently to insist on conciseness and relevancy of statement. Besides original articles the Journal will contain from time to time critical discussions of current controversial topics whether arising out of articles in journals or in consequence of the appearance of new books of importance. But it will not undertake regularly to review books, or to furnish abstracts of the contents of other journals, or to publish bibliographical lists. These are no doubt important matters, but they seem to be already amply provided for in existing periodicals.

In common with those of many other scientific periodicals the parts of the Journal of Psychology will be issued at irregular intervals: whether the completion of a volume is to occupy more than a year or less will depend primarily on the activity of our contributors.

J. W.

W. H. R. R.

Chapter 2 The rise of education

Christopher Arnold

Introduction

By the late nineteenth century psychology had both a research base and methods for helping people with some kind of mental disorder. The developments which were to follow came from different political initiatives in different countries to create access to free and universal education for children. In 1852 the state of Massachusetts started a process of compulsory and free education for primary aged pupils. Other states followed suit and by the early twentieth century all of the United States had similar legislation.

In England the 1870 Education Act paved the way for compulsory education of young people from five to 12 years (although a pupil could leave at the age of ten, if a satisfactory standard had been reached). The process was completed by 1880 (although not for all children until 1972 when education was provided for the most severely disabled children by the 1970 Education Act. See chapter 3 for more detail).

In France similar legislation was passed in 1882. Notably, the law of 28 March 1882 removed all explicitly religious teaching from the curriculum (Bergen, 1990). Universal education had arrived.

This chapter will describe the developments in education and psychology which provided a backdrop to the appointment of the first British educational psychologist in 1913.

The development of education

The arrival of compulsory and free education in many countries at the same time might be seen as a great leap forward for civilisation and motivated by high moral principles, but the evidence points to rather more practical and pragmatic motives – the need for a successful military. A flavour of these ideas can be found in the comments of a factory inspector to a workforce in the Ardennes after France's defeat at the hands of the Germans in the Franco-Prussian war of 1870-71:

> *that the Prussians could all read and write, and that those, like the brutes I had in front of me who were rotting in their ignorance, could only be bad Frenchmen and bad soldiers, who would run away on our day of revenge.*

Cited in Haywood (2001)

Education was seen as a way of improving the armed forces. Germany was the pacesetter in a number of ways. In 1619 the city of Weimar passed legislation that attempted to introduce compulsory education for all children aged from six to twelve. It failed mainly due to the shortage of teachers, but a Prussian defeat in 1806 rekindled interest in using education for national regeneration. By the mid nineteenth century 80 per cent of German children were attending school between the ages of six and fourteen. The aspiration was that the new generation would be more law abiding, make more productive factory workers and better soldiers.

Psychology and selection in education

With the introduction of universal education came new challenges. Children who previously would not have been considered to be educable were admitted to schools. It was clear that some children had difficulties not manifested by the vast majority of others. Medical practitioners had long been accustomed to diagnosing a wide range of handicapping conditions. It is difficult for the reader today not to feel some revulsion in the labels used to categorise children at the turn of the twentieth century. The terms 'idiot', 'imbecile', 'cretin', 'moron', 'retarded' and 'feeble minded' are extremely offensive to our ears, but at the time they were used to attempt to discriminate between different types of children with what we now might describe as having 'special needs'. In France special classes were available for those with such diagnoses. The allocation of children to these special classes was by physicians or medical practitioners. However, there were inconsistencies between practitioners and the criteria were not clear. Alfred Binet had developed an interest in intelligence after studying law in Paris in the 1870s and, rather than continue into medical school, he started to read books on psychology. He took a position in the Laboratory for Experimental Psychology at the Sorbonne and during this time he, and one of his students, Theodore Simon, became interested in children with learning difficulties and pointed to the inconsistencies around diagnosis when citing a comment by Dr Blinn, a physician of an Asylum in Vaucluse:

> *One child, called imbecile in the first certificate, is marked idiot in the second, feeble-minded*
> *(débile) in the third, and degenerate in the fourth.*

In Binet & Simon (1916/1980)

Binet had studied hypnotism under Charcot at Paris' Salpêtrière Hospital and then volunteered to work at the new Laboratory for Physiological Psychology at the Sorbonne in Paris in 1891. He observed that there were three essential problems with the practices adopted at the time for allocation of children to the special classes:
1. Ignorance of the physician to diagnose the condition.
2. The variability in the terms adopted.
3. The lack of precision in the description of the symptoms.

He asserted that confusion arises 'principally from a fault in the method of examination' and concludes: 'We do not think that we are going too far in saying that at the present time very few physicians would be able to cite with absolute precision the objective and invariable sign, or signs, by which they distinguish the degrees of inferior mentality' (in Binet & Simon, ibid) The solution was to establish a new method for measuring intelligence. Binet described previous methods as *medical* and *pedagogical*. The *medical* approach aimed to diagnose inferior intelligence by analysis of anatomical, physiological and pathological elements. The *pedagogical* method assessed the knowledge of the child and judged the intelligence from this, but his proposed *psychological* method used direct measurements and observations to assess intelligence.

Binet and Simon noted that physical and anatomical differences were not always present in children presenting with learning difficulties, so this alone could not be a satisfactory method. Equally the test of knowledge of the child is influenced by their experiences. Children who had not been to school or had not been raised in families speaking French as a first language would be disadvantaged and therefore this was not a satisfactory measure for diagnosing educational difficulties as it would select children who had simply not been to school. He noted that this method would favour the children from middle class, educated backgrounds. Some parents would not want their children to attend special classes because of the stigma that could result. He proposed and developed a series of tests which directly measured the intelligence of the child at that moment. Binet and Simon wrote:

> *It does this by experiments which oblige the subject to make an effort which shows his capability in*
> *the way of comprehension, judgement, reasoning and invention.*
> *The fundamental idea of this [psychological] method is the establishment of what we shall*

call a measuring scale of intelligence. This scale is composed of a series of tests of increasing difficulty, starting from the lowest intellectual level that can be observed, and ending with that of average normal intelligence. Each group in the series corresponds to a different mental level.

Ibid.

These ideas were not original. Ebbinghaus had been experimenting with intelligence testing of children in the 1880s using a word completion technique. In the United States, William James introduced the first university course in psychology and prepared a text book for students. His field covered perception, memory, instinct and emotion in systematic ways which reflected his interest in comparative anatomy. He also wrote about reasoning as a sign of mental functioning, defined as: 'Let us make this ability to deal with novel data the technical differential of reasoning' (James 1892).

He cited syllogisms such as

> M is P;
> S is M;

therefore   S is P

as examples of reasoning. He developed these ideas by describing 'Modes of Conceiving' which allowed the person to consider the same object in different ways according to function. Paper can be something to write on or start fires with. It remains paper, but is conceived in different ways. Sagacity allows the person to 'see into the situation – that is, they analyse it – with their first glance'. He argued that superior reasoning is facilitated by association and similarity. He started to categorise humans into one of at least three groups (genius, vulgarian and brute):

Highly gifted minds [operate] without any deliberation, spontaneously collecting analogous instances. Geniuses are, by common consent, considered to differ from ordinary minds by an unusual development of association by similarity. As the genius is to the vulgarian, so the vulgar human mind is to the intelligence of a brute. Compared with men, it is probable that brutes neither attend to abstract characters, nor have associations by similarity.

James (1905)

As far as we can tell, James' ideas in these matters were not put to the test. Binet and Simon, however, used such tests for *selection* of children for special education. It is a matter of debate as to whether the 'special classes' or 'special education' acted as ways of supporting children's learning or ways of separating such children because they were considered less than perfect.

There were long established facilities for people with mental disorders. Asylums existed and admissions were organised by medical practitioners. Reading Binet and Simon it is clear that they had misgivings about the selection proceedings used at the time and were suggesting alternatives designed not to favour any particular social group. The development of tests given in a standardised way was seen to be a fairer method of selection.

The tests were tried in both the asylum at Salpêtrière and primary schools in Paris. One essential element was to separate the measures of 'natural intelligence' from those assessing the outcomes of instruction. They were insistent that intelligence was not dependent on the senses, pointing to the cases of Helen Keller and Laura Bridgman who were both blind and deaf, but able to demonstrate intelligence. Nor was intelligence synonymous with memory. They cited an example of a girl with a very good memory (better than that of Binet or Simon) who, nonetheless, had demonstrable learning difficulties. They conclude that it was *judgement* that was the most significant manifestation of intelligence:

It seems to us that in intelligence there is a fundamental faculty, the alteration or the lack of which, is of the utmost importance for practical life. This faculty is judgement, otherwise called good sense, practical sense, initiative, the faculty of adapting one's self to circumstances. To judge well, to comprehend well, to reason well, these are the essential activities of intelligence.

Binet & Simon, op cit.

The tests were published in 1905 and involved an adult giving tasks to children and recording their responses. There were 30 items assessing elements such as comparison of weights, repetition of sentences, knowledge of objects and drawing a design from memory. Many of the items are still found in tests used by practising educational psychologists today.

A year later, the first volume reached the United States and coincided with the opening of the first institution for the study of 'feeblemindedness' – the Vineland Research Laboratory. Its first director, Henry Goddard, did a literature search to establish what was known about the subject. However, the Binet and Simon test was written in French, and so Goddard did not find it until a visit to Brussels in the spring of 1908. The tests were being trialled in local schools and clearly made an impression on Goddard who took them back to the United States and published an English version in December of the same year.

Meanwhile Binet and Simon were developing the tests further by establishing age gradings. Goddard wrote of his scepticism, finding the method 'too easy, too simple', but by 1910 he was convinced and published the scale in the United States. It became an instant success selling 22,000 copies of the test and 88,000 record sheets. Sales extended to Canada, England, Australia, New Zealand, South Africa, Germany, Switzerland, Italy, Russia and China, with translations into Japanese and Turkish. With this success came wider research and by 1914 there were already 254 titles about their testing published; however, the original was still not available in translation into English until 1916.

In the United States a young man, Lewis Terman, had published his doctoral dissertation in 1906 with the title *Genius and Stupidity: A study of some of the intellectual processes of seven bright and seven stupid boys*. He went on to work as an instructor at Los Angeles Normal School for four years before joining the faculty of Stanford University. He revised and developed Binet's work, expanding the scale from 54 items to 90 and in 1916 he published the celebrated Stanford Revision and extension of the Binet–Simon Intelligence Test (Teman, 1916). The test was put to use in a range of selection settings. The rush to recruit for the army produced opportunities to allocate different roles according to test results. Robert Yerkes produced written and verbally administered tests to determine which soldiers had leadership potential. At the same time Howard Knox developed tests for use in the Atlantic reception centre on Ellis Island to select those potential immigrants who were to be allowed to stay (Richardson, 2011).

The development of ways of measuring intelligence that seemed innovative and useful at the time allowed other areas of research to become more acceptable. Galton's influences have already been mentioned in the previous chapter, but in 1888 he published an article 'Co-relations and their measurement, chiefly from anthropomorphic data'. This introduced concepts of correlation, regression to the mean and median to psychology. This method of calculating measures of similarity in different populations was to open up a new area of research: the degree to which human attributes were inherited or learned from the environment. In 1907 Galton published *Inquiries into Human Faculty and its Development* with chapters on 'The History of Twins', 'Selection and Race' and 'Influence of Man on Race'.

Galton's researches into the similarity of twins were based on a survey of 80 pairs, of which 35 had sufficient detail to be of use. He looked for areas of similarity and found many. One father reported that if one had an illness the other would have it within a day or two. Furthermore, they would recover at the same time. Twins were cited as buying the same presents for each other in different towns whilst being quite unaware of it. Other examples covered similarities of growth and even head size. Galton also found examples of twins that were very different, in spite of being treated similarly by their parents. He concluded that there are 'identical' and 'complementary' twins. From this he inferred that identical twins are identical because they shared biological characteristics that complementary twins did not. He highlighted the role of innate biology by referring to the cuckoo, which is raised by other species, yet still retains the characteristic song:

> *But the cuckoo cannot or will not adopt that language, or any other of the habits of its foster-parents. It leaves its birthplace as soon as it is able, and finds out its own kith and kin, and identifies itself henceforth with them. So utterly are its earliest instructions in an alien bird-language neglected, and so completely is its new education successful, that the note of the cuckoo tribe is singularly correct.*

Galton (1907)

Galton's half-cousin was Charles Darwin and he started to apply Darwin's ideas of natural selection to the concept of race in humans. He described the processes of selective breeding adopted for horses and used it to warn of the dangers of over selection:

> *Overbred animals have little stamina; they resemble in this respect the 'weedy' colts so often reared from first-class racers.*

Ibid.

He further warned of 'diminished fertility' and 'some degree of sexual indifference'. However, he used these ideas and applied them to humans, although with some words of caution:

> *It will be easily understood that these difficulties, which are so formidable in the case of plants and animals, which we can mate as often as we please and destroy when we please, would make the maintenance of a highly-selected breed of men an impossibility.*

Ibid.

He proceeded to suggest a different application:

> *Whenever a low race is preserved under conditions of life that exact a high level of efficiency, it must be subject to rigorous selection. The few best specimens of that race can alone be allowed to become parents, and not many of their descendents can be allowed to live. On the other hand, if a higher race be substituted for the low one, all this terrible misery disappears. The most merciful form of what I ventured to call 'eugenics' would consist in watching for the indication of superior strains or races, and in so favouring them that their progeny shall outnumber and gradually replace that of the old one.*

Ibid.

He proposed that the study of immigrants would be productive as they had separated themselves from the society in which they had developed. It would be relatively easy to spot the strong. He wrote: '…exiles are also on the whole men of exceptional and energetic natures, and it is especially from such men as these that new strains of race are likely to proceed'.

These ideas were born in the mid nineteenth century, but were still alive in Burt's time. Burt was clearly aware of Eugenics and the possible application to different human problems. Other countries had similar ideas. In Italy Lombroso wrote in 1888:

> *Born criminals, including hopeless recidivists and the morally insane, should be considered as incurable; all of them should be confined for life in a criminal asylum, or relegated to a penal colony, or else condemned to death.*

Lombroso, cited in Burt (1927)

However Burt quickly rejected this stance and recognised them for what they were:

> ...*such [eugenic] measures would still be purely negative. They would, of necessity, be based primarily upon eugenic principles – to segregate or sterilize all who openly manifest, or carry in latent form, the seeds of a criminal disposition, until at last the breed becomes extinct.*

Burt (1927)

He suggested that there was 'no single and simple disposition to crime' and identified the differences between what is inherited and what is inborn. It would not be possible to identify a separate race which was responsible for criminal acts. Accordingly, he rejected any notion of the 'eugenic solution' in matters relating to humans.

Psychology and curriculum development

A key influence in educational psychology before the First World War was the Italian Maria Montessori, first publishing in Italy in 1909. Three years later saw the first English translation of her work, and her approach is still found in nurseries in Great Britain. The translation was sponsored by Harvard University and the original title *Il Metodo della Pedagogia Scientifica Applicato all'Educazione Infantile nelle Case dei Bambini*[1] was simply 'The Montessori Method'. Psychology was now being applied to curriculum development rather than simply selection.

The work set out the applications of the scientific method to teaching and suggested that the initiatives in other countries (particularly in France, England and America) had been behind the Italian researches:

> *In France, in England, and especially in America, experiments have been made in the elementary schools, based upon a study of anthropology and psychological pedagogy, in the hope of finding in anthropometry and psychometry, the regeneration of the school. In these attempts it has rarely been the teachers who have carried on the research; the experiments have been, in most cases, in the hands of physicians who have taken an interest in the especial science than in education. They have usually sought to get from their experiments some contribution to psychology, or anthropology, rather than to attempt to organise their work and their results toward the formation of the long-sought Scientific Pedagogy.*

Montessori (1912)

She laid down principles of collectivism, believing that schools should be run and owned by the community so that children would be able to leave the limitations of their families, yet enabling the family to view the work of the teacher 'in the accomplishment of her high mission.'

Her work set out both a basic curriculum and teaching methods. The senses were to be trained. There were ideas for vision, touch, smell, sounds, taste and smell. To teach sounds, children were presented with musical bells and whistles making graded sounds and shown how to discriminate sounds from each other. A class would sit with eyes closed in absolute silence to enable better concentration. Vision would be taught by inset puzzles with different geometric shapes. There were programmes for all aspects of sensory development.

Her ideas went further. In describing the common practice of seating children at desks as a manifestation of 'slavery', she was critical of other educators seating children at benches and desks:

> *It is incomprehensible that so-called science should have worked to perfect an instrument of slavery in the school without being enlightened by one ray from the movement of social liberation, growing and developing throughout the world. For the age of scientific benches was also the age of the redemption of the working classes from the yoke of unjust labour.*

Ibid.

---

[1] *The Scientific Method of Teaching Applied to the Education of Infants in the House of Children.*

She described the *spirit* of the child being killed from 'within' by other regimes. Children needed a libertarian regime. Even rewards and punishments were discouraged, with references to horses running faster if they run free rather than running to avoid being beaten by a stick or even rewarded with a piece of sugar. The brain must be at liberty to develop freely. Educators must be inspired by *'a deep worship of life'*, showing respect and reverence to the expansion of the life of a child. The book is comprehensive in recommending every aspect of schooling for children including diet and mealtimes. She recognised that children would have morning and evening meals at home, but did not hold back from recommendations:

> For the evening meal, a soup is to be advised (children should eat soups twice a day), and an egg à la coque or a cup of mild; or rice soup with a base of mild, and buttered bread, with cooked fruits, etc.

Ibid.

Montessori was describing a system of education for all children, but in the United States similar ideas were found in the Massachusetts Institution for the Feeble Minded at Waverly. This was attributed to Montessori basing her ideas on those of Seguin, who was the head of the Waverley school. So the link between special education and a *scientific* approach to teaching as described by Montessori was established.

These ideas were first published in English in the United States, but reached England via articles appearing in a journal, *World's Work*, before the book was produced in London in 1914.

Psychology as an academic discipline

Meanwhile London was becoming the English home to the academic study of psychology in the first decade of the twentieth century. The Psychological Society was founded in 1902 and in its first year had four meetings with the following papers:

15 February 1902	*The Evolution of Laughter*, by James Sully
	Fechner's Paradoxical Experiment, by W. McDougall
	Pathological Changes in Immediate Memory and Association, by W.G. Smith
3 May 1902	*Psychophysical Parallelism*, by James Ward
	A Contribution to the Analysis of the Process of Comparison, by F.N. Hales
	Colour Nomenclature, by W.H.R. Rivers
12 June 1902	*The Effect of Practice on Certain Simple Mental Activities*, by W.G. Smith
	A Study in Contrast, by C. Lloyd Morgan
	Remarks upon the Central Nervous Activity and Efferent Nerve Cells, by Francis Gotch
6 December 1902	*Time Judgment*, by Beatrice Edgell

This programme was published in the first edition of the *British Journal of Psychology* in January 1904.

So, at that time there were at least four separate aspects of what we call psychology:

1. Psychology was an area of academic study developing in universities. It had a long interest in studying and measuring the senses.
2. Psychology was also being used for selection within education as a means of allocating children to special classes.
3. Psychology was being applied to the development of a curriculum for children, particularly of those with some kind of disability.
4. Psychology was providing some service for people with some mental disorders.

The birth of educational psychology

The potential for psychology to become more closely aligned to education grew with the demands of the new education service. Around this time legislation was used to expand both the age of compulsory education and the range services offered by schools, ensuring that schools provided services for children with a range of medical conditions:

1893 Elementary Education (Blind and Deaf) Children Act – making provision for special schools for blind and deaf children.

1893 Elementary Education (Attendance) Act – raising the age of compulsory education from 10 to 11.

1899 Education Act (Defective and Epileptic Children) Act:

Section 1: A school authority may make such arrangements for ascertaining (a) what children in their district, not being imbecile, and not being merely dull or backward, are defective, that is to say, what children by reason of mental or physical defect are incapable of receiving proper benefit from instruction in the ordinary schools.

Some concern was evident about the selection of children for special schools. These concerns were articulated by a report presented to the London City Council in 1912. Note how similar the nature of these concerns were to those of Binet expressed much earlier:

Full committee 26.6.1912 and 3.7.1912

We have had under consideration the question of the examination of pupils in elementary schools nominated for admission to schools for mentally defective children, and after carefully considering proposals for appointment of additional medical officers in the public health department, we are convinced that such proposals will not entirely solve the difficulty. In our opinion, a careful examination by a psychologist of the pupils nominated for admission to the special schools would show that the admission of a number of these children to such schools might advantageously be delayed until they had been under special observation for a period.

The procedure proposed is as follows – In each department of an elementary school, a list of pupils suggested as fit for schools for mentally defective children will be compiled by the head teacher. The list will be presented to the school doctor on each visit, and to the psychologist on his visits. If the school doctor or the psychologist considers that any of the children on this list should be presented at once to the school medical officer for the statutory examination, the head teacher will place their names on the appropriate form and forward it to the school medical officer. The rest of the children on the list will undergo a period of special observation under the general supervision of the psychologist. It will also be open to the school doctor or the psychologist to add names to the special school list.

For the purpose outlined above, we are of the opinion that a psychologist should be appointed as a half-time officer in the education officer's department at a salary of £300 a year.[2] In order, however, that the value of the new procedure may be give a fair trial, we suggest that the appointment should be for a period of three years. Assuming that the appointment takes effect from August 1912, the additional expenditure to be incurred during the current financial year will be £180, and £300 during the succeeding financial years. There is sufficient provision for the expenditure in vote 134 of the annual maintenance votes 1912–13. We have communicated with the establishment and financial committees on the matter and we recommend:

That a psychologist working half-time be appointed in the education officer's department for a period of three years from 26th August 1912 at a salary of £300 a year.

---

[2] This was a substantial sum for a part-time post. In 1914 a 'second master' of Trinity Academy (the equivalent of a deputy head) was paid £230 a year, with the head (rector) earning £450 a year for full-time positions.

The psychologist was not appointed until later that year and the report to the Education Committee described the process:

> ...*on 22nd October 1912 [the Committee] decided that applications for the position would be invited by public advertisement, members of staff not being precluded from making application for the position. 38 applications were received in response to the advertisement, and we have interviewed six candidates.*
>
> *After careful consideration of the qualifications and experience of the candidates, we are of opinion that Mr C.L. Burt should be appointed. Mr Burt, who is 29 years of age, was educated at Christ's Hospital and Jesus College Oxford of which foundation he was a classical scholar. He obtained a second class in classical moderations in 1904 and a second class in the final classical school in 1906, and he was re elected a scholar of his college in that year in order that he might continue his psychological studies. He was elected 'John Locke' scholar in mental philosophy in 1908, and during the tenure of the scholarship devoted himself wholly to experimental research in tests of general intelligence in school children, the results of which were published in the* British Journal of Psychology *1909. He graduated M.A. in that year. He also studies under Professor Kulpe in the Psychological Institute at Wurtzburg, and he has visited Germany, Switzerland and Russia, with a view to obtaining experience of the work in the various universities and schools, and in psychological laboratories.*
>
> *During the last four years Mr Burt has held the position of lecturer in experimental psychology and assistant lecturer and demonstrator in physiology in the University of Liverpool.*
>
> *Mr Burt has also read psychological papers before the British Association and other learned societies, and has published various articles such as 'tests of general intelligence'* (British Journal of Psychology) '*The experimental study of general intelligence*' (Journal of Child Study) *'Experimental tests of higher mental processes'* (Journal of Experimental Pedagogy).
>
> *Mr Burt seems to us to be admirably qualified by training and experience for the post of psychologist, and we recommend:*
> *Education Committee 27th Nov 1912*
> *'That, Mr Cyril Lodowic Burt M.A. (Oxon) be appointed as a psychologist working half time in the education officer's department, at a salary of £300 a year, for a period not exceeding three years; that the appointment be held during the pleasure of the Council and be subject to three month's notice on either side for its termination; and that the Council be recommended accordingly.'*

LCC minutes (1912)

In a letter of congratulation to Mr Burt the Chief Inspector wrote:

> *We are arranging a physiological meeting at our Conference of Teachers this year. It is to be held on Friday morning, 3rd January, at 11 o'clock, at the Birkbeck College, and we are dealing with the subject of 'Attention'. Professor Spearman is presiding. Would it be possible for you to give a twenty minutes' paper on some special aspect of Attention? Professor Spearman will give an address on the general question; Professor Adamson, of King's will deal with 'Attention from the child's point of view'; and Mr Pear, of Manchester, will give us an account of recent researches.*

London Archive D191/2/5/1/1

This was the first appointment in any field of psychology outside a university. His mandate included selection and research. So, in this way the profession of applied psychology was born.

Vignette 2

Part of Cyril Burt's contract with the London County Council

Reproduced by kind permission of Liverpool University Archive

D336/2/2/10   CCC
Burt

SCHEME OF PSYCHOLOGIST IN LONDON COUNTY COUNCIL

EDUCATION OFFICER'S DEPARTMENT.

(Provisional and only first half year only).

I. TIME:-

    A. L.C.C.'s time:- to test children recommended for special schools
        or classes, deserving special attention either as subnormal or
        supernormal in general or special mental capacities.

        1. With Medical Inspector, (two days = twelve hours per week).
            One hour to each child, is possible testing each child
            on a second occasion.

            - 12 children per week for 26 weeks.

            - 312, say 300 children.

        2. Independently, (a) standardisation of tests (normals and abnormals)
            (b) Consultation (where non-medical matters are involved only)
            (b) Observation
            (c) Recording, statistical and administrative work.

    B. Own time:- laboratory work (elaboration of new tests, etc.)
               Oxford, Cambridge, or University College, London; (At least
               one night's residence out of London, per week, if required
               e.g. Friday)

II. PLACE:-

    For A. 1, various schools, to suit convenience of medical inspector.
    For A 2, (a) one or two schools to be selected.
            (b) Sorting school or provisional centre
            (c) L.C.C. offices.

    For B. ? Psychological Laboratories at University College or King's
          College, London; or at Oxford or Cambridge. (At least one
          night's residence (e.g. Friday) out of London per week, if
          required)

D336/2/2/10   2.

Eventually Psychological clinic and laboratory, with pedalogical museum and library. (Cf. Institute of Applied Psychology, Berlin.)

III. TESTS :-

1. Binet (non-experimental) tests as basis (to be re-standardised) to be supplemented and eventually superseded by
2. Experimental Tests, such as

(a) Burt-Moore tests   (J. Exp. Ped., 1912;   full description and Liverpool standardisation. Psych. Mon.1914)

(b) Abelson & Spearman tests (B.J.P.   )

(c) Addition Tests as required.

All tests to be restandardised.

D336/2/2/10   3.

Grant : -   1. Capital
            2. annual.

IV. APPARATUS.

1. Stop Watch.

Form board.

Printed blanks   (5000 x 10)

Pictures and toys
Photography &

2. Record Books.

Files.

Card index.

Statistical analysis books.

3. (If possible)

Apparatus for senses.   (   )

Apparatus for reaction time   (chronometer, etc.)

"   "   emotional tests.   (sphygmograph)

(pneumograph)

(galvanometer).

D336/2/2/10   4.

V.   STAFF.

     X (Shorthand recorder · (working in schools).

       (Clerk and Typist   (working in office)

   X X Assistant Experimenter. (research student from Cambridge or university later, or ? Eugenics lab.)

      (Nurse, or woman doctor.

      (Visitor, social worker, or female sanitary inspector.

      Philosopher.

     (Several of these capacities may be combined in one person.)

never dftd in Council : never ask more than pros.
either os di—

Chapter 3 An evolving discipline: Exploring the origins of educational psychology, educational selection and special education

Vivian Hill

Introduction

In reviewing the evolution of the profession of educational psychology it is crucial to understand the social, political, ideological and philosophical milieu in which it was conceived. The role and function of the educational psychologist (EP) has always been strongly influenced by these diverse factors, as well as those of the distinct philosophical orientations observed within the discipline of psychology. At times the discord between psychological and political/legislative influences has led to polarised views, opinions and practices within the profession. Furthermore the inherent tensions between being a professional psychologist and an employee of the state is not insignificant.

The *traditional model* places an emphasis on assessment and identification of needs linked to the allocation of appropriate provision, and is indicative of a belief that such needs are intractable, perhaps even fixed. Whereas alternative, more contemporary models of practice emphasise the notion of assessment and intervention, with the underlying premise that change is possible. Both the history of our profession and the changing political context exert a powerful influence on what is seen to be the dominant role for the EP. It is therefore necessary to understand the influence of the social and political ethos of the late nineteenth and early twentieth centuries in which the profession evolved, and to understand the ideological beliefs of those who led the development of both psychology as a discipline and the profession of educational psychology to understand the traditional model and its powerful legacy.

Building on the discussion in chapter two, in the post Darwinian, final years of the nineteenth century psychology emerged as an academic discipline in British universities. By 1939 there were six chairs in Psychology, three in London, and one each in Cambridge, Oxford and Manchester. It was during this period that educational psychology emerged as an independent discipline, and as a profession. This development was in part due to the challenging context of compulsory education, introduced by the 1870 Education Act, and the sense that psychology had an important part to play in responding to the immense diversity of need being witnessed, for the first time, within schools.

A brief summary of the rapidly changing educational and legislative context

In the post industrial era there was increasing political awareness of the need to educate the workforce in order to promote further industrial growth and to tackle the burden of poverty and ignorance. As a consequence, across Europe there was a focus on providing universal access to education, and in the United Kingdom Forster's Education Act (1870) introduced this entitlement. For the first time the education system was exposed to a diverse population of children with a range of additional needs. Teachers rapidly expressed concern about their ability to adapt the curriculum to respond the variety of pupil needs they were experiencing.

Quicke (1982) in his review of this period of legislation refers to Sutherland (1981) who reported that:

> *The London School Board in 1889 estimated that one child in eight was underfed and suffering from malnutrition, diseases and various disabilities. It was soon recognised that many of these children would have difficulties in coping with normal schooling even when fed.*

The Report of the Royal Commission (1889) acknowledged the necessity of making additional provision or resources available for those with exceptional needs. As a consequence, in the 1890s the first special schools were opened; however, these represented local rather than a national responses to the emerging profile of pupils' needs. The first government response was the 1899 Elementary Education Act (Defective and Epileptic Children), which acknowledged the need for special provision, although there was no requirement for local authorities to make such provision. Over time, as increasing numbers of children entered the school system the level of demand for specialist provision became evident. By 1903 there were special schools in London and 50 other local authorities, and the process of identifying pupils requiring special provision rested with the medical profession. The 1914 Education Act made the provision of special education the statutory responsibility of the local authority, they had the responsibility to ascertain 'children between seven and sixteen who were incapable of education in the ordinary school', and the 'local mental deficiency committees' had responsibility to determine provision suitable for their needs. In this context, in 1913 Cyril Burt had been appointed as the first Educational Psychologist to the London County Council (LCC). His role involved surveying the profile of pupils' needs in London schools and helping teachers respond to them.

The focus on education reform shifted with the start of the First World War and it remained a lesser priority during the economic down turn that followed. The 1929 Wood Committee provided evidence that considerable numbers of children with additional needs remained unidentified and as a consequence their needs were not being met (Wood, 1929). At this stage the influence of Burt's work for the LCC came to the fore as a means to better identify pupils requiring special provision. Burt had liaised with Alfred Binet, the French psychologist, who had developed a psychometric test to help identify pupils requiring special provision. The controversy about what this test actually measures will be considered later, but by 1929 it had been redeveloped, and was being used as a measure of intelligence with far reaching implications. The commitment to the value of this type of assessment is clear in Wood's recommendations. These were that:

> *Those children with IQs between 50 and 70 should be joined with those between 70 and 80 to form a new group known as the 'retarded' who should be given special consideration within the framework of the school system. A single system of special education was proposed … which was to be 'brought into closer relation with the public elementary school system and presented to parents as not something both distinct and humiliating but as a helpful variation of the ordinary school.*

Quicke (1982, p.12)

The 1944 Education Act established a national framework to educate all children according to their 'age, aptitude and ability'. This involved introducing the selective eleven-plus examination to facilitate this process. Furthermore, the 1944 Act, and subsequent Handicapped Pupils and School Health Service Regulations of 1945, increased the range of specialisation of special school provision, reflecting the new terminology of the Act, which described children as Educationally Subnormal and Maladjusted and redefining educationally subnormal children as those 'who by reason of limited ability or other conditions resulting in educational retardation require some form of education wholly or partly in substitution for education normally given in ordinary schools'. New categories included the blind, partially sighted, deaf, delicate and maladjusted. These categories reflected the growing influence of psychological and educational interpretations of need as opposed to medical diagnoses, and in this context the use of psychometric assessments grew to form a key element of placement decision making: Quicke (1982, p.14) concludes:

> *It is no exaggeration to suggest that the development of special education was not only assisted by but also in a sense made possible by the application of psychological techniques and findings. They served to legitimate diagnostic and assessment procedures and provided a rational for various definitions of handicap. This was the backdrop to the expansion in the EP profession in Local Authorities.*

The psychological context

As noted above, the milieu of the early twentieth century reflected intense social and political pressures to screen and classify individuals in order to rationalise resources, the development of psychology, and psychometric assessment techniques in particular, seemed to provide a robust and objective means to do so. In 1904 the French psychologist Alfred Binet developed a screening tool for the French education system to use to identify pupils requiring special education programmes. Binet's test did not aim to measure intelligence and the assessment tool he devised was not based on theoretical explanations of either intelligence or human ability; rather he developed a series of tests based on personal observations and teachers' evidence of how best to identify children likely to succeed educationally from those likely to need support. Consequently, the results of the Binet test, quite predictably, correlated well with scholastic outcomes, but the societal inference that the test measured intelligence or innate cognitive abilities was mistaken (Howe, 1997; Montagu, 1999; Richardson, 1996; 1999; Sternberg, 1984). This logical flaw is at the heart of the controversy about intelligence tests. At the time few psychologists seemed to be concerned by this issue and by 1910 Binet's test had been translated into English and was widely used in the United States, where in 1916 Terman made further developments to the test, creating the Stanford-Binet. His comments provide insight into his perception of purpose of the test:

> *It is safe to predict that in the near future intelligence tests will bring tens of thousands of these high-grade defectives under the surveillance and protection of society. This will ultimately result in curtailing the reproduction of feeblemindedness and the elimination of an enormous amount of crime, pauperism, and industrial inefficiency.*

Terman (1916, pp.6–7)

The erroneous belief that these tests measured innate and biologically determined intelligence meant that reasonable concerns about cultural specificity and consequent test bias were largely ignored, despite the strong challenge of environmental hypothesis advocates such as Walter Lippmann. Writing in *New Republic* in 1922, he challenged the belief that 'intelligence is innate, hereditary, and predetermined' and warned that 'Intelligence testing in the hands of men who hold this dogma could not but lead to an intellectual caste system' (Lippmann, 1922, in Montagu, 1999, p.33). These words predict the shameful links between the IQ test and the eugenics movement, and the resulting compulsory sterilisation of thousands of people within the United States, with those from different cultural and linguistic groups significantly over represented.

Stobart (2008) explains that Binet was quick to distance himself from hereditary views of intelligence, and to challenge the way his test was being misused:

> *Recent thinkers who have given their moral support to these deplorable verdicts by affirming that an individual's intelligence is a fixed quantity, a quantity that cannot be increased. We must protest and react against this brutal pessimism; we must try to demonstrate it is founded on nothing.*

Binet (1909), in Stobart (2008, p.54)

Binet demonstrated the use of his screening test to provide access to specialist resources and interventions for those experiencing difficulties promoted better learning, and increased ability:

> *It is in this practical sense, the only one accessible to us, that we say that the intelligence of these children has been increased. We have increased what constitutes the intelligence of a pupil, the capacity to learn and assimilate instruction.*

Ibid., p.54

Burt, although addressing similar issues to Binet held very different views and used psychometric tests with different objectives in mind:

> *The degree of intelligence with which any particular child is endowed is one of the most important factors determining his general efficiency all throughout life. In particular it sets an upper limit to what he can perform, especially in the educational vocational and intellectual fields.*

Burt (1955, p.281)

It is worth considering the factors that influenced Burt's position and the development of educational psychology in the United Kingdom. Whilst the education systems across Europe faced unprecedented challenges through the provision of universal education, and there was a need to help identify children requiring additional support, the attitudes and approach of Binet and Burt were in stark contrast and had major implications for further developments within their respective educations systems. Burt's influence in the United Kingdom was ultimately to lead to universal screening and selective education.

Ideological influences on Burt's educational psychology

Burt's orientation and beliefs were very much post Darwinian and he acknowledged that he was heavily influenced by the work of Sir Frances Galton, the half cousin of Charles Darwin. During his childhood Burt had regular contact with Galton, as his father, a GP often took him on his rounds and Galton was a patient. White (2006) provides a fascinating account of the influence of Galton on Burt's ideological beliefs:

> *I heard more about Francis Galton than anyone else. Next to Milton and Darwin, he was I think, my father's supreme example of the ideal man ... So it was that, on returning to school, I got from the library Galton's enquiries into Human Faculty, and I still recollect a superstitious thrill when I noticed on the title page that it first saw daylight in the same year that I was born.*

Burt (1952), in White (2006, p.11)

Thus the influence of Galton was evident from early in Burt's life and contributed to some of his most strongly held beliefs. Galton firmly believed that intelligence was innate, inherited and immutable. In the introduction to his book *Heredity Genius* he describes his position:

> *I propose to show in this book that a man's natural abilities are derived by inheritance, under exactly the same limitations as are the form and physical features of the whole organic world. Consequently, as it is easy, notwithstanding those limitations, to obtain by careful selection a permanent breed of dogs or horses gifted with peculiar powers of running, or of doing anything else, so it would be quite practicable to produce a highly gifted race of men by judicious marriages during several consecutive generations.*

Galton (1869), in White (2006, p.18)

Galton developed the term 'eugenics' and formed the Eugenics Society in 1908. Burt served as a member of the Consultative Council of the Eugenics Society in 1937 and 1957. It is likely that a number of factors, including Burt's upbringing, the belief in a ruling elite, his religious beliefs, including those of predestination, reported by White (2006) and his exposure to

Galton's work during his formative years, all contributed to his most controversial belief, that of hereditary intelligence. Furthermore, Burt remained in regular correspondence with Galton throughout his life and his appointment as educational psychologist to London County Council (LCC) in 1913 was in part a consequence of Galton's support of this initiative. The style of educational psychology that Burt developed was heavily influenced by that employed in Galton's assessment resource, and the principles that influenced his approach to service delivery at every level aimed to promote selection, and as a consequence de-selection. The wider social and political demands of the era and Burt's personal psychological orientation paved the way for radical educational reform.

Selection and special education

Towards the end of the nineteenth century the British education system was perceived to be falling behind that of European neighbours, due to reforms in the French and German education systems. In this context the British government set about a review of the antiquated and elitist British education system. A Consultative Committee, which included Burt, was set up after the first world war and produced three reports, the most influential and radical, *The Education of the Adolescent* (1927), known as the Hadow Report, is described by Burt (1959, p.100) thus:

> It was taken as axiomatic that no child should be precluded by financial handicaps from securing an education appropriate to his merits: The problem was to devise a workable machinery for attaining this goal.

Burt then describes the psychological principles that constituted the solution: 'to make a clean cut across our public education system at the age of 11-plus' and that 'it is vital to regard all types of post primary education as attempts to solve, by different means appropriate to different cases, what is essentially a single problem – namely the education of adolescent girls and boys' (Burt, 1959, p.100). He goes on to explain the planned solution on the basis of psychological evidence and in particular his own views about human intelligence:

> During childhood intellectual development progresses as if it were governed largely by a single central factor known as 'general intelligence' which may be described as 'innate, all-round, intellectual ability' and appears to enter into everything the child does and this seems the most important factor in determining his work in the classroom ... since the ratio of each child's mental age to his chronological remains approximately the same, at least up to the pubertal period, it follows that 'as age increases, the mental differences between one child and another will grow larger and larger, and reach a maximum towards adolescence. And by the age of eleven they will already have increased so much that it will no longer be sufficient to sort out different children into classes within the same school.
>
> Ibid.

He described the Consultative Committee's discussion of 'special abilities' and 'special disabilities', concluding that 'specific aptitudes for verbal, numerical, and manual or practical work' become evident at age 11 or later and concludes that:

> At or after that age different children will, if justice is to be done to their varying capacities, require types of education varying in certain important respects.
>
> Ibid.

This provided the rational for the development and implementation of 11-Plus; a test of abilities, it drew on elements of the IQ test and included three components: arithmetic, writing and general problem solving. Burt whole-heartedly supported this screening procedure.

Selective screening at 11-Plus

The 1944 Education Act introduced the 11-Plus examination, which was implemented nationally to help determine secondary school placements for children. The dominant provision was intended to be tripartite (modern, grammar, and technical schools), but was more often bipartite as few technical schools ever emerged. Entry to the different types of schooling was to be determined by the outcome of the 11-Plus. Whilst this selection process provided many socially and economically disadvantaged young people with unprecedented educational opportunities, including access to university which at the time required a grammar school education, it also meant that those unsuccessful in the test were placed in the modern schools. This ended their chances of receiving a university education. Burt defended this position, arguing:

> *It is essential in the interests alike of the children and the nation as a whole, that those who possess the highest ability – the cleverest of the clever – should be identified as accurately as possible. Of the methods hitherto tried out the so called 11-Plus examination has proved to be by far the most trustworthy.*

Burt (1959, p.117)

Wasted potential

By 1956 88 per cent of local authorities were using the 11-Plus at transition. Over time many educationalists and psychologists began to challenge the use of this selection process; they were concerned about the wasted potential of many children, who on the basis of a one-off assessment at age 11, were placed in different forms of schooling with life-long implications. Many, including Douglas (1964), felt that the test was socially biased in favour of the middle classes and blatantly excluded numerous children of good potential but from more disadvantaged backgrounds:

> *Social class differences in secondary education are marked. Fifty four per cent of upper-middle-class children, but only 11 per cent of lower manual working class children, go to grammar schools; and not all of the poor achievement of the working-class children is explained by their lower measured ability. If we compare secondary selection within groups of children whose eleven-year test scores are similar, the middle class children are consistently at an advantage until very high levels of ability are reached. With children in the top 2 per cent of ability, social background is unimportant, but below this it has a considerable influence on their chances of going to grammar schools. As an illustration consider children who score between 55 and 57 in the tests; among them grammar school places are awarded at the age of eleven to 51 per cent from the upper middle classes, and 34 per cent of the lower middle classes...*

Douglas (1964, pp.228–9)

Writing in 1959 Burt admitted the evidence of the Hadow Committee:

> *First 'there is no sharp demarcation, psychological or social, between pupils who attend grammar schools and those who attend modern schools'. Secondly, quite apart from any shortcomings in the method of examination or selection 'it is impossible to forecast with absolute certainty at the age of 11+ how each child is likely to develop. Time will therefore reveal a number of misfits' p103.*

Furthermore Burt felt that there should be considerable overlap in the curriculum across the two forms of school and he later suggested that after a year or two there should be a further review of the appropriateness of the placement. Despite these acknowledgements he still retorts that: 'Yet in practice less than two per cent of the pupils get retransferred from modern to grammar schools and less than 1% from grammar to modern'. Over time Burt was able to reflect on a number of areas of social injustice. He observed considerable geographic inconsistencies that were often related to social class differences:

> *Provision of grammar schools varies from one area to another; in some the percentages of*
> *grammar school places (or the equivalent) amounts barely to 10 per cent; in others it reaches*
> *nearly 45 per cent … only 25 per cent, about one quarter, of authorities provide GCE courses in*
> *modern schools and in most areas there are grave shortages of technical and other forms of higher*
> *education.*

Burt (1959, p.103)

Burt notes that to be sure of the top 3 per cent of pupils progressing to grammar school it is necessary for the top 25 per cent to make this transition. However, with this figure he acknowledged that:

> Eight per cent of those allocated to the modern school will prove to be just as bright as the 25 per cent who have been lucky enough to scrape into the grammar school … disappointed parents may be tempted to complain. Yet in many ways, I suggest they ought rather to rejoice: in all probability the child thus rejected would have had an anxious struggle to come up to the standard demanded...

Ibid., pp.113–14.

This seems to be very much in contradiction with earlier statements about the need for considerable overlap in the curriculum between the two forms of schooling, and the need for further review of placements and opportunities for transition between the two systems, these comments seem to betray Burt's class prejudice.

Towards the end of the 1950s and into the 1960s there was considerable disquiet about the 11-Plus, it's social bias and consequent wasted potential. It was phased out in most of the UK by 1976, apart from in a few counties that were determined to retain selective education. In reviewing the evidence against the 11-Plus Burt concluded that: 'The time for testing innate ability is not 11-plus but 11-minus' (1959, p.111) and he emphasised the importance of an earlier process of screening and streaming, one that is now well embedded in the current education system. Despite all the worthy rhetoric about the development of an educational meritocracy, Burt's beliefs about the genetic transmission of intelligence meant that he would have anticipated that very few socially and economically disadvantaged children would join the progeny of the professional classes within grammar schools and he was not overly motivated to change the system that delivered such a clear social divide:

> *One reason for the class differences in intelligence is obvious. To become a doctor, lawyer or*
> *teacher, it is necessary to pass certain qualifying examinations; and these demand a high level of*
> *innate ability. The ability of parents who have entered one of these professions tends to be*
> *transmitted to the children.*

Burt, cited in Cox & Dyson (1969)

Burt's defence of the 11-Plus, written in 1959, captures the often-contradictory messages that are encapsulated in his later work, particularly that written after his retirement. He was born in the Victorian era and was heavily influenced by the post Darwinian work of Galton. At times in his work on education committees, with progressive educationalists such as Sir Percy Nunn, the Principal of the Institute of Education and collaborator on the Hadow report, one senses that Burt was stimulated by the influence of psychological and scientific evidence. However, when this contradicted his own deeply held values and beliefs he reverted to them and selectively attended to the evidence, defaulting to his hereditary explanations.

One gains the sense that Burt's inability to fully justify and reconcile the issues in the psychological debate around intelligence and selection, in light of the emerging evidence of unfairness and wasteful exclusion, may even have provided the later *sense* of him potentially tailoring findings to fit his default theoretical beliefs about hereditary intelligence.

White refers to Hearnshaw (1987, p.121) who describes Burt thus:

> *He was never at heart a scientist. Much of the data he collected were hastily gathered and of doubtful quality. He was an able and ambitious man, who early came to regard the Galtonian tradition almost as gospel truth and himself as Galton's heir.*

However, in his early work Burt was more open to challenging and radical discoveries and his views about the relative contributions of the environment and inheritance were not always those he subscribed to in relation to intelligence. Burt was a complex individual and despite the shadows cast by his views on intelligence he did much to improve educational access for the socially disadvantaged, so much so that he was knighted by a Labour government in 1946.

Burt's diverse views about the contributions of environment and inheritance

Despite Burt's strong conviction that hereditary factors had the strongest influence on individual intelligence, his position on environmental issues is far from straight forward. Whilst he acknowledges the significance of environment, his position was that these factors might also have a genetic basis. Writing in 1921 he explained:

> *That children of better social status succeed better with the Binet–Simon scale is not necessarily an objection to that scale; nor is it necessarily a ground for constructing separate norms: for, by birth as well as by home training, children who are superior in social status may be equally superior in general ability. Conversely, if a child proves defective according to a scale that is otherwise authentic, the mere fact that his family is poor and his dwelling a hovel does not of itself condone his deficiency. His parents' home may be mean precisely because their hereditary intelligence is mean. Whether poverty and its accompaniments affect the child's performances in any direct fashion – whether, for example, in the Binet–Simon tests a child that inherits an abundance of natural ability may be handicapped through a lack of cultural opportunities – is a further and a separate issue.*
>
> Burt (1921, p.192)

However, it is of interest that when Burt writes about delinquency he takes a rather different view about the significance of environment. It seems that during his time at Liverpool University (1909–1913), he had direct personal experience of slum living conditions. The university had a housing project on the outskirts of a slum, the aim of which was to expose researchers to the impact of these living conditions (Rushton, 2002). These experiences led to a firm conviction that delinquency was not hereditary but indeed environmental: 'a contagion is all too often mistaken for heredity' (Burt, 1925). Likewise his views about race and intelligence reflect a more considered view of environmental influences. Rushton (2002) describes how Burt adhered to the prevalent views of the day that Europeans were intellectually superior to other races, but for Burt the difference was not considered to be purely genetic. Writing in the *Eugenics Review* in 1912, Burt explains: 'In the case of the individual we found the influence of heredity large and indisputable; in the case of the race, small and controversial.'

Burt also studied gender differences in intellectual ability, and when considering the dominant societal views of his day he reached what must have been very controversial findings: 'with few exceptions innate sex differences in mental constitution are astonishingly small – far smaller than common belief and common practice would lead us to expect' (Burt & Moore, 1912). His later studies highlighted female superiority in linguistic abilities and a number of developmental stages where females demonstrate intellectual superiority over males, however, he concluded that overall gender differences to be negligible (Burt, 1922, p.193). Hearnshaw (1979) concludes that Burt's work would have facilitated greater gender equality in both schools and in access to universities.

Conclusions

What is of interest in reviewing Burt's contribution to psychology is, how on occasions, he appears open to the influence of environment on aspects of functioning (for example, behaviour) and is able to challenge dominant societal views. However, throughout his life he appears quite intransigent about environmental influences on intelligence, maintaining a staunch belief in the heritability of intelligence. White (2006) provides an interesting hypothesis that traces the influence of Burt's life long commitment to Galton's work, but also his core religious beliefs. White identifies that within the leading research figures of the time the Puritan views of predestination dominated. Perhaps the seeming inconsistencies in Burt's views are attributable to these entrenched beliefs; that these two influences combined to make it an act of supreme cognitive dissonance for Burt to change his opinions and beliefs.

> *The innateness of intelligence was Burt's idée fixe. When he tuned his intellectual skills to other areas, he reasoned well, subtly, and often with great insight. When he considered the innateness of intelligence, blinders descended and his rational thinking evaporated before the hereditarian dogma that won his fame and eventually sealed his intellectual doom.*
>
> Gould (1981, p.279)

More recently, reviews of Burt's contribution to psychology have been less harsh. He was working at a time of immense social, industrial and political change, within a new and fast growing discipline. He was under pressure to help the government respond to the challenges of fully inclusive education, to help improve the efficiency of our education system and to make use of advances in psychology to support teachers in responding to diverse pupil needs. In addition to his advocacy of psychometric testing, he was also enjoying working in a much more therapeutic way with children and their families within child guidance settings. His personal values and beliefs undoubtedly penetrated his work and presented him with challenges and dilemmas; in some situations he adopted hereditary views and in others he dismissed them in favour of environmental explanations. Burt energetically straddled three distinct levels of applied educational psychology: individual; school level; and systemic and policy level. The pressures and demands of each level are significantly different, as were the psychological theories and models that informed them. These often conflicting demands and alternative paradigms are still evident in the work of EPs to this very day, and as noted in the introduction create tension and potential dissonance in EPs trying to work within each of the distinct strands. Burt's role in shaping the British education system and securing the growth and continuation of professional educational psychology is without question. Burt's own defence of the legislative underpinnings of the 1944 Education Act, and its consequences is illuminating:

> *Our English educational system, like our cathedrals, has grown by a slow process of irregular accretion; and the real crux of the matter has been to reorganise the existing system, with its oddly assorted relics of unrelated efforts in the past, and reshape it and readjust it so as to meet the complex needs of a new age which has already experienced a swift succession of social, industrial, and technological changes.*
>
> Burt (1959, p.99)

The 1944 Act was intended to establish a tripartite education system with an academic, a technical and a functional route. The aim of the 11-Plus was to match the child and their abilities to the most appropriate route. However, few technical schools were ever developed and the 11-

Plus began to fulfil a very different purpose. Rather than allocating children to schools on the basis of need or ability, it became a matter of them passing or failing the examination, and those 11-year-olds who failed were denied many life opportunities. In the 1940s, an era of fast-moving legislation and post-war austerity, one can see how the 11–Plus examination system seemed like an effective solution to the government's problems. Presented as a system of meritocracy – providing an objective measure to achieve greater educational efficiency by selecting the highest achieving pupils to access elite grammar schools – it represented a radical step forward in education. Sadly, over time it became clear that this process ultimately precluded many young people from reaching their full educational potential, with tragic consequences for individuals and a dreadful waste of intellectual resource for the nation.

Vignette 3
Edited extract from the transcript of Burt's 1964 speech, made on being made a Patron of the Association of Educational Psychologists

The School Psychological Service: Its History and Development

Teachers and educationists had been getting more and more convinced that the work carried out on a limited but unofficial basis by Galton and his co-workers at the Anthropometric Laboratory should be taken over by the Education Authority as part of their school system. Of the many problems which, as Sully argued, required attention from the trained psychologist, the one which in those days worried education officers and education committees most of all was the problem of selecting and certifying so-called defectives for transference to special schools. The certifying doctors, not unnaturally, at first tended to pass on every backwards youngster who might profit by the smaller classes, the individual teaching, and the more practical curriculum. And many children were consequently certified, who in a year or two's time, were returned to the ordinary school as cured.

The net cost of maintaining a pupil at one of these special schools was nearly three times that of the cost of maintaining him at an ordinary elementary school. The Education Committee complained of the expense, the parents complained of the stigma, and the inspectors and the teachers complained of the faulty diagnoses. Different doctors had different standards. A child who was "normal" in [working class] Stepney might be certified as 'feeble-minded' in [middle class] St Pancras, and excluded as an 'imbecile' in [professional class] Hampstead. Justice plainly required that, from one end of the county to the other, there should be one weight and one measure. Furthermore, said the teachers, the task of deciding whether a pupil was (in the phrase of the Act), "capable of benefiting by the education given in the ordinary school' was a question which should be decided by someone with educational or psychological experience, not by someone with a merely medical training.

Eventually in 1913, the London County Council – which in those days preened itself on being the most progressive educational authority in the most progressive capital in the world – decided to appoint an official psychologist. He was to be a member, not of the medical department, but of the school inspectorate. He was assigned an office at headquarters and allowed a small fund for equipping it on the lines of Galton's laboratory. This was the first official Child Guidance Clinic set up in this country and indeed I think in the whole world.

The appointment, which in the first instance was to run for three years or so, was to be half time only. Thus the psychologist was free to devote the other half of his time to psychological research. This had one tremendous advantage. Hitherto, anybody who (like myself at Oxford and Liverpool) wanted to investigate the problems of child psychology, had to enter schools from the outside, and certainly could not venture to disarrange the time-tables or the procedures of the teachers. But now, as a member of the inspectorate, the psychologist was able to organise surveys and experiments from within the school system with all the authority of an Edwardian school inspector. He had access to private files, to medical records and the like, which in those days had to be kept as secret as formulae for a new explosive bomb in the eyes of outsiders, and he could also call on the help of doctors, social workers, and even introduce voluntary research students from various university departments to aid him in his work.

And, with a remarkable stroke of generosity, the Council itself handsomely financed the publication of the psychologist's reports – with statistical tables, correlations, factor analyses, diagrams in two colours, all of which would have been much too expensive either for a scientific journal or for a commercial publisher to set up in print. Educational psychology is indeed deeply indebted to the munificence of the Council of those days.

On the first day of my appointment, I duly appeared in top hat and striped trousers in the doorway of the Education Officer's private room, asking, very humbly asking, for my terms of reference. I was greeted (in his Aberdonian accent), with a curt 'Young man, you've all London at your feet, go away and draw 'em up yerself.' I went away. I drew them up. And, as finally approved by the Education Committee, my general plan of campaign was very roughly, as follows.

First, to report on problematic cases referred by teachers, doctors, or magistrates for individual investigation. These cases fell into several fairly distinctive categories. By far the most important were the borderline cases of mental deficiency, which had already aroused such heated controversy. On collecting the relevant data I found surprising variations from one electoral district to another. In [working class] Stepney and Bethnal Green, for instance, the proportion of defectives was nearly three times as large as in [middle and professional class] Lewisham and Hampstead. And one naturally asked, was this due to differences in subjective standards of the local medical officers? If so, how was it that, in the very areas where defectives were most numerous, the scholarship winners were also few and far between? What were the causes? Poverty? Other environmental handicaps? The inheritable dullness of the family or the stock? Or perhaps a combination of the two? Or, finally, some causal factor hitherto unsuspected? It seemed clear that my first job must be to study the pupils attending the special schools and the varying procedures governing their certification.

I well remember how, at the Educational Officer's suggestion, I was taken round the schools a week or two later by a rather pompous member of the Education Committee and presented to the various Headmasters. His opening introduction, which I found alarmingly ambiguous, was always the same, 'Mr Smith, this is Dr Burt, who is responsible for all the mentally defective children born within the County of London.'

The immediate need was plainly some objective method for determining the borderline. The borderline itself naturally depended on the amount of school accommodation actually available, and that was in those days, just under two percent, which, of course, corresponds with a standard deviation of minus two; or on the conventional scale (decided by percentiles not mental ages) with an IQ or mental ratio of almost exactly 70. In deciding the fate of each questionable case, the method we adopted was to compile a short but systematic case history. This always included an assessment based on a test of intelligence, but (as you may have gathered from our reports), it also covered half a dozen other items as well. The purpose of the intelligence test was two-fold: to exclude educational handicaps resulting from an illiterate home or inadequate schooling; and to provide a method of equating the different standards adopted by different doctors or teachers.

However, in recent years, educational psychologists have come under heavy fire from a number of younger writers, like Dr Stott, and Dr Campbell, and Dr McLeish, for our 'naive reliance', as they call it, on tests. 'The Educational Authorities of those days,' said Dr Stott, 'were only too glad to hand on their headaches to a pseudo-scientist and meekly accept the findings of a pseudo-test.' In a book published only a few months ago, Dr McLeish (1963) sharply attacked what he calls the educational psychologist's conception of ''an immutable, adamantine IQ'. Tests constructed by an academic psychologist, he says, are bound to display an academic bias. As a result, 'the working class child' is badly penalised – prevented from following a university career, and often relegated, quite unfairly, to a school for the feeble-minded, all on the basis of ten minutes' testing. Well, since Dr McLeish's criticisms have been widely publicised, may I, as your patron or advocate, be permitted in passing, just a word or two of reply?

I find it difficult to avoid the conclusion that these younger critics glean their notions of what went on in those early days from each other rather than from the contemporary reports. So far from meekly accepting the psychologist and his methods, educational authorities were acutely skeptical, and their medical officers were outspoken opponents. My own appointment was strictly probationary, and was disarmingly announced as an experiment only. Had my diagnoses been as inaccurate as Dr McLeish and others suggest, I should have lost my job at the end of three years, if not before.

I have kept careful record of the after-histories of almost every case referred to me. Indeed, after half a century, I still am in touch with quite a number of them. And a year or two after my appointment I learnt that my most active antagonist – Dr Shrubsall, the school medical officer, had been doing the same – keeping a private check on all my decisions as, indeed, I had been doing on his. Later on he confessed to me that he and his colleagues were quite unable to catch me out, at any rate in any serious error. And, when my initial period of appointment expired, he became one of my warmest supporters. And here if I may, I should like to take this opportunity of expressing my deep indebtedness to all those who at first eyed me askance as a rival, but later came to give me and my various helpers all the co-operation I could desire.

As to the use of 'quotients', or 'ratios', they were introduced because they were fairly intelligible to the teacher, whereas of course, percentiles and standard deviations would not have been. From the outset, however, we insisted that the IQ was not invariably constant, and certainly not suited for purposes of research. As for class bias, the aim and effect of the intelligence tests were exactly the reverse. The Education Officer himself pointed out in one of his farewell reviews (and he supported his statements with figures), that the new psychological methods must have saved, these are his words, 'Hundreds of children who had been handicapped by a home in the slums from a stigma of mental deficiency, helped other hundreds who were dull and backward, and enabled almost as many from the working classes to get to a grammar school and even to a university when under the older procedure they would undoubtedly have failed.'

So much then for the first type of case, the borderline defective. The second type, to which we paid increasing attention as time went on, were those suffering from some special disability: inability to read, spell, to learn arithmetic, as well as other less familiar deficiencies; defective mechanical memory; defective imagery; as well as various tempera- mental hindrances. And it was here that our remedial methods were often most effective.

The third group of cases I've already briefly mentioned – cases at the top end of the intellectual scale. Quite frequently teachers would appeal to the psychologist's judgment in regard to gifted or supernormal pupils. Pupils may be considered definitely worthy of a scholarship but, who, nevertheless, had come to grief in the one day that the scholarship examination which was formerly known in those days as the eleven-plus.

Nor were we interested solely in general intelligence. There were occasional instances of high specific ability or talent: pupils with exceptional artistic, musical or technical gifts. Teachers, I think, are not quite quick enough to spot children who are specialized in ways outside the narrow scope of the traditional curriculum. At least half a dozen were awarded by the Council, what were called 'Special Talent Scholarships', and several of them have since made their name.

Another group, my fifth, also I think failed to get adequate attention; mainly youngsters who were emotionally rather than intellectually subnormal – the potential neurotics and the maladjusted.

Last of all there were the children who seemed morally subnormal, that is, the potentially delinquent. Every war is followed by a marked increase in delinquency and crime, and the First World War was no exception. As a result, the attention of both psychologists and educationists was now turned into a fresh direction. The delinquent youngsters and teenagers, however, proved a far more elusive problem than the intellectually subnormal.

We've all of us, I suppose, been reading recently Professor Vernon's latest book (1964) on personality assessment, and all of us I expect, would readily endorse the conclusion he has so convincingly maintained, that the assessment of moral qualities is infinitely more difficult than the measurement of intellectual ability or school attainments. And I for one would here agree with Dr McLeish (1963) that the academic psychologist is often at a disadvantage. The academic psychologist – particularly of those early days – would have been quite at home with Little Eric, as Dean Farrar drew him, or with Kipling's Stalky and Beetle; but the habits and outlooks of the Artful Dodger were as unfamiliar to him as those of the Trobriand Islanders. My first step therefore was to try and know these people in their own social and family environments. I lodged first at a settlement in the slums; I spent weekends as a guest in the homes of dock-labourers and once of a burglar; and I even for a while got accepted as a member of a criminal gang in Soho. Fortunately, I was not detected or thought of as a 'copper's nark', but I did hear afterwards that I was popularly known as 'Charlie the Parson'.

Born as I was within the sound of Bow Bells and educated in a school just opposite Newgate Jail, I could drop into Cockney whenever I pleased. And although our school was residential, we were always free on half-holidays to roam where we liked without any parents to criticise. When we got tired of the Abbey, or the Tower of London, we set out to explore the purlieus of China Town and Limehouse, and find Fagan's Hideouts in Hoxton and the Docks. And this background knowledge was invaluable to me 20 years later when I came to study the young London delinquent (Burt, 1925). I recommend every educational psychologist to start by actually living among his cases and with their families. Well, from all this, you'll readily understand that during my first few years with the Council most of my working days were occupied with these individual case studies. Whatever the problem might be, instead of calling each child up to the office, I always found it far more effective to study him, as it were, *in situ*, and that of course meant visiting him in the school, calling at his home, and watching him with his play-fellows larking in the streets.

Copies of the full transcript are available from:
The Burt Archives, University of Liverpool Library, Special Collections and Archives, catalogue no. D191/13/1. A transcript is also included in Rushton (2002).

Chapter 4 'Challenging behaviour' and the challenges for educational psychologists

Adrian Faupel & Julia Hardy

Why 'challenging behaviour' challenges EPs?

Any historical review of the first hundred years will inevitably be selective and reflects the experiences and biases of the authors. This is certainly true in this review of the educational psychologist (EP) in relation to emotional and behavioural difficulties. Both authors have experience exclusively in the south of England, for example, and coincidentally both underwent training as EPs in the same institution. The ideas in this chapter are inevitably influenced by our own experience as EPs over a few decades, as well as our interest in the topic of 'challenging behaviour'.

A strong case can be made that of all the types of special educational needs, those arising from emotional and behavioural difficulties are the most problematic. If this is the case then this area poses considerable challenges to the EP profession in terms of its role and theoretical understandings. To begin we suggest the following four challenges.

Changes to the terminology

The first challenge is that this area is the most difficult to define: 'maladjustment' became emotional and behavioural difficulty (EBD), then social, emotional and behavioural difficulty (SEBD) which became behaviour, social and emotional difficulties (BSED) in its relatively short history. The label 'EBD' is itself extremely problematic – is it emotional *and* behavioural, emotional *or* behavioural, or even emotional *and/or* behavioural. This is not simply a matter of fussy semantics: children with purely behavioural difficulties were historically construed as simply 'naughty' and best dealt with, first within Tutorial Units, which later became PRUs and with additional requirement for Pastoral Support Plans within mainstream. These were the disaffected, disturbing/troubling children and were not included within the special educational needs procedures. The notion of a special educational need seemed to require an additional emotional component since these were the disturbed and troubled children. They needed Statements of Special Educational Need and Individual Educational Plans (IEPs). So where did 'delinquency' fit in? For many years, the education of delinquents was in Approved Schools which were not subject to the Department of Education but, first, to the Home Office and later to social services departments. EP involvement with this group was generally very marginal. There were some notable exceptions where School Psychological Services had EPs with time allocated to working in approved schools, for example Tennal School in Birmingham.

Behaviour – a subjective concept

Secondly, there is a degree of subjectivity in the assessment of emotional and behavioural difficulties that is not matched by other areas of special need. Cognitive, visual, auditory and physical functioning have measurement tools which are much more 'objective'. Measurement of the degree of EBD[1] is usually via checklists completed by adults – and the way these are completed

---

[1] We will use the term EBD since this is currently referred to in the literature (Jackson et al., 2010)

probably says more about the rater (their norms, beliefs and values) than about the child. This fact of much greater subjectivity in the assessment of the seriousness of EBD has been very important historically, particularly in times when EPs were either 'gatekeepers' to special schooling or when, after the 1981 Education Act, they were burdened by LEAs to contributing to decisions about the determination of whether a statement of SEN was appropriate or/and to the allocation of resources more generally. This situation not infrequently led to a kind of 'blackmail' by headteachers, who could threaten to exclude a pupil if resources were not forth-coming. It was much easier for headteachers to adopt a righteousness about excluding a pupil for behavioural problems than they could do for other areas of SEN. In the post 1981 Educa-tion Act period the values of equity and fairness, surely hallmarks of EP practice, were frequently put under great pressure in the advice regarding provision for SEN; the term EBD has threat-ened these values in ways which other areas of SEN have not. Additionally, this area of work could potentially lead both individual EPs and EP services into 'confrontational' rather than supportive roles with senior management of schools and with LEAs.

Ethics and the area of EBD

The issue of ethics and values is linked to a consideration of the third area specifically related to EBD and not to other areas of SEN: behaviour can be described as good or bad and 'badness' has moral overtones and can provoke teacher reactions which are often highly emotional. EBD is an emotional area to a degree and intensity not associated with other areas of SEN. The sensitivity required by EPs to interact with adults in highly charged emotional situ-ations requires counselling, supportive and other interpersonal skills. This was perhaps a particular challenge to the profession in the 1960s and 70s, which had been largely child guid-ance based and where the bread-and-butter-work and skills developed by EPs centred on inter-acting with children. The skills and expertise needed by the profession at that time were primarily child focused, rather than working with teachers and school staff. We will see that this changed quite markedly towards the end of the 1970s and with the introduction of the 1981 Education Act.

The personal challenge to teachers themselves

Finally, EBD poses challenges to teachers which are generally unique to EBD. It is part of the self-image and self-esteem of teachers that they are competent to relate to children and feel that they are able to manage and lead classrooms. But a child with behavioural difficulties is often a direct challenge to such beliefs because here is a situation in which the teacher is frequently unable to exert appropriate control. To preserve their own self image of compe-tence, teachers are seemingly tempted to 'demonise' the badly behaved child. Andy Miller (1996) has shown that teachers, and here they are probably no different from the rest of us, tend to attribute successful pupil learning and behaviour to their own effort and competences, whereas they attribute any failure to be due to the characteristics of the pupil. Children with emotional and behavioural difficulties affect the ethos of the classroom and interfere with the learning and attainments of other pupils to an extent not experienced in other areas of SEN. All of this requires that EPs, in relating to teachers about behavioural issues, have needed to be highly sensitive to the emotional resilience of teachers and to consider how best, particu-larly in consultative approaches, to help teachers cope with their own emotional insecurities. One of the major contributions to teacher stress is classroom management, and when feeling stressed the purely rational and logical approaches become less salient.

Thus far, we have attempted to show that the area of EBD poses particular challenges to the role and practice of EPs. It would not be surprising to find therefore that in the course of the history of educational psychology, there have been highs and lows, successes and failures in this area.

How dominant world-views influence EPs in changing eras

What EPs have done, and even more importantly how they think about EBD, has been heavily influenced by two aspects of their history. EPs have been men and women of their times, and the times have changed dramatically and exponentially over the last hundred years. The way they have construed EBD has been affected by a series of changes in the dominant paradigms or world-views, so it is these that we will first review. What they have actually done, their actual practice, has been determined by changes in societal expectations, manifested in the particular legislation in place at a particular time.

People as farmers

The period of the last 100 years starts towards the end of the Industrial Revolution. For many thousands of years previously the dominant world-view was agricultural, so that the framework adopted to understand how and why people felt and behaved in the way they did was essentially an agricultural one, with the four major elements of air, fire, wind and water central to thinking. Human beings were thought to be made up of four essential elements and their behaviour was an expression of their temperament, determined by the relative balance of these elements to produce four personality types: choleric, phlegmatic, sanguine and melancholic. In that pre-scientific, pre-Enlightenment age, there was clearly no place for educational psychology.

People as steam engines

When Freud in the late nineteenth and early twentieth centuries was attempting to construct a model for understanding why we behave as we do, he naturally turned to the dominant technology of coal, iron and steel of the industrial revolution. His model was essentially a steam engine one, characterised by 'drives' with the 'id' seen as a cauldron or boiler driving the whole process. Based on ideas of 'pressure', suppression and repression were used to explain the behavioural maladjustment which were seen as symptoms, rather like steam escaping from a lid too tightly applied to the boiler. Simply preventing the steam escaping only increases the problem, for the underlying neuroses will simply find another behavioural expression. Taking the lid off (catharsis) might be one way to reduce the amount and intensity of the feelings and so reduce the deviant behaviour. Psychology at the time of the birth and early development of educational psychology was dominated by this psychodynamic model.

The early history of educational provision for children and young people exhibiting EBD had very little EP involvement – provision was mainly in residential schools for the maladjusted and by 1962 it could be said that

> *virtually all the pioneer research work in the treatment of maladjusted children has been done in private or independent schools. In these schools one outstandingly gifted individual has built around himself a therapeutic environment and treatment team, and has been able to conceptualise and communicate what is being done.*
>
> Shields (1962), quoted in Bridgeland (1971)

The treatment of 'maladjustment' was heavily dominated by psychiatry and this remained true right up to the 1970s and found expression in the Child Guidance movement, which was frequently the birthplace of educational psychology services.

People as monkeys

In the late nineteenth century, a new paradigm slowly emerged. Such changes in dominant ways of thinking do not usually emerge out of the blue and do not immediately replace existing paradigms. However, individual thinkers may assume a critical importance in the development of a new paradigm. Charles Darwin, in *On the Origin of Species* (1859), presented a very different understanding of human emotions and behaviours. His was an essentially biological model and, like all science, depends upon rigorous description and classification. It is not surprising, therefore, that in psychological terms this led to the development of psychometrics as the way of classifying cognitive and personality dimensions. Educational psychologists were employed to classify cognitive functioning and became the qualified users of psychometric instruments measuring 'intelligence'. There was not as much initial emphasis on classifying emotions and behaviour, though psychometric instruments became available in later years (e.g. Cattel's 16 PF, 1946). Given a child guidance model, psychiatrists leading a team of psychiatric social workers (PSWs) and educational psychologists, the major function of the latter was to eliminate the possibility of intellectual dysfunction as a cause of the problematical behaviour. Generally speaking, though always with notable exceptions, the EP role in child guidance clinics was a subordinate one. The psychiatrist carried out the mental health assessment of the child, the PSW assessed the family dynamics (usually focusing on the mother!), whilst the EP carried out a psychometric assessment of the child's intellectual functioning. This model of service provision for children in the mainstream remained dominant at the time of the Underwood Report (Ministry of Education, 1955), which described the EP role under the section dealing with child guidance.

People as economists

The interwar years were characterised by economic issues. Karl Marx had published *Das Kapital* in 1867 and this became the inspiration for the setting up of the Communist political and economic system in the Soviet Union after 1917. The rivalry between this and the capitalist system of the West dominated the middle half of the 20th century. The new paradigm emerging in the West construed emotions and behaviour in economic terms and found psychological expression in behaviourism. Human behaviour is developed and maintained by the operation of credits (rewards) and debits (punishments). This understanding of the origins of behaviour became very important in classroom management systems, and the way behaviour was managed within schools was at least often loosely conceived in terms of token economies where good behaviour resulted in rewards and privileges and bad behaviour in punishments and sanctions. Beginning in the late 60s, behavioural approaches gradually became the wellspring of EP understandings and practices and competed with the more general psychometric approach. 'Behaviour modification' was eagerly taken on board by many educational practitioners, often without a great deal of psychological understanding and expertise. By focusing simply on rewards and punishments, the individual pupil became the object of intervention and sometimes of manipulation. It became the task of EPs to put this over-simplistic and incomplete picture of behavioural approaches into its proper context by emphasising the importance of the environment in cueing appropriate and inappropriate behaviour using an applied Analysis of Behaviour Model (Wheldall et al., 1986; Solity & Bull, 1996).

Despite the abuses and the over-simplistic nature of some of the behavioural approaches, with its psychological narrowness of focusing solely on behaviour to the neglect of cognitive and emotional dimensions, the period of behavioural dominance produced very creative EP work. One of the essential elements of the approach was the emphasis it placed on accurate collection of data and of the rigorous application of the applied scientific methodology (see Thomas & Walter, 1973; Westmacott & Cameron, 1981). Behaviour change was now not simply a matter of the intuition gained by experience or due to the charisma of the adult, but the application of a problem-solving framework. To be an applied scientist became one of the hallmarks of good EP practice (see Cameron & Stratford, 1987; Miller et al., 1992; Monsen et al., 1998). Not only did this framework enable the development of a consultative way of working with teachers regarding individual pupils, but it enabled EPs to engage in relevant in-service training of teachers and this led to a change of emphasis away from simply working with individual children in many EP services.

The emphasis on 'research' and data driven decisions (see *The Fourth R* by Haring et al., 1978) led to a number of exciting and innovative approaches pioneered almost exclusively by EPs. The learning hierarchy developed by Haring (Acquisition, Fluency, Generalisation, Adaptation) fed into the development of Precision Teaching, which, although primarily applied to academic learning, in for example DataPac (Ackerman et al., 1983), also had implications for behaviour, such as SNAP in Coventry (Muncey & Ainscow, 1983).

EPs played a vital part in the development of the Portage Programme which over a short period of time developed into a national response to the learning and behavioural needs of preschool children with disabilities. The Portage Programme was based on behavioural principles and at the heart of the weekly interaction between home visitor and parent was the 'activity chart' which explicitly applied the scientific methodology to behaviour change.

One of the major assumptions of the behavioural approach was that social behaviour is governed by the same laws of learning as any other form of learning, for example, academic learning. Thus emotional difficulties began to be construed as skill and competence problems and not simply a matter of a regime of rewards and punishments. Task analysis could be applied to interpersonal and pro-social behaviour just as much as to any other learning. This was particularly important for the development of curricula in special schools for moderate and, especially, severe learning difficulties. Coincidentally, at around this time (1970) it was accepted that every child, no matter how severe their intellectual disabilities, should become part of the educational system and not governed by health authorities. EPs were at the forefront of initiatives in this area (see Chapter 7).

People as automata

Up to this point in history the dominant paradigms have been essentially concerned with the individual pupil exhibiting EBD. For its first 50 years EP practice was mainly focused on individual pupils using psychodynamic approaches, psychometric assessment and behavioural analysis. The Second World War was fundamentally not so much about soldiers, but about technology and the growth of mass production of tanks, planes and ships. It led to the development of large, complex factories, characterised by long assembly lines with the individual worker but a cog in a complex machine, (cf. Charlie Chaplin's *Modern Times*). Big became beautiful and this industrial model was applied to schools in the 1970s, with the development of the large comprehensive school. This was the paradigm where 'systems' became increasingly dominant and was reflected, following Rutter and Mortimer's work (Rutter et al., 1979) with an emphasis moving away from assessment of the individual pupil to the assessment of the system – the school (see Provis, 1992). Working at the whole school level became the preferred option, though it was very difficult to realise in practice. Materials designed to help in this process were developed or taken up by EPs , such as Myers 'System Supplied Information' (SSI: Myers et al., 1989) and techniques using soft systems methodology, for example 'rich pictures'. There was a renewed interest in whole school behaviour policies, for example Galvin & Costa: *Building The Better Behaved School* (1994) and the assessment of classroom climate and ethos as in *My Class Inventory* (Fraser et al., 1982). Although theoretically EPs were frequently committed to working at whole school levels, the reality of achieving this was problematic, particularly at secondary level where systems issues seemed most acute, (Stratford, 2000). Difficulties facing EPs at the time included their generally low status amongst secondary school staff; the propensity for teachers to attribute success to their own efforts but pupil failure to the pupil or the family; and to the sometimes perceived 'arrogance' of EPs, who rightly stopped blaming the pupil but were felt now to be blaming and judging the teacher and the school.

People as greens

The next development in changing world-views seems to have been linked psychologically to the technology of space travel and satellite technology. For the first time our planet could be seen from the outside. The notion of the Earth being a very fragile ecosystem had been gaining ground since the publication of Rachel Carson's *Silent Spring* in 1962. Planet Earth became increasingly seen as an ecosystem with interdependent and interlocking parts. A butterfly flapping its wings off the coast of West Africa 'causes' a hurricane in the Gulf of Mexico. What happens in equatorial rainforests has profound implications for what happens in the Arctic thousands of miles away. The application of Kurt Lewin's (1936) famous dictum expressed in his equation B = fPE (behaviour is a function of the reciprocal interaction between the person and the environment) now begun to be realised in psychological practice. Ecology is the study of the relationships between organisms, not the study of organisms themselves, and it shocks us out of the either/or dilemma of whether we should blame the child or the teacher/family for emotional and behavioural difficulties. It forces us into an essentially interactional both/and model. Klaus Weddell summed up this new understanding: Psychological difficulties should not be attributed to the weakness of the individual, nor to the deficiencies within the environment which shapes him or her, but to the inappropriate matching of one to the other. Problems are not seen as the 'fault' of children, nor of schools, but as a mismatch in the interactions between a child and his family and the teacher in a particular classroom in a particular school in a particular community. Whether a child can cope in school depends on the interaction between the resources and deficiencies of the child's setting – both at home and at school. The teacher's ability to 'cope' with the child's needs similarly depends on the outcome of such interactions.

The interactional perspective operates at different levels. At the individual person level, the three components of the individual (cognitive, emotional and behavioural), hitherto often identified in the different schools of psychology as the sole source of behavioural difficulties, were now seen as essentially reciprocally interacting. This has paved the way for rapprochement between previously conflicting understandings. Behavioural approaches were transformed into cognitive behavioural ones with the emphasis in its early days on the cognitive, but now increasingly recognising the importance of the earliest schemas laid down in the early years. On the whole, EPs have come relatively late into the cognitive behavioural arena, but they pioneered the renewed importance of emotions in the crucial aspect of secure attachment to both academic and interpersonal functioning (Bennathan & Boxall, 1996), and the establishment of nurture groups to develop that emotional security which was seen as an essential precursor of effective learning in schools. Building on this systemic and interactional paradigm have been interventions developed by EPs, such as the No Blame approach to bullying (Maines & Robinson, 1992) and Circle of Friends (Newton et al., 1996), which are at the heart of good consultative frameworks widely adopted by EP services. Although a contemporary paradigm, it is under threat from the excessive medicalisation of behavioural difficulties (see chapter 12), and the misunderstandings of the relationships between genes and gene expression and an oversimplification of the first findings of neuroscience.

People as computers

Present-day life is dominated as never before by the computer and information technology. We live in the computer age and it is not surprising that attempts to understand human functioning now frequently employ computer analogies. The computer is essentially a technology for processing information and the brain, like a computer, consists of hardware (the biological structures of the brain) and software (the operating system managing the hardware) to process information. To understand and predict behaviour, social information-processing models construe interpersonal functioning as having a task to perform, reading the situation (getting input), generating alternative solutions (scanning a database), executing a routine and applying a solution (Crick & Dodge, 1996). The results of this process in solving the task give iterative feedback to influence the database of preferred options for future interactions. As an integrative model, it brings together problem solving, planning, and social skills and competences, elements which are perhaps exemplified by the SEAL curriculum DfE, 2005), the construction of which EPs played a uniquely dominant role.

Since this model is about tasks to be achieved, it has a future orientation and to that extent is part of a more general paradigm shift which focuses on the future rather than on the past, on the solution rather than the problem, on the positive rather than a negative, on strengths rather than weaknesses. EP work in the EBD area now frequently reflects this shift – with solution focused approaches, appreciative enquiry and a new emphasis on developing well-being as the preferred 'antidote' to emotional and behavioural difficulties (Hooper, 2012).

Models have been described as being beautiful creations but very difficult to live with and there are some perhaps even more fundamental paradigm shifts over the past hundred years, including that from modernism to post-modernism. The work of Tom Ravenette in creatively integrating the social constructivist principles of Kelly's Personal Construct Psychology in working with pupils with EBD has had an enduring impact on EP practice (Beaver, 2011).

The impact of legislation and government initiatives on EP practice

However, whatever the underlying constructs of the way EPs construe EBD, what EPs actually do is to a great extent constrained by changes in society's expectations of their role embodied in government legislation. From the 1870s, with the introduction of compulsory universal education, until the Warnock Report and the 1981 Education Act, there was a steady 'removal' of children with disabilities from mainstream schooling. This can be interpreted positively (an attempt to meet the needs of individual pupils in the most effective and efficient way) or negatively (the needs of teachers and the majority being met at the expense and exclusion of minorities). The number of categories of children excluded from mainstream schooling and placed in special schools increased to 10 by the time of the 1944 Education Act and its 1945 Regulations. Perhaps surprisingly, the category of 'maladjusted' appears for the first time in 1945. Some maintain that with mass evacuations of inner-city children from socially deprived areas in the war years, it was the experience of teachers in the leafy glades of rural England that exposed the fact that there were children not able to access a normal curriculum because of their bad behaviour. What is clear, however, is that the number of categorised 'maladjusted' children increased rapidly in the immediate post-war years and such was the concern that a special committee, of which Cyril Burt was a member, was set up in 1950 which reported as the Underwood Report (Ministry of Education, 1955) five years later. This had a very important impact on the numbers of EPs, their training and their employment base, as LEAs were charged with developing appropriate provision and LEAs structures to operationalise these. However, we have seen that the Underwood Report firmly placed EPs very much within a child guidance structure, although it charged LEAs, rather than health services, with responsibility for setting these up where they did not already exist.

Following the Underwood Report the EP became increasingly responsible for identifying and assessing 'candidates' for special schooling, so their role in its assessments became secure. The downside was perhaps an overemphasis on assessment at the expense of intervention and the problem of being essentially 'gatekeepers' to special schooling. By the end of the 70s, the pressure for 'normalisation' and for integration rather than exclusion led to a committee being set up by Mary Warnock which reported in 1978. This recommended the abolition of 'categories of handicap', developed the notion of a continuum of special educational needs

(SEN) with the responsibility given to mainstream schooling to meet these needs, arguing in principle for integration rather than special schooling. Incidentally, although not liking the term 'maladjusted' it did not recommend that it be replaced. The 1981 Education Act embodied many of the recommendations of the Warnock Report and led to a rapid growth in the employment of EPs who now had precise legal responsibilities within the drawing up of Statements of Special Educational Need. The emphasis on provision for EBD within mainstream schooling was taken up by EPs with an increased role in INSET and in the provision of materials for use in mainstream schools in helping teachers not only to identify pupils experiencing EBD, but in developing within teachers an understanding and the skills to help pupils with behavioural problems to access the curriculum. The work of David Tweddle leading a group of EPs in the production of Preventive Approaches to Disruption (PAD; Lake, 1985) was for example highlighted as good practice in the Elton report (1989). The latter report was well received by EPs with its emphasis on the importance of whole school policies and procedures in relation to pupil behaviour.

Terminology may change but some priorities remain

Anti-bullying

In the early 1990s with government funding for 'Elton Projects', EPs were given unique opportunities to work systemically within and between schools. At that time Olweus's (1993) action research into bullying was significant in its influence: EPs worked with schools to reflect on the whole school responsibilities to overcome bullying. Indeed, the theme of anti-bullying initiatives in schools is one of the many themes that remains a priority for EP work over the decades (Smith et al., 2012). Our more recent focus should be that of cyberbullying: EPs still have a key role here, particularly in hearing the views and experiences of children and young people (Ackers, 2012).

Whole school culture and work with individuals

The awareness of the influence of whole school culture is another recurring theme; of all the areas of research that EPs have been influenced by, Miller's 1996 findings on pupil behaviour and teacher culture have been and continue to be crucial to EP practice (Miller, 2003) in the field of 'behaviour'. Fox (2003) describes the 'EP Flip' in their movement from espoused theories to theories in use, and this can be seen in the iterative movements between a focus on individual students and whole school approaches. EPs do work with school staff and directly with young people, and in the area of behaviour in particular we continue to need to help take a nuanced approach. In the 1970s we were influenced by Egan (1990) to think about both school staff and our own role as 'skilled helper(s)'. Egan was ahead of his time, arguing for the need for positive psychology by not just in focusing on problems but on the 'opportunity development process', through understanding scenarios, considering the preferred scenario and strategic planning to move from action towards valued outcomes. Moving on from Egan's work is the use of Solution-Focused Brief Therapy (de Shazer, 1985), with EPs developing the language used in their consultations using specific techniques (Rhodes, 1993). Perhaps over the decades the movement has been for an increased focus on systems work, but the application of systemic thinking with families has come full circle (Fox, 2009). Three decades ago many EPs worked within child guidance settings, collaborating with family therapists and others in applying systems thinking. Today we have returned to this partnership through EPs' work within CAMHS settings; many EPs are delivering cognitive behaviour therapy (CBT) and some are designing tools for the measurement of school-based interventions and their influences on schoolchildren's well-being, such as Ivens' (2007) School Children's Happiness Inventory.

Integration to inclusion

Although Warnock brought us the concept of 'integration', EPs still focus on inclusion and their role in promoting this right for the most vulnerable children/young people. One way that EPs have promoted more inclusive practices in schools was through the Index for Inclusion (2000), designed as a vehicle for consultation and self-reflection by headteachers and their staff. Hick's (2005) study of EPs acting as 'critical friends' to schools outlines the important potential role of the EP in helping schools reflect on their own institutions' inclusive policies and practice.

Iterations in the area of EBD

As EPs we have seen the language change (Thomas et al., 1978) although the focus may have remained the same (Swinson & Knight, 2007). We have seen a welcomed increase in EPs' use of consultations and systemic work in schools, with fewer EPs as experts, giving solutions to others. Many key areas of focus and concern for EPs remain constant: being aware of our role in promoting the inclusion of those with challenging behaviour through whole-school approaches; supporting schools change through a systemic focus with action research and yet still being aware of the needs of vulnerable young people who may be experiencing specific issues such as cyber-bullying. The contexts change with advances in information technology and the political rhetoric is that of 'evidence-base'; EPs will, where appropriate, apply evidence-based approaches such as CBT, but they also we all need to take up the role of helping hear the voice of children and young people in schools.

Vignette 4

An encounter with Sir Cyril Burt

Alan Labram

It was into the golden age of expanding public sector opportunities in 1970 that I was one of two educational psychologists appointed to the London Borough of Croydon, the other being Sheila Wolfendale. Croydon's education service was gifted with an impressive number of very able school inspectors, educational psychologists and advisory teachers who formed an intellectual community which was highly regarded by Croydon's schools and teachers. In later years many members of that Croydon group went on to become education leaders in Her Majesty's Inspectorate, schools, universities and local authorities.

Bob Reid, a burly Scot, was the Principal Educational Psychologist in Croydon and part of a coterie of similarly aged male PEPs who had, a generation earlier, formed the Association of Educational Psychologists. Bob disliked psychiatrists intensely and (to the frustration of our Education Directorate) spent a lot of his professional time and effort needling any child psychiatrist who strayed into his domain. Bob was also editor of the *AEP Journal* but all submitted articles were sent on for comment or correction to none other than Sir Cyril Burt, Patron of the AEP.

At that time Burt was an awesome figure within psychology and, as the first LEA appointed EP to the London County Council in 1913, a guru of the profession. Bob and Sir Cyril also shared a common birthday, March 3, so when Bob invited Sheila and me to accompany him on his birthday to an editorial meeting with Sir Cyril at his Hampstead home, we jumped at the chance.

On the day, we drove across London to Primrose Hill where Burt lived with his (I think) Austrian housekeeper who ushered us into a large study/lounge where Sheila and I were introduced to a smallish, bespectacled man whose sprightly manner belied his considerable age. After settling us in comfortable leather chairs, Burt sprang across the room to a table, poured out four glasses of Moselle wine, then cut and passed round four pieces of birthday cake. We toasted the birthday boys and settled down to whatever might follow.

The 'business' bit of the meeting was pretty brief as Burt had long in advance read carefully all of the manuscripts, made comments and suggestions, as well as having checked for typos.

Burt was charming, socially facilitating and totally non-egocentric, enquiring about our (Sheila and my) backgrounds and about which aspects of psychology held our interest. It was a bit like a friendly student tutorial. Burt appeared to know every important figure in psychology. He was also very knowledgeable about many other branches of science. I also remember him using a phrase I had not heard before but which became popular within academia and the media soon afterwards: 'The ghost in the machine', i.e. the debate about whether or not the brain creates or somehow receives consciousness.

To me as a young man Burt seemed like the stereotypic academic, cloistered and remote, one of those people who were defined almost entirely by the day job and whose social life was largely contained within that work context. Therefore I did not deem it appropriate to ask if he had seen George Best's incredible goal at White Hart Lane some time before. But it was not lost on me that within the confines of his intellectual metaworld he could exert considerable power and control over many of the people he met. They were, after all, on his territory.

A few years later, significantly after his death, when the storm broke over his falsified research, issues about Burt the person had to be addressed. Was he just a lonely old man hanging on to his past, becoming more fearful that his secret would come out? An emperor without any clothes? In those pre-information technology days it was perhaps possible to fool some of the people for quite a lot of the time. One remembers the philosopher C.E.M. Joad's fall from grace with his train fare avoidance and it is just possible that Burt was similarly flawed in believing that his reputation rendered him unassailable.

There are, of course, ironies galore with Burt's legacy. He had a significant influence in shaping education policy over a 20-year period up to the 1944 Education Act. He believed in the notion of generally fixed intellectual ability. With hindsight we can see that his views confirmed him as an academic with a highly privileged family background linking him to Galton and Darwin. But nearly 70 years on from the1944 Act, with upward social mobility all but stalled in Britain, we can look back to Burt's time when whole cohorts of working class children passed the 11-Plus, swept into universities and the professions to become the property-owning middle class. Nice one, Cyril.

Chapter 5 From ascertainment to reconstruction: 1944–1978

Harriet Martin

The post-Second World War years were formative ones for the profession of educational psychology. While there have been subsequent influential events, reports and research that have altered the direction of the profession's development, the post-war years set a pattern of practice, role, training and status that still has a hold today. Many of the barriers to development of the profession in all its aspects in more recent years can be traced to this period. Inevitably, some of the crucial factors, such as social and political change, developments in educational theory, legislation and availability of resources, were beyond the direct control of educational psychologists. Nevertheless, there is also an argument that not enough educational psychologists had the confidence, knowledge and motivation to take control of their own destinies and be drivers rather than passengers in these post-war years.

Before the Second World War there had been some advances in the education of disabled children, particularly where their difficulties were clearly defined, for example the deaf and the blind. There were special schools for those deemed 'mentally defective' and considerable work done on the identification of such children through mental testing. By 1944 there were also about 70 child guidance clinics in the UK. These centres, usually staffed by a psychiatrist, psychologist and psychiatric social worker, worked with 'maladjusted' children, who, although they might have been of normal intelligence, were difficult to manage in some way or another. The Second World War provided further impetus and requirement for child guidance clinics, and therefore for psychologists, to cope with the increase in children with emotional and behavioural difficulties resulting from their experiences during the war. Agatha H. Bowley, a senior psychologist in the Leicester Schools Psychological Service, wrote that the service was responsible 'for the welfare of all children who are dull, backward or maladjusted, who show difficulties in development or behaviour' (Bowley, 1948). The final chapter of her book is devoted to how knowledge of child psychology can help children who were affected by the Second World War. It includes information on evacuation, air raids and the effect of a father's absence. Bowley concludes by arguing that the work of her service is largely preventive and educational and that her psychological service adequately fulfills the requirements of the 1944 Education Act. It is interesting to note that the Leicester School Board provided the first special class for 'feeble-minded' children in 1892 and was the first local education authority to appoint a psychologist, after Cyril Burt in London, in 1931, which may explain why Bowley's book reflects a surprisingly well developed understanding, for the time, of the potential of psychological services for children. Much of the language is clearly dated and would be deemed inappropriate and politically incorrect today but the underlying content would seem familiar to today's educational psychologists.

The 1944 Education Act provided a framework for a reformed national system of education designed to meet the needs of a post-war world. Previous legislation regarded the education of handicapped children as a separate category of provision and children had to be 'certified' as defective before being sent to a special school. Certification was the responsibility of the medical profession. Not surprisingly parents resented this stigma and teachers complained that the diagnosis was often faulty. There was also little adequate provision for those children with difficulties who did not meet the criteria for certification. The 1944 Act stipulated that local education authorities must meet the needs of these children within their general duty to provide sufficient schools. Now any child considered educable would have the right to schooling. The local education authority had a duty to ascertain which children required special educational treatment. This applied to all 'pupils who suffer from any disability of mind or body'. The process of ascertainment was ultimately the responsibility of a medical officer but educational psychologists were usually responsible for the mental testing aspects of the assessment. There was an official set of forms (Handicapped Pupil Forms: HP1, 2, etc.) to be completed. The Ministry of Education pamphlet *The Nation's Schools: Their Plan and Purpose* (Ministry of Education, 1945), which was effectively the implementation plan for the 1944 Education Act, indicated: 'Children found to be suffering from educational, personal or social maladjustment should be referred to a psychologist, or child guidance centre or clinic, which will advise on the special educational treatment required. This may include treatment by the psychologist, or at the clinic, and also appropriate handling of the child's difficulties by his teacher in the course of his school work.' This was a great improvement on the previous situation but still left some children, deemed uneducable, in the hands of the health authorities under the Mental Deficiency Act 1913. However, the role of the educational psychologist as assessor established the stereotypical image of the educational psychologist as the man (it was usually a man in those days) in a suit with a suitcase who retreated into broom cupboards to subject children to a barrage of tests.

By 1950 the model of child guidance clinic and school psychological services working together was well established. The educational psychologist divided his or her time between the two. The Report of the Committee on Maladjusted Education (the Underwood Report; Ministry of Education, 1955) considered the child guidance clinic, working in conjunction with the school psychological and school health services, to be the most effective way of working. However, throughout the 1940s and 1950s and into the 1960s, educational psychologists worked mainly under the direction of the psychiatrist and they spent much of their time administering psychological tests to children to help with the psychiatrist's diagnosis. The theoretical basis for work within a child guidance clinic was firmly psychoanalysis and psychometrics, and many educational psychologists did rather less of the former. The more confident would see children within the clinic and might initiate therapeutic treatment but generally under the direction of the psychiatrist. My mother worked in a child guidance clinic in Bristol around 1950 and would speak with a tinge of awe of the clinic psychiatrist, and could not imagine any reason why she would be absent from the weekly referral discussion meeting. Some more rebellious psychologists, I suspect, became difficult and tried to spend more time in schools. Nevertheless, despite occasional attempts to broaden their role – Cyril Burt himself emphasised the importance of research – educational psychologists remained stubbornly entrenched as assessors of children. For my mother the test of choice was the Stanford-Binet (the edition she would have used was published in 1937). The Wechsler Intelligence Scale for Children (WISC), first published in 1949, does not appear to have become popular until later. However, both my mother and father, also an educational psychologist, did regard their role as therapist as important. My father had a particular interest in sand tray (play) therapy. Many years later, when I was training to be an educational psychologist, he stressed to me the importance of listening to the stories of everyone involved in a case. This seemed to me an early example of taking a social constructionist approach. Later reports, such as the Chief Medical Officer's to the Ministry of Education 1956/57, boosted the status of educational psychologists but did not question their role as assessors. This report argued that in the case of educationally subnormal pupils, the appropriate special educational treatment to be provided must be settled largely on the advice of 'other persons', i.e. not only on the medical officer's report. It was not until the mid 1970s when educational psychologists became fully employed by local education authorities while psychiatrists remained within health, that the ties could truly begin to be dissolved. However, I believe, that, even now, educational psychologists can trace some of their current struggles back to the culture of the child guidance clinic.

In 1959 the Mental Health Act reinforced parental rights to query the labelling of their children, and also enforced the cooperation of health and education services by statute. However, this did not change the situation for those children who had been deemed not fit for education. The Education (Handicapped Children) Act 1970 responded to increasing criticism that children were being designated uneducable and confined to health training institutions by declaring that local education authorities should be responsible for all children's education whether or not they had a mental handicap. At a stroke 24,000 children in junior training centres, 8,000 in hospitals, and an unknown number of others at home became entitled to special education. These children were given the description severely educationally subnormal (ESN(S)), compared to those with difficulties who were already in schools who were described as moderately educationally subnormal (ESN(M)). Some 400 new special schools were created nationally which opened up opportunities for educational psychologists and properly started the discussion about inclusion/integration. I have a personal recollection of the effects of the segregationist view of pupils with disabilities (as we would now term them) which gave me cause for disquiet even before I had studied psychology, let alone trained as an educational psychologist. As a teenager I spent one summer holiday volunteering at the Chailey Heritage School in Sussex. This institution was opened by Dame Grace Kimmins in 1903 as part of her work as founder of the Guild of Poor Brave Things, established in 1894, which aimed to provide some education for 'crippled' children. Chailey Heritage was a relatively enlightened place for its day, and I am sure did provide some children with opportunities they would not otherwise have had, but I can still remember being concerned at how some of the children had actually found their way there, why no-one considered they could be educated alongside their non-disabled peers and what would happen to them as adults. In particular I can still picture a four-year-old boy with mild spina bifida (he could walk with crutches), who did not appear to have particularly significant learning difficulties and a six-year-old girl with a cleft palate, but no other apparent difficulty, both of whom had fully residential places at the school.

There was no recognisable route for training to be an educational psychologist in the 1940s, 1950s and early 1960s. Educational psychologists commonly had a degree in psychology (but most would have studied philosophy or social sciences as well), teaching experience and some kind of postgraduate training. However, this was not universal. My parents, both of whom were educational psychologists starting out in about 1950, illustrate this well. My mother, who grew up in Scotland, took a degree in history and after working in London during the war returned to Aberdeen to do an MEd. This gave her a teaching qualification and some psychology. She then taught for a while before applying for her first job in a child guidance clinic. My father, on the other hand, took a degree in psychology and philosophy, taught for a short while and then studied, more as a clinical psychologist, in the psychiatry department at Guy's Hospital. Those who did take the most obviously related postgraduate course of the time, the Diploma in Educational Psychology, would have been exposed to a curriculum the content of which would sound familiar to educational psychologists now, even if the language is uncomfortable. When ferreting around in my father's papers I discovered his lecture notes for such a course, dated 1961/62 (at the time he was teaching at the University of Wales in Bangor). These include such topics as: the history of psychology, special education, the educationally subnormal child (ESN) and remedial teaching, and child development in relationship to stages of schooling. In the lecture on topics of educational psychology, which includes learning, personality development and individual differences, he even makes a note in the margin: 'These are topics which a psychologist must know about; not necessarily what is most relevant and useful for teachers', thus presaging the often stated view that the perspectives of teachers and educational psychologists are different and that it is not always easy for a teacher to make the shift to become a psychologist. However, it is worth noting that a study of the training of educational psychologists in 1972 revealed that while all six institutions questioned provided instruction on, for example, child development and the techniques of assessment, only one appeared to provide anything substantial on research and statistical design.

The absence of a clear training route for educational psychologists at a time when their number was expanding and when there was an apparent acceptance by local authority employers that teaching experience was sufficient to perform the role expected of a psychologist has set a pattern that has had far reaching effects in 1965/66 when the information was collected for the Summerfield Report (see below). Most educational psychologists had trained and/or worked as teachers but 40 per cent had no specific training in educational psychology and 20 per cent had not studied psychology at undergraduate level. The discussion about whether educational psychologists need a teaching background remains to this day, still a debatable point. However, the legacy of the early cohorts of educational psychologists who, on paper at least, appeared not to have a detailed knowledge and understanding of psychology may be more enduring than the profession has been willing to acknowledge. It may have hindered the efforts of the profession to establish itself as applied psychology and to broaden the range of its activities. In his speech to the Association of Educational Psychologists (AEP) in 1964 Cyril Burt said: 'the science of applied physiology, medicine as we call it, has largely been built up on the basis of first hand observations by the practising doctors themselves' and argues that applied psychology and 'educational psychology perhaps most of all' should follow the same path and practitioners work as scientific investigators. Not all of the early educational psychologists may have had the initial training or further professional development which would have given them the confidence and knowledge to pursue this way forward.

A turning point for the training and role of educational psychologists came in 1968 with the publication of *Psychologists in Education Services* (the Summerfield Report: DES, 1968) which made recommendations regarding the duties, training and supply of educational psychologists. The Underwood Report (Ministry of Education, 1955) had suggested that there should be one educational psychologist per 22,000 school children; the Summerfield Report recommended one educational psychologist per 10,000 children and a trebling of the number of educational psychologists in 20 years. In 1965, when the working party that resulted in the Summerfield Report was set up, there were 36 identified specialist postgraduate training places for educational psychologists in England and Wales. (Thus, a trebling of places would bring the total not far off the number of funded training places available today.) While the focus of the duties of an educational psychologist was still assumed to be to assess and treat individual children, there were hints of a wider role. For example, the report indicates that educational psychologists should be available not just to education services but to other services concerned with children and young people, for example pre-schools, training centres, provision for children in care and young people going before the courts and careers guidance. While the report did not suggest that the required training for an educational psychologist should be set out by statute, it did recommend that Government should take central responsibility for the planning and co-coordinating of training facilities. Memos between government officials of the time clearly state that there should be 'immediate' expansion of existing training arrangements. It suggested that two new two-year courses should be established, though financial considerations meant that in the end a one-year Masters course of further training for teachers with psychology degrees became the more common route. While reading the numerous memos flying between officials at the Department of Education, Treasury and those in charge of local government, I was struck by the fact that much of the correspondence involved discussion about finance. This included discussion of the fact that the Local Government Act 1966 contained a specific clause to enable the pooling of local authority expenditure incurred 'in the training of persons to ... become educational psychologists'. Finance, and the mechanisms for identifying funds, are still, of course, the major barrier to establishing a sustainable training route for educational psychologists today.

Following the Summerfield Report there was an expansion of specialist training for educational psychologists and the postgraduate masters qualification replaced the diploma course. Courses were already established at the London Child Guidance Clinic at the Tavistock, Manchester, Birmingham, Swansea and University College London for example. The University of Nottingham established a course in 1967, others started in Exeter and Essex in 1972 and the first two-year Masters course opened at the University of Sussex in 1969.

Throughout the 1940s and 1950s the educational psychologist was, to all intents and purposes, regarded as a technician, carrying out procedures (assessments and sometimes treatments) assisting in decision-making (ascertainment) and, to a lesser extent, contributing to the provision resulting from the decision. However, by the 1960s educational psychologists began to gain confidence and to broaden the scope of their thinking, and their areas of work, both within and without the arena of child guidance clinics. At this time one of the few opportunities professionals working with children had to meet nationally was at the annual Child Guidance Inter-Clinic Conference. The foreword to the proceedings of the 19th of such conferences, held in 1963, notes: 'Psychologists seemed, to many people, to have played a more active role in the conference and this bears out the growing impression that clinic teams are really beginning to deserve that title' (NAMH, 1963). Unfortunately this sentiment was slightly marred by the introductory words of D. Evans, a senior psychologist at the Horsham and Crawley Child Guidance Clinic, who said: 'One of the wise things Dr Kahn [the consultant in charge at Horsham] said last night I think was this: 'Every adult views himself at times as a small and inadequate child.' He is right! ... This is quite an ordeal! Fortunately Dr Pringle says I can be as critical as I like.' Dr Pringle refers to Mia Kelmer Pringle, at the time a senior lecturer in education at the University of Birmingham, previously an educational psychologist in Hertfordshire, who went on to become the first director of the National Children's Bureau.

Dr Pringle was one of a number of educational psychologists in the early 1960s who had grown up from the 'small and inadequate child' to become the challenging adolescent. A number of these psychologists were responsible for founding the Association of Educational Psychologists (AEP). The inaugural meeting of the AEP was held in 1962 at the London School of Economics. Seventy-eight educational psychologists attended and 266 did not attend but signed up to join the new group. Cyril Burt was appointed patron of the AEP in 1964. He was 81 and suffering from 'a passing disability' at the time and so had to send a tape recording of his inaugural speech rather than attend the meeting in person. In his speech Burt stated that 'the work of the educational psychologist is essentially that of a scientific investigator; in a word it is research'. He went on to suggest that causes were probably pretty well understood and so 'the real need is for further research into methods of treatment, particularly the different value of treatment for different cases'. The records of the minutes of AEP committee meetings and the contents of the early issues of the newsletter and then the *AEP Journal* clearly show how, at least, those educational psychologists on the AEP committee were confident and determined to raise both the profile of educational psychologists and establish clearly who they were and what they could do. At every meeting applications to join the AEP were carefully scrutinised. Whilst at the time a significant minority of people working as educational psychologists did not have one or more of the following – a degree in psychology, teaching experience and a post-graduate qualification, no-one would be admitted as a full member unless they met all these criteria. Even Dr Pringle was only able to take up affiliate status, as she was no longer practising as an educational psychologist. Those setting up new courses wrote to the AEP with curriculum details for comment. My father, who was responsible for developing the course at the University of Sussex, sent in his proposed curriculum in April 1968, comments were sent back to him in September and he duly thanked the AEP committee. Unfortunately a year or two later he was in trouble with the AEP for taking on a student who did not have the required teaching experience. The matter was resolved and the committee minutes record that my father, ever the gentleman, had sent in a letter of apology.

In an article entitled 'Child psychology and local government' in the *AEP Journal* in 1976 (Sutton, 1976), Sutton writes: 'Thus there has been increasing concern of late in the continuing high level of school illiteracy, about willful non-attendance and about teachers' inability to control pupils. Immigration from countries of vastly different cultural development has provided problems for the education system which it was totally unprepared to meet.' Sutton goes on to lament the fact that educational psychologists do not seem to be much in evidence in tackling these problems. In 1978 Reid, in an article titled 'Drums in the jungle' (Reid, 1978) talks about educational psychologists 'advancing from the colonial status in which we were held by the medical profession'. Issues of the *AEP Journal* of the late 1960s and early 1970s carry reports on the work going on in various school psychological services. These show that the drive to broaden the reach of services provided by educational psychologists seems to be working. For example, there are references to parent workshops, counseling in secondary schools, research, toy libraries and even radio broadcasts to the community. Titles of the AEP annual courses also reflect the developing reach of educational psychologists. The first course held in 1971 has the relatively bland title of *The Severely Subnormal Child and the Educational Psychologist*. 1972 looks a little more contemporary – *Maladjustment: Clinical Concept or Administrative Convenience*. By 1976 and 1977 we have *Prevention* and *Collaboration beyond the Educational Service* respectively. Strong criticism of the attitude of local authorities to psychology and, by implication, their attitude to educational psychology, was provided by Howells in his book *Remember Maria* (as cited in Gilham, 1978). This title refers to Maria Colwell who was killed by her stepfather in 1973. Howells suggests that Maria's death largely resulted from 'a misconceived professional notion of emotional development'. The contention is that decisions are not made with due reference to research and an up-to-date understanding of child psychology. The potential contribution of local authority educational psychologists was, at best, not recognised and, at worst, ignored.

Alongside the development of the AEP came the rise of child and educational psychology at the British Psychology Society (BPS). The BPS was founded in 1901 as the Psychological Society, changing its name to the BPS in 1906. It was granted a Royal Charter in 1965. This had important implications for the AEP, founded only two years before. As an organisation with a royal charter the Society was no longer allowed to represent its members for negotiations around pay or conditions. This therefore meant that the AEP took on this role representing educational psychologists in negotiations with the Soulbury Committee, still the employers' organisation today. This turned the AEP towards a union role as well as one of a professional association. As early as 1950 the BPS had a committee on the training of psychologists. In 1959 the Committee of Professional Psychologists (CPP) was formed. This gave rise to separate English and Scottish Divisions of Professional Psychologists (EDPP and SDPP). In 1966 the Division of Clinical Psychology was formed and in 1967 the EDPP became the Division of Educational and Child Psychology (DECP). In response to the call for more specific routes to train educational psychologists following the Summerfield Report, the Society introduced the

Diploma in Developmental and Educational Psychology. The BPS did not provide the teaching required but offered an opportunity for psychology graduates to qualify as educational psychologists by passing exams set by the BPS. The first candidates sat the exam in 1978. It is interesting to note that AEP committee minutes of the time show that the AEP had made representations to the BPS to drop 'developmental' from the title of the diploma.

While training, the role of educational psychologists, and the structures and organisations that supported educational psychology in the UK were developing, elsewhere psychologists were working on ideas and doing research that would influence the future development of educational psychologists' professional practice. In 1963 the National Society for the Study of Education in the USA devoted its yearbook to child psychology. Among the contributors were Bandura, writing about aggression and social modeling; Bronfenbrenner, who writes about a possible convergence of Piaget's thinking and social learning; and Kohlberg who sets out his ideas on the development of morality in children. In 1966 Bruner published his book of essays, *Towards a Theory of Instruction*. Piaget published *The Psychology of Intelligence* in 1950 and continued to produce a range of books into the 1960s and 1970s. Vygotsky's *Thought and Language* appeared in 1962, which introduced the now much used social learning theory and 'zone of proximal development'. Here in the UK Bowlby's influential *Maternal Care and Mental Health* was published in 1952. Bowlby's ideas were almost instantly picked up by the psychologists of the day; perhaps because they resonated with the thinking common in child guidance clinics. The others mentioned would take a little while to filter through. They were not so easily assimilated into the thinking that dominated educational psychology in the 1950s and 1960s.

Examples of other ideas that would subsequently influence the practice of educational psychologists emerging at this time included Feuerstein's work with refugee children (as described in Feuerstein, 19809), which would lead to the development of dynamic assessment, and the notion of 'community psychology' already appearing quite frequently as a term in the *Bulletin of the British Psychological Society* by the 1970s. Although Feuerstein first started his work in the 1950s the use of a dynamic assessment model did not become common in educational psychology practice in the UK until the 1980s and 1990s. While some educational psychologists had been expressing dissatisfaction with psychometric assessment for some time, the use of standardised testing was so ingrained in educational psychology practice and so much a key part of the image that other professionals and the public had of them that it would have been difficult to shake off. In the same way, while there were some examples in the 1970s of educational psychologists trying to move their work into the community, this was limited; the effect of the more medical within child deficit approach was, and continues to be, still strong.

The challenging adolescence of the educational psychologists who were more radical, for example some of those who started up the AEP, turned into young adulthood with the publication of *Reconstructing Educational Psychology* edited by Bill Gilham in 1978. In the forward to this book Jack Tizard, Professor of Child Development at the Thomas Coram Research Unit, University of London Institute of Education, lists the three main sources of dissatisfaction with their imposed role (stemming from the Summerfield Report) for educational psychologists at the time: waiting lists and, hence, an individual referral system; disillusionment with the diagnosis/treatment model and a growing realisation that their real clients should be schools and the community, not individual children. The content of the book reflects the potential ways forward: criticism of psychometrics, greater emphasis on an interactionist approach; systems analysis; community psychology and 'giving away psychology'; increase in knowledge and use of research evidence. In the final overview chapter of *Reconstructing Educational Psychology* (1978), Leyden ends: 'The ground clearing of the last five to ten years has made it possible for growth to occur at the level of both infrastructure and superstructure so there are unusual opportunities for development across age levels and hierarchies. Dare we take it – and the responsibility of defining what we mean and what we contribute as psychologists? Or will we remain content in our discontent, forever attributing our condition to the restrictions we perceive to be imposed on us by others?'

The period 1944 to 1978 saw an expansion in the number of educational psychologists but not necessarily an expansion of educational psychologists doing a range of psychology. Those lucky enough to work within a confident school psychological service had more opportunity to do their own thing and develop their practice than those still confined to the hierarchy of the child guidance clinic. This period in the history of educational psychology serves to show how strong the influences of social and political attitudes, the legal framework and the institutions within which people work can be on the development of a profession. The backgrounds of those who first emerged to take on the role of the newly designated profession of educational psychology may also have had a long lasting influence on the attitudes of later educational psychologists and those of the public they serve. The educational psychologists of the reconstruction movement attempted revolution but, as a profession, educational psychology has still not entirely thrown off the shackles that were imposed on it after the Second World War. Educational psychologists are still seen by many as assessors and their primary task that of assessment; the medical profession still sometimes regards itself, and is regarded by others, as of higher status; the debate about whether teaching experience is essential to being an educational psychologist still rages, though reduced by the advent of the three-year doctoral training which does not require a teaching qualification. There is some evidence to suggest that, as Leyden wrote in 1978, educational psychologists are still too 'content in their discontent' to find successful, sustainable ways of navigating the barriers and traps in their path.

Vignette 5
Memories of training in the 1960s

Chris Reeve

The Child Guidance Training Centre was funded by the North West Regional Hospital Board as a child guidance clinic serving the community of north London. It had a couple of full-time psychiatrists who were very eminent – I worked in Lionel Hursove's team (he was editor of the *Journal of Child Psychiatry and Psychology*) – and then there were psychiatric social workers on the staff, trainees from the London School of Economics, two psychologists and four trainee psychologists. It quite appealed to me that the qualification would be recognised by the Department of Education and Skills, it covered children's psychology as well as educational psychology. In theory I could have worked in CAMHS when such things became prevalent as a clinical psychologist working with children.

Well, off Josie and I went to London and lived in one room off the Finchley Road. I've never really stopped to think whether I would have gone to the Child Guidance Centre if I'd had the choice. I've never really regretted taking the option that I did and above anything else I wanted to know all about psychoanalytic methods and see how these people applied them to children's behaviour problems, anxieties and that sort of thing. The way it worked was sort of orthodox child guidance practice of the time with psychiatrists as medical directors and then a psychiatric social worker, two psychologists and one of the trainees doing the assessment report. The traditional psychoanalytic model of child guidance was that the social worker interviewed the parent, the psychologist saw the child and did all sorts of psychometric tests and also carried out liaison with school. Sometimes projective tests were used such as the Bene Anthony Family Relations Test. You did not discuss with the child the reasons for him coming there because the psychiatrists would argue that this might interfere with transference with the child. You were quite often sitting there doing these nice puzzles with a little boy who had been soiling himself all his life. He was fairly happy because he had been expecting a lot worse when his mother had brought him down there and had never discussed that. When he came back to see the psychiatrist a fortnight later he would have a big smile on his face and it had worked. He cured me, those puzzles cured me. I had quite a few smiles at that sort of thing. When you got to the diagnostic case conference for the formulation of a treatment plan, it was quite democratic and well conducted, but I can tell you it's quite challenging to hear you read your report and present what should be happening when you'd got no idea what the other people round the table (and there could be nine or so including observers and visitors) were thinking or going to say. Once the plan was formulated the possibilities opened up quite a lot for people like myself. I helped with the running of some groups with a Jungian therapist and we all had five or six cases of children with learning difficulties that we saw on a weekly basis; one case of mine was an adult aged 22. Interesting things happened during the visits. For example, I spent time in a cerebral palsy clinic and we joined the Tavistock EP trainees for classes in administering and scoring the Rorschach test. Very interesting, the Rorschach test. I don't think I ever used one. I did use the Bene Anthony Family Relations test a few times. We also joined the UCL people for seminars from Grace Rawlings on the assessment of reading, which was interesting, but to this day I remain convinced that EPs know quite a lot about the assessment of reading performance but not enough about the cognitive and perceptual development that underlies that performance.

Chapter 6 Psychology for all: Everything you need to know about why it all went wrong and how to put it right

Jonathan Solity

I worked as a local authority educational psychologist for five years, from September 1979 until September 1984. With the benefit of over almost 30 years' hindsight this was probably the optimal time to work as an educational psychologist. Gillham (1978) edited what became a landmark publication, Leach and Raybould (1977) mapped out a curriculum-based approach for assessing children's difficulties in mainstream schools that explicitly rejected the test-based methodologies of the past and Ainscow and Tweddle (1979) outlined an objectives based curriculum for raising the attainments of lower performing pupils. It all seemed a far cry from the established traditions of I.Q. testing and assessing pupils' suitability for special education.

I was fortunate to find myself working in Walsall which had acquired a reputation for innovative, research-based practice through the pioneering work of its educational psychologists who became national figures in their respective fields of expertise. Jill Gardner, (Gardner et al., 1983) established new ways of working with children who at the time were labelled as having severe learning difficulties. Curricula were mapped out which were based on skill sequences rather than the conventional view of following developmental trajectories. Shirley Bull developed a comparable approach with pre-school children and effectively reframed Portage in terms of the sequences through which identified skills were best taught. Ted Raybould and Dave Tweddle also worked in Walsall alongside Chris Reeve, the Principal Educational Psychologist, who in his early career published a thoughtful book about Freud (McGlashan & Reeve, 1970). Together they provided astute and inspiring leadership to the young and relatively inexperienced psychologists that they recruited.

In terms of behaviour management Kevin Wheldall, a senior lecturer at the University of Birmingham (Wheldall & Merrett, 1984) reported research on how children's behaviour was managed largely through altering the consequences that were seen to maintain unwanted behaviour and replace them with alternatives that would facilitate more acceptable behaviour. Over time there was a gradual shift in emphasis that marked a departure from practice that was associated with behaviour modification to a greater focus on the antecedents of behaviour and how they could be organised to encourage acceptable behaviour from the outset and effectively prevent unwanted behaviour. Bull and Solity (1989) was one of the first published accounts in the UK to represent this change in focus, which was also reflected in Merrett and Wheldall (1990) and reinforced through Wheldall and Glynn (1988) and Wheldall and Carter's (1996) behavioural interactionist perspective.

The challenge for educational psychology at this time was to apply the new confidence that emerged to mainstream education and the education of all children, not only to those perceived to experience difficulties. There was a sense of optimism that EPs had the means to achieve something significant and acquire a reputation for being more than psychometricians who controlled children's access to special schools.

In many ways EPs were in the ideal position to demonstrate the value of the knowledge base they brought to the classroom. If they were able to highlight the benefits of the theories on which they drew through their work with the lowest achieving pupils, it seemed eminently plausible, and only a short step, to apply any recommended methodologies to a wider population within mainstream schools. This would have served three potential goals through: (i) reinforcing the value and impact of informing the teaching and learning process with psychological theory and research; (ii) raising the attainments of all children; and (iii) formulating a strategy aimed at preventing the occurrence of difficulties in learning. Ultimately realising such goals would not only have had a huge impact on all aspects of the professional practice of EPs but also had significant implications for schools, their perceptions of lower achieving pupils and the teaching and learning process within Key Stages 1 and 2. So why were the aspirations of many EPs to apply psychological theory, research and instructional principles to teaching more widely not fulfilled?

This chapter will examine why educational psychologists have worked almost exclusively within the field of special education and outline an alternative scenario and the knowledge base required to facilitate such a change. Although this chapter focuses on the contribution and influence of EPs within mainstream education, in particular the way that all pupils throughout Key Stages 1 and 2 are taught reading, writing, spelling and maths, no judgements should be inferred about their contributions elsewhere. Whether or not they have impacted significantly within the field of special education and teaching children perceived to have disabilities is another matter and not the focus of what follows. However, their endeavours in these areas would have been enhanced had they worked more constructively and systematically within the mainstream sector and applied psychology more effectively to a wider range of children than those perceived to have problems.

Why have the activities of educational psychologists been confined to special education?

EPs have devoted much of their professional lives to identifying and assessing the needs of children thought to be experiencing difficulties in learning and to determining the most appropriate provision to meet those needs. This has invariably involved making decisions about whether children were best placed in mainstream schools or would benefit from the help on offer within the special school sector through their smaller classes and the greater individual support available. The 'Special Education' forms (SE1-4) introduced in the mid-1970s and the 1981 Education Act reinforced this role formally through their assessment requirements. Although this view may not reflect the full extent of the professional practice of EPs there is little doubt that they have devoted much of their time to the needs of children who are failing or experiencing difficulties in learning in one form or another.

EPs' focus on those with problems has effectively confined their sphere of influence to the field of special education. It has been argued (Solity & Shapiro, 2008) that they are effectively no more than glorified SENCOs and allowed themselves to become marginalised within the field of education. It has also been suggested that the concept of special needs is a convenient psychological defence mechanism and that the whole concept of special education is potentially discriminatory (Solity, 1991; 1992). It allows those working within the field of education (politicians, administrators, teachers and EPs) to ignore the shortcomings within the system, and in what and how children are taught, and claim that children fail to learn because of their difficulties.

Theoretical models underpinning the work of educational psychologists

EPs have been sucked into the world of special education, in part, because of the theoretical models that have informed their practice. Cognitive psychology has focussed on within child factors to explain academic success and failure. It was assumed that children's learning was determined, to a considerable extent, by their ability and overall capacity to learn and that measures of children's cognitive functioning and IQ would provide a reliable guide to their potential learning outcomes. A failure to learn would lead to a variety of cognitive assessments and should children perform poorly, it was assumed that a lack of progress was attributable to them having a difficulty in learning. So the psychological frameworks and explanations for low attainments were articulated within a deficit model; children failed to learn because they lacked the essential abilities to master core literacy and numeracy skills (Solity & Raybould, 1988).

Skinner (1966) was for many years a lone voice in suggesting that a child's failure to learn was the responsibility of the teacher and their chosen methodology. He was concerned to develop methods of teaching that would prevent the occurrence of learning difficulties. His optimistic starting point, that every child would learn if the teaching was right, was rarely endorsed or accepted within the educational community. In the late 1970s Yorkshire Television made a documentary about Skinner, *A Change in Mind: The Autobiography of a Non-person*, in which he consented to a series of interviews with journalist Austin Mitchell, who later became a long-serving Labour MP. Skinner believed that the key to understanding behaviour was to understand the environment.

> *If you want to be a good teacher you have got to have the student teach you what to do. The student is always right. If the student isn't learning it isn't the student's fault it is the teacher's fault. If the student isn't learning the teacher has not created an environment in which students learn. You must let the student specify the conditions under which the student will then actually learn.*

Skinner's position appealed as it offered an alternative explanation for learning failure that reflected concerns about the practice of many EPs who devoted their time to conducting IQ tests on children perceived to have difficulties to determine whether they had the potential to be taught successfully within the mainstream sector. Brian Simon's eloquent critiques of IQ testing (1978, 1985) were persuasive and offered a theoretical motive for developing alternative approaches to working with lower achieving pupils and identifying and assessing their educational needs. So EPs increasingly explored the potential role of behavioural psychology in their work in schools.

Task Analysis, behavioural objectives and precision teaching

Skinner's approach had an enormous impact on the practice of EPs who embraced its philosophy and developed methodologies to reflect its positive outlook. These focussed on getting the curriculum right, which was attempted through a process known as task analysis. Here curriculum objectives were analysed and broken down into a series of small, manageable steps which were expressed in terms of clearly identifiable observable behaviour with explicit criterion for success. The approach was initially described by Leach and Raybould (1977) and was then followed by Ainscow and Tweddle's (1979) account of how they had developed objectives-based curricula in a special school in Walsall, where Mel Ainscow was the headteacher and Dave Tweddle the visiting the psychologist. Both books were highly influential, and although they could be seen to be focussing on children with difficulties, the implications for mainstream education, and teaching all children, were inescapable.

Paradoxically, had these initiatives appeared 25 years later they may have had a greater impact in the mainstream sector. Unfortunately, they emerged at a time when there was a backlash against objectives-based curricula and clearly specified learning outcomes. Curriculum theorists such as Kelly (1982) and Stenhouse (1975) argued that it was impossible to reduce learning to read or write to a series of sequentially arranged objectives. Ultimately it was felt that they failed to capture the essence of what it is to be a true 'reader' or 'writer.' It was also argued that teaching phonics was reductionist and contradicted the theories of Smith (1973, 1978) and Goodman (1986) who were increasingly persuasive in stating the merits of whole language approaches to teaching reading rather than phonics. Thus, there was considerable resistance within the mainstream sector amongst local authority advisors and inspectors to the behaviourally orientated approaches being advocated by EPs.

A potentially less contentious manifestation of behavioural psychology in mainstream schools was the use of Precision Teaching. The first UK accounts of Precision Teaching appeared in the early 1980s (Raybould, 1984; Raybould & Solity, 1982; Solity & Bull, 1987) following its introduction into the UK by Brian Roberts who was a tutor on the University of Birmingham Educational Psychology Training Course. He had been on a sabbatical at the University of British Columbia in Vancouver and while there met Marg Csapo who had both written about Precision Teaching and developed materials to be used by teachers. Brian Roberts had a strong sense that Precision Teaching could be of value to psychologists in the UK and so returned from Canada with articles and materials which he passed on to his fellow tutor, Ted Raybould, who then explored its potential role in schools.

The immediate appeal of Precision Teaching was that it mapped on to schools' existing curricula and did not require them to make whole sale changes in either what or how they taught. Precision Teaching, despite its name, is not a method of teaching but a way of evaluating whether or not what is being taught is impacting on children's learning. When used creatively it was possible to identify appropriate learning outcomes, irrespective of the educational philosophy being pursued by teachers, which could be monitored through the timed assessments that were integral to Precision Teaching.

Precision Teaching is a term that accurately describes the processes that it embraces. The philosophy it extolled was to refine and improve the quality of what was taught and the teaching methodology, in response to evidence collected in the classroom on children's learning. Teachers were effectively being shown how to become classroom-based researchers so that they could adapt and amend their teaching in response to children's learning. Ultimately the quality of teaching improved and became more 'precise' and effective in meeting children's needs. Unfortunately, the name also caused confusion as it was not a teaching approach and so some psychologists argued that it might be better called Precision Recording to reflect what it actually did; help teachers to record children's progress.

Therein lay a fundamental problem with the practice of EPs in attempting to exert an influence on mainstream education. Paradoxically, through trying to make an approach to teaching and learning more accessible for teachers they changed its fundamental nature, which it can be argued then made it less likely to be adopted on a wide basis. In part this was because the instructional principles on which Precision Teaching is based were effectively ignored and so were less likely to be applied in mainstream classrooms.

Assessment-through-teaching and finding out what works

Precision Teaching reflected a broader approach to assessing the impact of teaching which was known as assessment-through-teaching (or curriculum-based assessment) that offered an alternative, and potentially psychologically more rigorous approach to assessment than that addressed through one-off psychometric and normative assessments. Here it was argued that in the absence of clear, definitive, information on a child's learning history and how they had been taught, low attainments could not in themselves be taken as evidence that a child had a difficulty in learning (Solity, 1993, 1996). This could only be done through monitoring a child's progress over time in response to: (i) an appropriate curriculum; (ii) theoretically rigorous teaching methodologies; and (iii) regular and systematic assessments of children's progress.

These areas were all addressed within assessment-through-teaching, where it was accepted that if the teaching was right, children would learn. Only in the event of them failing to progress in response to the best possible teaching could it be suggested that they had a difficulty in learning. This of course then raised the question of what is the most effective instruction available to mainstream teachers. This was as ever a highly contentious issue because the conventional wisdom within the field of education is that there is no such thing as a one size fits all and that what works for one child may well not work for another. Furthermore, it was also argued that conducting randomised controlled trials within the field of education to establish the most effective curricula and teaching methodologies was incredibly problematic (Hammersley, 2002; Hargreaves, 1994, 1997). So not only was it claimed that there was no evidence that one way of teaching was more effective than another, the means through which this could potentially be demonstrated, were dismissed as impractical and unrealistic.

This may explain why the National Literacy Strategy (NLS: DfEE, 1998) was introduced to all schools in 1998 without any experimental empirical evidence to suggest that it would be effective. Similarly all the changes and programmes that were subsequently introduced (Playing with Sounds, Progression in Phonics, Letters and Sounds) also lacked a strong evidential base. Equally all but one of the synthetic phonics programmes which are eligible for matched government funding of up to £3000 in the Phonics Catalogue (ESPO, 2011) have no research to support their claims for their efficacy. In fact this is effectively acknowledged by Oxford University Press (OUP), the publisher of Read Write Inc, one of the programmes in the Phonics Catalogue, who only claim that the relationship between Read Write Inc and improved SATs performance is correlational rather than causal. The research underpinning the one programme (*Phonics Bug*, Johnson & Watson, 2010) that has been researched (Johnson & Watson, 2004, 2005) has been heavily criticised (Wyse & Styles, 2007) on numerous grounds but particularly in relation to its methodology, assessment methods and the legitimacy of the conclusions that were drawn.

The lack of experimental research to support educational interventions has been well documented over the years by David Hargreaves (1994) amongst others. He highlighted numerous limitations in much educational research. His most trenchant criticisms targeted the (i) lack of experimental evidence to support teachers' classroom practice where 'there is rarely any scientific basis for what the teacher chooses to do', and (ii) various government's reluctance to test out educational policies before implementing them. Interestingly the report on the project that piloted the NLS did recommend that it should be trialled experimentally but the advice was never accepted by the newly elected Labour government of 1997 (Ofsted, 1998). It is inconceivable that we would give our children medicine that had not been subjected to randomised controlled trials. It is difficult to understand why comparable requirements are not demanded of educational interventions, especially when so much public money was invested in the literacy and numeracy strategies over the years and is now being pumped into synthetic phonics programmes.

Direct Instruction and DataPac (Daily Teaching and Assessment – Primary Aged Children)

However, there have been large scale evaluations in the United States, particularly of interventions to raise standards of students from financially disadvantaged backgrounds. Headstart in the 1960s targeted preschool interventions to boost children's attainments before they entered formal education and this was followed by Project Follow Through which focussed on interventions for school-aged students (Rhine, 1984). Project Follow Through compared different programmes and looked at students' attainments across a range of measures that included reading, maths and language. Overall the most effective interventions were those based on the principles of Direct Instruction which consistently outperformed the others on all the dimensions measured. The Direct Instruction programmes used in the research were published commercially and appeared under the name DISTAR (Direct Instruction Systems for Teaching Arithmetic and Reading) and covered the teaching of reading, maths, spelling and language. They incorporate scripted lessons so that teachers were told what to say and how children were expected to respond. However, although hugely successful and highly economical, because all the teaching was conducted on a whole class basis and supported by quasi-experimental research, it was generally felt that Direct Instruction programmes in the form of DISTAR would have a limited appeal in the UK due to their prescriptive nature.

Perceptions about the potential applicability of instructional materials based on the principles of Direct Instruction were substantially revised following two seminal conferences on Direct Instruction at the Worcester College of Education in the early 1980s, organised by Roger Cocks, who had been an educational psychologist in Walsall before becoming a lecturer in educational psychology at the college. He invited the authors of the DISTAR programmes to talk about the principles of Direct Instruction rather than the programmes themselves. The conferences were memorable for three reasons. First of all the principles of Direct Instruction were made explicit in such a way that it became clear how they could be applied to classroom practice in the UK in the absence of the DISTAR programmes. Secondly, the individual principles themselves were supported by a wealth of experimental data. Thirdly, the principles addressed one major limitation in programmes derived from a typical, behavioural task analysis through enabling students to generalise and apply their knowledge to different problems or contexts in a way that task analytic programmes could not.

A typical task analysis examined skills in isolation and did not make potential connections explicit. So for example, when teaching maths, separate analyses were conducted for addition, subtraction, multiplication and division. An analysis of these four skills based on the principles of Direct Instruction had a different starting point. The first step in the analysis was to identify what was common to all four operations and then devise a teaching methodology to teach the features of addition, subtraction, multiplication and division that were the same and essential component skills of each operation. This led to the development of an instructional strategy that had a series of initial steps that were the same for teaching addition, subtraction, multiplication and division. This different starting point meant that it was possible to teach children to generalise and apply their knowledge; it was built into the instructional design in a way that was not addressed within task analysis.

Engelmann and his colleagues reinforced Skinner's general message about academic failure and probably went further than any other group of researchers and psychologists in arguing that a failure to learn reflected the quality of the learning environment rather than a child's inherent difficulties. They argued that if the teaching was right children would learn and wrote persuasively on this theme. Engelmann (1992) referred to learning difficulties as a form of 'academic child abuse' and the book that he co-wrote with Doug Carnine (Engelmann & Carnine, 1982) became a seminal text for EPs wanting to apply the principles of Direct Instruction to the classroom. Two other authoritative books also had a significant effect on the thinking of a number of psychologists and guided EPs through the complexities of instructional theory as they explored its consequences and implications for the everyday practice of teachers; one was on Direct Instruction Reading (Carnine et al., 1997) and the other on Direct Instruction Maths (Stein et al., 1997).

The courses in Worcester, the growing recognition that instructional principles could be applied to the classroom without recourse to DISTAR materials and feelings of unease about the potential impact of curricula based on behavioural objectives, provided the impetus for one of the most highly ambitious attempts to influence the practice of EPs and steer them towards assessment-through-teaching and curricula derived from Direct Instruction. In 1981

Dave Tweddle was appointed to a new lectureship at the University of Birmingham to coordinate the in-service training opportunities for experienced psychologists. It was the first post of its kind nationally and represented a bold and innovative attempt to develop the practice of EPs across the country. One of the first projects undertaken was the preparation of materials known as DataPac (Ackerman et al., 1983), that were developed over a two-year period with psychologists drawn largely from local authorities in the West Midlands. Their task was to develop curricula for teaching, reading, spelling, and maths, based on the principles of Direct Instruction, that could also serve as a basis for the systematic, formative assessment of children's learning.

Two groups of psychologists were seconded from their local authorities to work at Birmingham University in developing, trialling and then training their colleagues in the use of the materials. It was a major undertaking and no mean feat to train psychologists nationally in this way, to introduce them to the principles of assessment-through-teaching and Direct Instruction across the country. Until this point a number of psychologists (for example, Tim Jewell and Steve Booth in Oldham who developed PETSL – Precise Educational Techniques for Slow Learners: Booth & Jewell, 1983; Booth, 1984) attempted something comparable in their own authorities but they never had the wide-scale reach and impact of DataPac.

Thus, by the mid-1980s the practice of EPs was beginning to look quite different from 10 years earlier. Psychometric assessments were viewed less favourably and were less likely to be undertaken, particularly by newly trained EPs; high quality materials had been developed and disseminated to educational psychology services around the country; there was a growing body of research employing randomised controlled trials that was highlighting the major difficulties experienced by children failing to learn to read and Precision Teaching was seen to be a helpful approach that readily mapped on to a school's existing curricula and teaching approaches.

Where did it all go wrong?

The sense of optimism that emerged in the 1980s in response to these developments was relatively short lived and never led to a sustained change in the practice of EPs as far as mainstream schools were concerned. So where did it all go wrong? It is interesting to speculate on how many psychologists trained over the last 15–20 years have ever heard about DataPac, let alone become familiar with its contents. Some possible reasons are now offered.

The wrong theory?

It began to go wrong from the outset when EPs learnt the 'words' associated with Direct Instruction but not the 'tune.' They knew what to say and how to implement DataPac programmes as a result of the high quality training that accompanied their introduction, but they did not embrace its theoretical origins and underpinnings. Similarly, they were perfectly competent when introducing behavioural programmes involving the use of task analysis and Precision Teaching but never fully accepted the accompanying explanation that the reason that children failed to make progress was because of what and how they were being taught. Too often when children's progress on a DataPac programme was not satisfactory they were seen to be the problem rather than there being any possible limitations in DataPac or the way in which it was implemented. This was in part because many EPs were still wedded to a theoretical model of teaching and learning that focussed on the individual cognitive differences between children as the probable explanation for their learning failure.

Uncomfortable assumptions

There is always an uncomfortable implication associated with Direct Instruction and behavioural curricula which is possibly why they were not endorsed long-term, since ultimately teachers are responsible for children's learning. A failure to learn is seen as a failure to teach, which was far less comfortable than to assume that a failure to learn was in fact attributable to limitations in the capacity of children to learn. This was not to imply that it was the teachers' fault. They were invariably doing their best and were at the end of a long line of professionals who were responsible for the quality of teaching and what children learned. Just as today, the ultimate responsibility for what and how children learn lies with government Ministers, authors of synthetic phonics programmes, reading schemes and maths programmes and their publishers. Equally, where psychologists were advising teachers about what and how to teach they too were directly responsible for children's learning and were potentially 'the cause' of learning failure.

1981 Education Act
The period of optimism coincided with the introduction of the 1981 Education Act which followed the Warnock Report (DES, 1978) that estimated that approximately 20 per cent of pupils would have special needs at some point during their school careers. The Act led to a rapid increase in the number of psychologists required by local authorities to fulfil their statutory role: to complete an assessment of children's needs and advise on the nature of any difficulties and the most appropriate provision to meet them. The Act, from the perspective of instructional psychology, took psychologists away from preventive work and curriculum development with schools towards identifying and assessing individual needs which consolidated their role within the field of special education.

The 1981 Education Act was a major factor in EPs spending an increasing amount of their allocated mainstream time on children perceived to have difficulties which potentially reduced any tensions with local authority advisors and inspectors who saw it as their territory and role to advise schools on the teaching of reading and maths. This was a view that was probably shared by the majority of teachers and local authority administrators as well. Psychologists were seen to be the experts in child development and learning difficulties and not how to teach and assess reading or maths, except where low achieving pupils were concerned.

The National Literacy and Numeracy Strategies and the myth of one-to-one teaching
The launch of the NLS in 1998 and National Numeracy Strategy (NNS: DfEE, 1999) in 1999 only reinforced the general view that teaching reading and maths were nothing to do with EPs. Significant funds accompanied the introduction of the strategies so that local authorities could appoint large numbers of literacy and numeracy consultants to train and advise teachers.

The strategies also embraced a three-wave intervention model for meeting the diverse range of educational needs that teachers were expected to encounter in schools. Wave 1 comprised the delivery of the literacy hour on a whole class basis, Wave 2 were group-based interventions for children that failed to make adequate progress and Wave 3 were individual interventions for the lowest performing children, which is where EPs focussed their attention. Remarkably, yet again, the universal panacea for the lowest achievers was seen to be one-to-one teaching. Has there been a more enduring myth in the fields of special education than the belief than children perceived to have difficulties need individual teaching? To my knowledge there is no published research that has demonstrated this to be the case. On the contrary, Reading Recovery which is a highly expensive, one-to-one intervention has been the subject of considerable controversy as its benefits are open to question (Reynolds & Wheldall, 2007) and research into the impact of teaching assistants (TAs), who typically deliver interventions to low achieving pupils, has suggested that they are largely ineffective (Blatchford et al., 2011; Hattie, 2009). From an instructional perspective the progress of all children, not only the lowest achievers, is dependent on what and how they are taught, not the availability of one-to-one teaching and additional resources. Yet the majority of EPs endorsed the use of one-to-one teaching without question and left decisions about what and how to teach to central government, schools, teachers, literacy and numeracy consultants, local authority advisors and inspectors and publishers of reading, phonics and maths programmes. In many ways it is remarkable that EPs colluded with practices for which there was no evidence, only conventional wisdoms, and generally ignored the fact that in the few instances where credible evidence informed the literacy strategy it was conducted by psychologists.

Educational psychologists and teaching reading: 'That's nothing to do with us'
It is unclear why EPs were so willing to allow all those working in local authorities to hi-jack the responsibility for teaching reading and maths and position themselves firmly in the special needs world. There are few areas where psychologists have undertaken more detailed and systematic research than in reading and yet EPs did not appear to grasp the potential opportunities that this created. For example, Stannard and Huxford (2007) who were instrumental in launching the NLS have written somewhat defensively about its origins. Many of the methods and programmes it introduced to schools were not supported by any experimental evidence and yet at no point during the 15-year life of the NLS did local authority EPs publish articles challenging the practices that it introduced to schools, identify its flaws from an instructional perspective or argue that it was the cause of learning failure. In fact it was left to Ofsted (2012) to draw attention to the fact that methods such as guided reading were blindly adopted by schools without there being any evidence on their impact.

Yet the psychological research (for example, Bradley & Bryant, 1978; Goswami & Bryant, 1990; Snowling & Hulme, 2011) went a long way towards identifying the critical skills involved in learning to read, and Siegel (1992), Stanovich (1991, 1994) and Stanovich and Siegel (1994) questioned the validity of IQ testing and adopting discrepancy definitions of dyslexia. EPs have probably never had a better opportunity to question the non-experimental research methods on which much classroom practice was based and offer a psychologically rigorous, research based alternative derived from experimental and quasi-experimental studies.

What's the alternative? Instructional psychology: A different theoretical starting point

I have argued that despite their best efforts EPs have had little impact on how children are taught reading, writing, spelling, language or maths in mainstream schools. In fact the profession seems to be in pretty much the same position now as it was when I left almost 30 years ago. Although training is longer and most psychological services undergo what seems like an annual reorganisation, what EPs are doing in mainstream schools is pretty much the same as they have always done. Presumably this scenario exists out of choice and the majority of EPs would prefer to be located within the field of special education. Working more broadly within mainstream schools would be both challenging and demanding and require EPs to acquire considerably greater knowledge of theory and research into teaching reading, writing, language, spelling and maths. Yet the need for coherence, clarity and evidence based practice in mainstream schools has never been greater. The rationale for government led curriculum change is as capricious as ever and reflects a swinging pendulum with methods coming in and out of fashion with predictable regularity. The gap between the attainments of children from higher and lower income families has increased and attempts to raise standards all too often focus on school structures and organisational change, although the evidence from international studies into effective school systems (Jensen et al., 2012; Mourshed et al., 2010) indicates that focusing on the quality of teaching and learning should be the priority when attempting to bring about substantial changes in children's learning.

So will the practice of EPs look any different in 2113? My talk at the annual DECP Conference of 2003 ('How Many Educational Psychologists Does It Take to Change a Lightbulb?') asked whether EPs would ever change their practice in mainstream schools and I concluded that the answer was probably not. Ten years down the line I have not heard or read anything by EPs to lead me to revise my prediction. Nevertheless, I remain convinced that EPs could have a significant impact on the learning opportunities and experiences of children in mainstream schools. However, this will probably not happen until it is recognised that the low attainments of the majority of children perceived to have difficulties are the result of their educational and financial backgrounds, and the way they have been taught, not their capacity to learn.

I have described in various books (Solity & Bull, 1987; Solity & Raybould, 1988; Powell & Solity, 1989; Solity, 2008) and articles (Solity & Vousden, 2009; Solity & Shapiro, 2008; Vousden et al., 2011) how instructional psychology offers a different starting point for the professional practice of EPs and that it is underpinned by theory and nearly 20 years of classroom-based research. Most significantly it attempts to meet the educational and learning needs of all children, rather than just those identified as potentially having learning difficulties. The following section summarises its theoretical origins, highlights a number of key research outcomes and then considers the implications of instructional psychology for the future practice of EPs and the advice they offer to schools.

Instructional psychology and teaching reading: Origins and rationale

Instructional psychology has its origins in areas of psychology that focus on the teaching environment in attempting to understand human cognition. It draws on 'rational analysis', which shifts the emphasis from inducing what happens 'in the mind' to looking at the structure of the environment and how it influences cognition (Anderson, 1990) and so is entirely compatible with both Direct Instruction and behavioural psychology. Anderson argues that what we learn mirrors the structure of the world and that we adapt to the environment in a predictable and statistical manner. Thus, competent readers develop skills in such a way that what they learn reflects the structure of written English and the frequency of occurrence of graphemes and the phonemes that they represent. It follows that a key task in teaching reading is how best to characterise the (statistical) regularities in written English and represent them to those learning to read so that their performance becomes statistically optimal. This reflects the optimal reading hypothesis and Pareto's law (also known as the '80/20 principle') which proposes that 'a minority of causes, inputs or effort usually leads to the majority of the results, outputs or rewards'. It appears that there is a large corpus of written English that is far more consistent, regular and predictable than is typically assumed and can be read by acquiring a relatively small number of high-frequency words and grapheme–phoneme correspondences (GPCs). Equally there is a small component of written English that is far less consistent and predictable and can only be read through acquiring a large number of high-frequency words and GPCs.

One area of research within instructional psychology has focussed on an analysis of the knowledge that children have to be taught so that it can be organised and structured in such a way to facilitate children's learning, in particular their capacity to understand, generalise and apply their knowledge. It is this analysis that provides a different, and distinctive starting point for the practice of educational psychologist. As will be seen, interventions derived from instructional psychology have little in common with the advice that EPs typically offer teachers when assessing children's educational needs. This can be seen quite clear in the area of reading.

Solity and Vousden (2009) report an analysis of databases containing adult literature, children's real books and three reading schemes with slightly different underlying philosophies. The 100 most frequently occurring words in written English accounted for approximately 50 per cent of the word tokens in the databases and occurred as often in the children's real books as reading schemes and surprisingly most often in adult fiction and non-fiction. Similarly, the most frequently occurring GPCs occurred as often in the adult literature and children's real books as the reading schemes that had specifically been written to include examples of these skills for children to practise. The database of children's real books has now been extended and currently includes almost 1000 books and contains approximately 700,000 words. Again 100 words account for over 50 per cent of the word tokens and a relatively small number of GPCs account for the majority of phonically regular words.

These findings were unexpected given the conventional wisdom that reading schemes, rather than real books, give children the necessary opportunities to practise reading high-frequency words and commonly occurring GPCs. Furthermore, real books: (i) expose children to a wider vocabulary and broader general knowledge than can ever be achieved through reading schemes and so go some way towards helping children from language impoverished backgrounds to bridge the 32 million word gap that exists with their peers from more language rich backgrounds (Wolf, 2008); (ii) enable lower achieving pupils to access the texts they most want to read so that reading is no longer a chore (see Ofsted, 2004); and (iii) foster a love of reading which has been identified by Ofsted (2012) as a major problem in current practice in teaching reading. Finally, the real books database has not only provided an analysis of children's literature and identified the core skills that children need to be taught but also identified the books that give children the most opportunities to practise any specific phonic or whole word reading skills that they are being taught.

The clear instructional implication is that it is preferable to teach children to read exclusively through real books rather than reading schemes. Yet how often is this recommended by EPs? Is it likely to happen in the future now that schools receive government funding to use synthetic phonic programmes whose authors have confirmed that:

> *This product ensures that, as pupils move through the early stages of acquiring phonics, they are invited to practise by reading texts which are entirely decodable for them, so that they experience success and learn to rely on phonemic strategies.*
>
> Department for Education (2012)

An instructional analysis of children's real books also has implications for which skills are best taught and which might be redundant. The frequency of word tokens and GPCs in children's real books reflects Pareto's 80/20 principle which means that children are best taught a relatively small number of core skills. Whereas teaching 100 high frequency words account for over 50 per cent of word tokens, the next 50 most frequently occurring words only enable children to read a further 9 per cent of word tokens. Similarly the analysis revealed that in addition to 26 letter sounds the optimal number of letter combinations (where one phoneme is represented by a grapheme with two or more letters) to teach is 30. However, some popular phonic programmes such as Jolly Phonics, Read Write Inc and Letters and Sounds teach up to 30 additional letter combinations which occur infrequently in children's real books. So although they are necessary to progress through the reading scheme they are largely redundant in relation to the books that children will read that are not part of a scheme. The time spent teaching them is potentially wasted and better spent teaching skills that are useful and widely used, for example, children's language and vocabulary knowledge. The clear implication from instructional psychology is to teach a small, optimal number of high frequency words to be read on sight as well as a relatively small, optimal number of phonic skills. How often is this recommended by EPs?

Instructional psychology and lower-achieving pupils

The instructional paradox states that the only way it is possible to establish whether or not children have a difficulty in learning is to base all teaching on the assumption that they do not. Low attainments cannot be taken as evidence that children have difficulties and that the way they have been taught may well be contributing to their perceived difficulties, if for example, they are taught through reading schemes, never get to read books of their own choice or are taught too many redundant sight words and GPCs. Many children thought to have difficulties have few books at home (Clark & Poulton, 2011) and may have relatively limited experiences of written and spoken language. This starting point is then compounded by asking them to read phonically regular books that are also language impoverished, devoid of meaning and which do nothing to develop their curiosity, imaginations, general knowledge or love of reading. Yet how often do EPs recommend that lower achieving pupils are taught not only exclusively through real books but also where there is no attempt to grade, level or band books according to their hypothesised level of difficulty?

We all know the maxim, 'practice makes perfect' and many will be aware that the figure of 10,000 hours (Gladwell, 2008) is frequently seen to be the minimum amount of time required to perform at the highest levels. However, lower-achieving children when taught through reading schemes have fewer opportunities to read books than their more competent peers. It is usually the case when using reading schemes that children are required to read all the words in any book in isolation before actually receiving the book. By definition, the lower achieving pupils will take longer to master the necessary GPCs and whole word reading skills than their peers and will therefore read fewer books and have fewer opportunities to apply their skills to written English. This then invariably leads to the depressing outcomes reported by Ofsted (2004) about lower-achieving pupils' negative perception of reading and goes some way to explaining England's low standing in international tables when it comes to children reporting whether they read for pleasure (Twist et al., 2003; Twist et al., 2007).

A further challenge to conventional practice and the potential advice of EPs is the finding that lower achieving pupils make better progress, not only in reading, but in maths and writing as well, when taught through differentiated whole class teaching rather than small group or one-to-one teaching (Shapiro & Solity, 2008). This is a consequence of the instructional principles that underpin teaching programmes and methods based on instructional psychology impacting on all children and so enabling higher achievers to make better progress than they would through small group or one-to-one teaching. Yet how often do EPs ever recommend that lower-achieving pupils are taught alongside their peers at all times and not withdrawn or taught on a one-to-one basis?

It is likely that the only way the needs of lower-achieving children will be met is if there is a dramatic change in the way that they are taught and it is clear that in the past EPs have colluded with existing practice and rarely challenged the use of reading schemes and the role of small group and one-to-one teaching. Too often meeting the needs of lower-achieving pupils becomes a resource issue and a matter of securing the funding to provide the 'intensive support' that they are perceived to require rather than (i) focussing on what and how children are taught, in particular the more effective use of differentiated whole class teaching, and (ii) underpinning classroom practice with appropriate psychological theory. Ultimately all the arguments in favour of how the needs of lower-achieving pupils have typically been met are questioned through practice based on instructional psychology.

The instructional analysis conducted in reading has also been undertaken when teaching spelling, writing and maths. In each subject essential, core skills have been identified which enable children to understand, generalise and apply their knowledge broadly in varying contexts. For example, in maths these skills include being taught: (i) that the key task is to balance equations rather than 'get the right answer'; (ii) the equality principle; (iii) where to start balancing an equation; and (iv) how to check an equation balances. In teaching writing our analysis has identified seven generalisable skills that underpin any type of writing. Finally, if EPs are ever to apply their expertise to all children they will have to accept that an essential feature of their professional practice is a thorough knowledge of what and how to teach from a psychological perspective. This is not about acquiring expertise in materials and resources but developing (i) an understanding of instructional psychology and instructional principles and (ii) the ability to analyse and identify the strengths, weaknesses and limitations in how children are typically taught from a psychological perspective. This was illustrated in a recently completed study in a midlands local authority.

The impact of instructional psychology

The project was a three-year evaluation of KRM Reading, which is a substantially revised and updated version of the Early Reading Research (ERR) framework for teaching reading, due to its greater focus on teaching reading through real books, the introduction of a vocabulary component and whole class assessments and the use of a timed PowerPoint presentation. This helps teachers to differentiate their teaching, develop fluency levels and ensure that all skills teaching is effectively interleaved. The aim was to explore whether the results from previous studies could be replicated and so: (i) raise the attainments of both higher- and lower-achieving children; (ii) reduce the incidence of difficulties from approximately 20–25 per cent to less than 2 per cent; (iii) raise the percentage of children with reading ages 12 months or more ahead of their chronological ages; and (iv) demonstrate that differentiated whole-class teaching raised the attainments of lower-achieving pupils to a greater extent that individual or small group teaching.

The progress of children who were taught through KRM Reading in 16 schools was compared to those in 10 schools following a variety of other programmes that reflected the traditional three-wave intervention framework favoured within the NLS. A crucial element in all the training that teachers receive in KRM Reading is follow-up observations in the classroom on treatment fidelity, following the six half-day workshops that take place each academic year (Hattie, 2009). During the first two years of the project when, children were in Years R and 1, all the teachers in the experimental group were observed by EPs with considerable experience in Precision Teaching and Direct Instruction but with one exception, not instructional psychology and teaching reading.

All the observations were completed in Year R but when the children were in Year 1 only 57.39 per cent of the visits were undertaken. When the children progressed to Year 2 it was therefore decided to involve extra EPs with considerable expertise in instructional psychology and teaching reading to ensure all the follow-up observations were completed so that teachers received the essential feedback to ensure treatment fidelity. Thus, the 16 schools in the experimental group were divided into two smaller groups. The first contained the ten larger schools and were supported by the EPs with more experience in instructional psychology and its application to teaching reading. The second group contained six smaller schools that were supported by the EPs with less experience in instructional psychology and teaching reading.

Table 1 shows the results of the baseline and end-of-year assessments on the BAS and Table 2 shows the progress made each year by the experimental and comparison groups. The experimental group made more progress than the comparison group in Year R (10 months compared to 7 months) and Year 2 (17 months compared to 15 months) when all the observations were undertaken whereas the experimental group experienced a dip in progress in Year 1 (13 months compared to the comparison group's 16 months) when nearly half the teachers did not receive the required visits and feedback.

Table 1: KRM and comparison group baseline and end-of-year reading ages

	Baseline	Year R	Year 1	Year 2
KRM Experimental Group	5 years 1 month	5 years 11 months	7 years 0 months	8 years 5 months
Comparison Group	5 years 4 months	5 years 11 months	7 years 3 months	8 years 6 months

Table 2: KRM and comparison group progress (months)

	Year R	Year 1	Year 2
KRM Experimental Group	10	13	17
Comparison Group	7	16	15

However, the significance of the project is the progress made by the experimental group whose teachers were observed by the EPs with greater expertise. Children in their ten schools made 18 months' progress in Year 2 whereas the children in the six schools supported by the less experienced EPs made 14 months' progress. It seems most likely that the enhanced performance of the schools visited by the more experienced EPs could be attributable to their greater knowledge.

Of course there are numerous alternative explanations for the results, one being that throughout the three years of the project the children in the comparison group had more adult contact time than those in the experimental group. In Year 1 the comparison group had almost twice the contact time (93 per cent) than the experimental group, which when coupled with the lack of feedback to teachers in the experimental group, may have contributed to the observed outcomes. Although this is a plausible explanation, it is questionable given the progress made by children in a similar project in an east of England authority over the same time scale. All teachers were observed as required following each workshop. The outcomes in this authority were the same in Years R and 2 as in the Midlands authority but considerably higher in Year 1.

The research results in reading have been replicated by those in maths and writing where interventions based on instructional psychology have enabled all children – higher, middle- and lower achievers – to attain to higher levels than those following the NNS and NLS approaches to teaching writing. Of particular relevance to EPs in potential debates with teachers is the fact that the maths intervention enabled lower achievers in the experimental group to achieve to higher levels than the higher achievers in the control group in division which has been shown to be a predictor of later mathematical success in Key Stages 3 and 4 (Siegler et al., 2012). Finally, children at all attainments levels in the experimental group were better able to generalise and apply their mathematical knowledge than those in the comparison group. So again there is further evidence that teaching a small number of critical skills, directly and explicitly, in ways that are rarely observed in mainstream schools, enable children to attain to higher levels than conventional practice. Results such as these are potentially of great value in meeting children's needs, yet how often do EPs work with teachers to raise standards in maths and writing?

Instructional psychology and the role of the educational psychologist

Instructional psychology provides EPs with the opportunity to work in very different ways with schools largely because the assumptions and practices typically associated with the field of special education are challenged and seen to be highly questionable. The research in rational analysis and the optimal reading hypothesis offer an alternative perspective on the teaching and learning process, the development of inclusive practice and ultimately the role of the educational psychologist. Instead of focussing on children's cognitive development or examining the individual differences between children to provide an explanation for lower attainments, understanding what and how to teach starts with an analysis of what children are expected to learn, which it turns out leads to some surprising and counter-intuitive outcomes.

Given this starting point, how might psychologists work with schools? A pilot project researching an alternative form of service delivery has been conducted in a local authority in the north of England. The EPs participating in the project operate a consultation model and offer schools between 7.5 and 12 hours of visits a year, depending on the perceived needs and size of the schools. Usually this involves holding similar conversations about the cause of children's difficulties, methods of assessment and suitable interventions with requests for advice rarely, if ever, being accompanied by data on the progress and educational needs of either the 'referred' child, or his or her peers.

The EPs, when faced with this scenario began to explore alternative models of offering psychological knowledge and expertise, not only to the children that schools were initially concerned about but to other pupils in their classes. It was felt that a starting point for a different way of working would be to train staff in each school in instructional psychology, instructional principles and assessment-through-teaching so that they could evaluate the impact of their chosen curricula for teaching and assessing reading, writing, spelling and maths, meeting the needs of all children and managing children's behaviour. It was decided to aggregate the time that had been allocated for individual school visits and instead organise fortnightly, half-day, in-service workshops throughout the year that would be available to representatives from all schools. The workshops covered: an assessment of the teaching environment for teaching reading, writing, spelling and maths; baseline assessments of all the children's reading and maths skills; baseline assessments of children's oral reading and capacity to generalise their phonic and whole-word reading skills; an overview of the psychological research on teaching reading, writing, spelling and maths; an analysis of DfE and Ofsted reports on teaching reading, English, reading for pleasure, and teaching maths; a description of the core instructional principles associated with effective teaching; and an overview of managing children's behaviour. Schools were given written materials to support the course content and completed various tasks between workshops that were reviewed at the beginning of each session.

Course participants were informed that the starting point for any intervention is an assessment of the teaching environment, coupled with baseline assessments of children's skills in reading, writing, spelling and maths. These would then form the basis of an intervention using the schools' current approaches to teaching and learning. Where appropriate these could be informed by core principles derived from instructional psychology. Schools were told that if they chose not to participate in the workshops that they would still be required to undertake exactly the same baseline assessments of the teaching environment and children's skills. However, within this scenario schools would only receive their allotted 7.5–12 hours to discuss the results and plan appropriate interventions compared with approximately 50 hours through the in-service workshops. The project has been extremely well received by schools which have been able to meet the needs of lower-achieving pupils but also had the opportunity to increase the attainments of all children. The one consistent comment from all participants is that they feel more confident in their own practice through their understanding of instructional psychology.

There are two final and potentially significant implications of EPs working on a whole school basis. The first is financial and the cost effectiveness of programmes based on instructional psychology. For example the Midlands authority that participated in the evaluation of KRM Reading could save well over £100m each academic year through moving towards differentiated, whole class teaching and away from a three-wave intervention and one-to-one support for lower-achieving pupils. The second is the consequence of dramatically reducing the incidence of pupils seen to have literacy or numeracy difficulties. It considerably increases the EPs' capacity to work with students who have severe and complex needs and not be distracted by all the 'false positive,' who are referred as a result of how they have been taught, not because they genuinely experience difficulties in learning.

Conclusion

This chapter has offered a perspective and critique of how psychologists have worked within mainstream schools over nearly half a century. I have highlighted and questioned the assumptions on which past practice was based and its potential limitations for those wishing to apply psychological theory and research to raising the attainments of all children and not only those perceived to have difficulties. I have suggested that this goal will, in all probability, only be achieved through underpinning practice with instructional psychology and indicated that there are a number of potential barriers for those EPs who wish to develop their practice in this way. In part these relate to their role within the field of special education, the assumptions on which their practice is typically based and their unfamiliarity with instructional psychology and its application to curriculum analysis and the teaching and learning process.

EPs have invariably allowed others working within the field of education to define their professional role within mainstream schools. The contexts in which EPs are now working are very different from any point in the past and many of the local authority staff who challenged EPs' right to talk about the teaching of reading, writing and maths, such as advisors, inspectors and literacy and numeracy consultants are no longer employed by local authorities. It is difficult to predict what the future might look like for EPs. It would be unfortunate if they did not recognise the opportunities that exist for developing and applying their knowledge and expertise widely within mainstream schools. It is potentially significant that Snowling and Hulme (2011) implicitly reinforced the process of assessment-through-teaching, and in so doing partially bridged the gap between cognitive and instructional psychology, in suggesting that recent trends in identifying literacy difficulties have focused on children's 'response to instruction' and 'well founded interventions.' Ultimately, EPs now, as in the past, are potentially the best qualified, most knowledgeable professional group working in schools with considerable knowledge of relevant theory, research and practice. It would be encouraging to think that in the coming years EPs will be able to challenge conventional wisdoms and educational mythology and develop their practice so that they impact significantly on the attainments of all children, to enable them to achieve to levels that will enhance their educational and life opportunities.

Vignette 6

Memories of practice in the 1970s: Was this indeed the optimal time to work as an educational psychologist?

Sue Morris

Memories are, of course dangerous things, comprising merely selective, retrospective constructions of past events, viewed through an inherently distorting lens with some very oblique camera angles and, no doubt, many of the important action sequences missed altogether, or subsequently taped over. This brief personal narrative does not therefore constitute a reliable or necessarily representative account of the way things were. However, I'd agree with Jonathan Solity that the 1970s was a wonderful decade in which to join the EP profession: ours was the 'reconstructing' generation; we were the (appropriately circumspect) hero innovators who shared the vision set out in Gillham's celebrated 1978 text, willingly, and perhaps rather arrogantly, accepting the mantle of responsibility to contribute to the transformation of the profession, within an era relatively untrammelled by intrusive central or local government control over education, or constraints on EPs' interpretation of their role. We aspired to work preventively, in community settings, making our psychologically based knowledge and skills relevant at population level in order to contribute to improved quality of life and outcomes for children and families!

In my current role in the initial training of EPs at the University of Birmingham, I find myself surprised and, indeed, sometimes irritated to read the accounts of contemporary trainees who, while acknowledging the vision of the 'Reconstructing Movement', position my generation, and indeed even EPs of the recent past, as blinkered determinists, focusing exclusively on 'within child' factors, wedded to their psychometric tests, to the exclusion of virtually all else. I can, I'm afraid, recognise this caricature, and indeed, in my postgraduate teaching in the early 1970s I had direct experience of EP practice which conformed to this stereotype. To me, it appeared that both assessment and intervention did indeed often focus on understanding and treating the child as an independent entity, with scant attention to ecological influences on either the lifespan developmental trajectory or current family and school environments. 'Treatment' too was decontextualised, with children referred to child guidance clinics for individual or small group therapy – perhaps with parallels to assumptions underpinning contemporary Health Service Child and Adolescent Mental Health Service delivery.

Meanwhile, as a teacher, I had learned the power of the impact of environmental influences on children's life trajectories, and the leverage of what was later termed 'the school effect' in compensating for both early and enduring disadvantage. I learned, too, how potent was parental partnership in supporting changes in children's lives outside school, and the contingent impact on their presentation and performance in school. Students made great progress in our school; their rate of learning made a mockery of their psychometrically based 'ascertainment' as 'educationally subnormal', and experience suggested that we tended to achieve conspicuously better results in addressing 'maladjusted' behaviour than did the child guidance therapy which was, I regret to say, widely ridiculed by colleagues in my own and other schools.

So much then for my own direct experience of the tyranny of psychometric assessment as the dominant paradigm informing decisions about children's learning capacity and needs for special provision, and dissatisfaction with the value of the clinic-based treatment in which many EPs engaged at this time. These were, however, times of seismic change within the profession: local government reorganisation in 1974 saw EPs emerge from the child guidance clinics to form distinctive School or Educational Psychology Services, while in parallel, in anticipation of and following the 1978 publication of the Warnock Report, the graduated, school-based approach to assessment heralded a shift in professional responsibilities for assessing special needs from health to education professionals, and an emphasis on evaluating learning contexts alongside any assessment of children's attributes.

In the midst of these changes and striking differences in practices within and between EP services, I began my postgraduate professional training year alongside Jonathan at the University of Birmingham in 1978, joining a programme which was both innovative and rigorous: we were steeped in behavioural psychology and its many areas of application within instructional psychology, functional analysis, single case design, and classroom management – to name but a few examples. Moreover, applied behaviour analysis afforded a theoretical framework and repertoire of methods through which EPs could support developments in teaching children with severe, profound and multiple learning difficulties, whose entitlement to education had begun with the start of the decade: a development that has since been transcended, but which was, I think, a significant contribution in its time.

Our ecological and interactionist orientation to practice was further supported by our introduction to systems theory, largely thanks to the pioneering work of Bob Burden, John Thacker and colleagues at the University of Exeter. Placement work and subsequent qualified experience gave many opportunities to develop and apply this theoretical orientation in problem analysis and intervention with individuals, families and groups and, albeit less frequently, in contributing to organisational development projects.

Jonathan has described the vibrant orientation of the University of Birmingham programme at this time, complemented by dynamic and transformational developments in a number of EP services within the West Midlands which were characterised by the confidence, energy, creativity and innovation redolent of the Left Bank during the Impressionist era! The region seemed awash with impassioned practitioner scientists, and evidence of impact of (mostly behaviourally based) curricular innovation, teaching technologies, classroom management practices, social skills programmes, and many other developments was impressive! These were communities of practice which we trainee EPs felt privileged to join, where recently qualified EPs formed accessible role models, many of whom, in my experience and judgment, have kept the flame burning over intervening decades.

However, 1970s EP service norms were not above reproach, even when at their best! I have no recall of receiving or being offered professional supervision in my first years in post, and any consideration of a career-long entitlement to, or requirement for, continuing professional development would have been considered radical indeed.

Importantly, too, in these days before child sexual abuse media scandals and contingent policy development within the UK, while we 1970s EPs were schooled to exclude sensory impairment and medical factors in early investigations of reported difficulties in children's learning or behaviour, it was not until the 1980s that it became routine to weigh risks of abuse, neglect or maltreatment as precipitating factors in our problem analyses. Our contribution to safeguarding children's well-being had some way to go.

Jonathan asks, 'Where did it all go wrong?' It would be my contention that it has not: the profession established some important principles and values in the 1970s which have laid secure foundations for its subsequent development. While I agree that there have been lost opportunities and uneven progress thereafter, and while the current landscape brings unprecedented challenge, from my perspective the profession continues to flourish; I continue to feel privileged to be an EP, enjoying the intellectual rigour, scope for creativity and diversity of practice within different domains and at different levels, and appreciating the great personal professional rewards that are integral to our practice; my commitment, enthusiasm and belief in the potential and actual impact of educational psychology as an art, a science, a craft and a vocation remain undimmed!

Chapter 7 The changing nature of assessment by educational psychologists: Yesterday, today and tomorrow

R.J. (Sean) Cameron & Julia Hardy

'The past is a foreign country: they do things differently there.' L.P. Hartley's opening sentence of *The Go-Between* could also be used to set the scene for any chapter which sought to identify historical trends and milestones in a rapidly developing discipline like psychology. Indeed, in their introductory textbook for undergraduates, published in association with the British Psychological Society, Hewstone, Fincham & Foster (2005) were able to present the convincing argument that psychology had 'lost its mind' with the advent of Watsonian 'Behaviourism' in the post-World War II period, then 'regained it' in 1967 with the publication of Neisser's seminal book *Cognitive Psychology*.

In educational psychology, the appointment of Cyril Burt in 1913 as psychologist to the London County Council (part-time) was clearly a major milestone for the profession. Burt's brief was to advise the educational decision-makers of the day about the education of those children and young people who were 'backward', maladjusted and delinquent, and to these ends he produced several influential reports and policy documents on these groups, together with two highly regarded books that were included in all teacher training programmes for many decades: *The Young Delinquent* (1925) and *The Backward Child* (1933).

In the World War I period and for some years afterwards, Burt advocated the use of a relatively new intelligence test to select out those children who would attend special education schools and those who should be capable of benefitting from a grammar school education, irrespective of the socio-economic status of their families and/or their early childhood learning opportunities. In the early 1920s Burt started to assess the performance of all children in schools, collecting an enormous amount of data based upon teachers' reports, and the Stanford-Binet intelligence test for his research into the genetic-environmental components of human ability, a quest which was later to end in a blaze of controversy, accusations and counter arguments,

From intelligence to cognitive abilities

The intelligence test which Burt had employed for his research had begun to take shape in the earlier part of the century when the French government commissioned the psychologist, Alfred Binet, to develop a method of identifying 'intellectually deficient' children who could be placed in special education. To begin to create their measure of intelligence, Binet and his colleague Theodore Simon had used a list of about 25 'abstract questions' and provided 'appropriate' answers to these. To obtain these responses from children, Binet and Simon (1905) wrote: 'One of us interrogated (the child) while the other wrote the responses or noted the attitude, the play of the facial expressions of the child on the stool. The interrogatory had, moreover, less the appearance of the examination, more of a game which was made with good nature, without dry formulae and during which the child was continually encouraged...' (p.296).

For the completed version, items were grouped into age levels and a child's mental age was deemed to correspond to the highest age level that he or she could complete successfully. Later, when the American version of the Binet–Simon intelligence scale appeared (see Terman et al., 1915), the concept of an intelligence quotient (IQ) was introduced and this gave a measure which was independent of the chronological age of the child, since it was the ratio between 'mental' and chronological ages multiplied by 100 (see Terman & Merrill, 1961).

Clive James, author and TV personality, was on the receiving end of this selection process, and in his autobiography *Always Unreliable* he described the outcome as follows:

> *The big change I could not get out of was being sent to a special school. In Fourth Class at Kogarah, when we were all about ten years old, we took an IQ test. t was the Stanford Binet on which I score about 140. On the more searching Wechsler-Bellevue, I got about 135. Such results are enough to put me into the 98 percentile, meaning that 97 per cent of any given population is likely to be less good at doing these tests than I am. This is nothing to boast about. Intelligence starts being original only in the next percentile up from mine where the scores go zooming off the scale. Time has taught me, too slowly alas, that there is nothing extraordinary about my mental capacities. In my romantic phase, which lasted for too long, I was fond of blaming my sense of loneliness on superior intellect. In fact, were, the causes were, and are, psychological.*

> James (2001, p.55)

In the USA, shortly after the end of World War II, David Wechsler (1896–1981) began to develop a series of standardised intelligence scales that became widely used by psychologists across the world. As well as providing a general IQ score, the Wechsler Intelligence Scale for children (WISC) provided two other measures: verbal ability and performance (Wechsler, 1949). Many of the verbal tasks were similar to those developed by Binet and Simon in the earlier part of the century and most of the performance items had their roots in the non-verbal test batteries which were used for selection by the American Army during World War I. Despite some concerns about adapting adult test material for use by children (see Keir, 1949), the WISC, which appeared in the same year, was a downward extension of the original Wechsler–Bellevue Intelligence Scale for Adults and covered the age range 5–15 years. There were 12 sub-tests (six verbal and six perform-ance) with an optional performance scale sub-test (Mazes) and differences between the IQ figure for an individual child and those of a similar aged sample could be compared by standard scores which had been adjusted to a mean of 100 and the standard deviation of 15.

In 1967 the Wechsler Pre-School and Primary Scale of Intelligence (WPPSI) was published; this was a downward extension of the WISC and designed for children aged 4 to 6½ years. The first UK version of the WISC appeared in 1974 and the most recent (the WISC III UK) was published near 30 years later (Wechsler, 2004).

In the 1950s, 60s and early 70s the cognitive ability testing of individual children and young people seemed to have been central to educational psychology practice, as well as a major component of the procedures that paved children's roads to special school placement, and also an important component of most professional training courses for EPs.

One interesting variant of this process that encouraged the teachers to carry out their own assessments in their classroom emerged from the West Sussex County Educational Committee Psychological Service, which introduced an information booklet for teachers entitled *Assess-ment of Intelligence*. As well as describing the uses of intelligence measures, in this booklet, Labon (1974) was also careful to point out the drawbacks and went on to review a number of intelligence tests for children which were available to teachers in UK schools.

While standardised measures of behaviour problems were less common than measures of intelligence, one interesting attempt to link items on a rating scale with psychopathological problems resulted in the Bristol Social Adjustment Guides (BSAG). These scales were designed to describe a child's behaviour in a number of different settings and items were grouped together into a number of 'syndromes' which included unforthcomingness, withdrawal, depression, hostility towards adults, anxiety, writing off adults and adults' standards, anxiety for acceptance by children, hostility towards children, restlessness, inconsequential behaviour, miscellaneous symptoms, and miscellaneous 'nervous' symptoms (Stott, 1963). All of these previously listed syndromes could be added together to provide a 'total behavioural deviance'. An adaption of the BSAG was included in the first and second of the National Child Development Studies, while a critique of the theoretical model on which the BSAG was based, together with a number of statistical considerations was provided by Ghodsian (1977).

After a 12-year incubation period, the National Foundation for Educational Research published the British Ability Scales, an intelligence test which was standardised on British children aged 2–17 years drawn from various parts of England, Wales and Scotland (Elliott, Murray & Pearson, 1979). Through its 20 sub-tests, each measuring specific types of knowledge, thinking and reasoning and key skills (matching, verbal and visual recall), the BAS attempted to identify the cognitive strengths and weaknesses of children and young people. A unique feature of the BAS was the introduction of Item Sets, based on the use of the Rasch psychometric model. For practitioners, Item Sets had two advantages. The first was time efficiency for the examiner. The second was that, when item sets were used, children's experience of failure was minimised, and their experience of success was maximised.

An example of how the BAS might have been used in the late 1970s to assess the cognitive profile of a child in a school setting, is provided in the case history opposite. Almost 20 years later, a revised version (BAS II) was published (Elliot, Smith & McCullough, 1997) and the most recent version (BAS III) appeared in 2011 (Elliott & Smith, 2011).

The shift from a narrow focus on IQ to a wider spread of cognitive abilities has been reflected in a more recent instrument which is closely linked with a number of contemporary theoretical models in psychology. The Cognitive Abilities Profile (Deutch & Mohammed, 2009) drew its material from Vygotsky's 'Zone of Proximal Development', Luria's (1976) description of mental processes, and Feuerstein's influential ideas on 'dynamic assessment' (Feuerstein, 1990) and focused on three main areas of learning and development: the cognitive abilities of the learner, the learner response to teacher and mediation and an analysis of the task(s).

With the advent of the CAP, it would appear that the historical, single 'g' factor in intelligence has been finally superseded by the new multi-factor, interactive perspective as a psychological explanation of the problems faced by children and young people .

An over-concern with 'within-child' variables?

Constructs such as IQ have remained modest but consistent predictors of success in school attainment; however, they have a number of inherent features that often make applied psychologists feel uncomfortable with their use. By the mid-1970s, debates over the use of IQ and other psychometric tests led to a spate of journal articles with professionally challenging titles such as 'If we throw tests out of the window, what is there left to do?' (Burden, 1973), and 'Silk purses into sow's ears: The decline of psychological testing and a suggestion for its redemption' (Bersoff, 1973). In 1975, Ward summed up the situation as follows:

> For well over a decade, educational psychologists in this country have questioned the dominance played by traditional psychometry in their routine work. Criticisms of the ritualistic use of tests are made at every level of the profession and in a wide variety of context: The cry for less testing and more remediation or treatment echoes at almost every conference and workshop.
>
> Ward (1975, p.380)

In his highly influential book *Reconstructing Educational Psychology* Gillham (1975) raised a number of professional and ethical issues which at first began to challenge (and later to undermine) traditional EP practice and eventually created a movement away from uncritical, within-child assessment. By the 1980s, discomfort with the 'medical' or 'psychometric' model had

---

Case history: Graham (poor speed of information processing)

Graham was ten when he was referred and was attending his local primary school. His teachers were convinced that he had generally above average ability and scholastic achievement. He had good general knowledge, was able to converse at an above-average level with a good vocabulary and was above average at mathematics. However, in class he was very slow at getting work done and frequently complained that the teacher went too fast.

His teacher had kept him in on many occasions during break, lunch time and at the end of school so that he could finish off work. He became very distressed at this and considered he was being punished and he began developing emotional symptoms at home to such an extent that his parents discussed the matter with the class teacher. There was nothing in his behaviour to suggest he was not a generally pleasant and cooperative boy.

Information collected:

On the British Ability Scales, his T scores on various scales were as follows:
Speed of Information Processing – 35
Matrices – 60
Similarities – 71
Basic Number Skills – 67
Word Reading – 63

Discussion

The test results confirmed the school's observation about his above average scholastic and other abilities. He had an unusually low score on Speed of Information Processing, however. Could his problems be related to a specific difficulty in processing information rapidly? The Speed of Information Processing scale was given again, with greatly increased emphasis on speed of performance. He did no better and he made more errors. He was then given a piece of prose to copy, under three conditions: no time stress, moderate time stress and extreme time stress. The number of words written in two minutes under each of the three conditions was obtained and it was found that when under time stress the number of words written did not increase, but the size and untidiness of his writing increased markedly. In other words, in an effort to process the information and copy it more quickly, his pen moved faster but the amount of information actually processed remained much the same.

Recommendations

Brief counselling for all parties concerned – teacher, parent and boy. Reduce pressure on him to allow him time to do work in a non-punitive way. Be prepared for possible trouble with later external examinations which are timed, and pay attention to the most efficient form of strategies.

---

reached increasingly high levels of concern, much of which had come from within the profession itself, where many argued that this approach led to widespread stigmatising labelling of children and concentrated measurement on variables which were not directly related to the learning situation. The latter claim was strongly backed up by the personality theorist Walter Mischel, who declared: 'if human behaviour is determined by many interacting vehicles – both in the person and in the environment – then a focus on any one of them is likely to lead to limited predictions and generalisations...' (Michel, 1977, p.246).

The split among educational psychology practitioners at that time is well illustrated by the response from Jack Wright, Principal Educational Psychologist in Hampshire, to a letter of concern about the introduction of the Cognitive Abilities Test as a countywide screening test from Tim Jewell, then a Southampton University EP in training (and later to become the PEP for the London Borough of Southwark). Both these EPs were highly principled, professional psychologists who held contrasting views of how best to help children succeed in school: the former, who had studied under Burt, believing that positive social change could be brought about by providing education appropriate to a child's measured ability, the latter focusing on the flip-side of ability testing which could lead to labelling, stigma and spoiled identity, and offer few guidelines to improved support.

> *... I agree that if a school is doing its job very well the screening procedure we have suggested, which is minimal, will not add any new information. What it does do is make sure that all our schools look at the various aspects which the screening procedure draws to their attention. We have discussed this question of rating between schools. The kinds of rating scales that we use are only effective in identifying children within schools. This, of course, is their major purpose. The idea is to help the teachers identify the children within their own school for whom more help might be given by them in their own school situation. For a minority, however, the screening will identify them as possibly needing help beyond that which can be provided in a school through using facilities in special education, etc. When we wish to make comparisons from one school to another, as when a secondary school takes in pupils from a wide catchment area, some form of objective normed test is needed. No rating scales, I think, can easily be used in a way that is fair to schools with very differing catchment areas. We have had many comments on our screening and will be revising this in the near future – we are not happy with the present scheme.*
>
> *I note the comments you make that some teachers say it will be difficult to devise a school programme based on the CAT results. I would think it amazing if they could. It would be equally impossible to base a school programme on a child's age, as is suggested in the Education Act, but clearly both age and ability are factors that help one in the complex task of devising an adequate curriculum for a child. Indeed, the Education Act makes it clear that Education Authorities should provide education according to a pupil's age, ability and aptitude. I imagine if the Act were written today the terminology might well be in terms of educational need (which would subsume the older concepts). I have met this criticism of tests on innumerable occasions. As I once commented to Sean, the planning of a curriculum and the techniques by which teachers can help children to learn, and indeed to learn how to learn, are resolved not by tests but by a three-year, at least, initial training, some years of experience, and some further in-service education, including, if children have difficulties, a one-year special course as recommended by Warnock. I would find it a miracle if any tests could in fact achieve such profound objectives. This, however, is not to argue that the tests haven't a quite valuable and useful contributory role to play in providing some background information around which the planning occurs and provided that they are clearly seen as 'means to an end' not ends in themselves...*
>
> Yours sincerely, H.J. Wright, Principal (dated 28 December 1978)

The arguments in Bill Gillham's book also coincided with similar concerns from outside the profession: in an increasingly diverse population, many cognitive ability tests were viewed as culturally unfair, since a child from a different cultural background might not have had the previous Western-biased experiences that were taken for granted in these tests, nor were they likely possess a competent mastery of the language used in an assessment situation, and they might even lack the language conventions required for an encounter with an interviewer. The role of psychometric testing in special education came under increasing pressure due to the over-representation of African Caribbean pupils in schools for children with moderate learning difficulties in Inner London, where local councillors and policy makers began to lay the blame for this unacceptable situation squarely on decision making which depended to a considerable extent on psychometric testing.

More graphically, some psychologists argued that colleagues who viewed problems as mainly stemming from within the child were ignoring the lack of evidence for their apparent belief that 'filling imaginary holes in children's heads' enabled them to perform better in school (Cameron et al., 1986, p.3). An exclusive focus on within-child variables was viewed as diverting attention away from other features of the living-learning context which were more amenable to change; for example the quality of teaching or parenting, classroom organisation, the selection of appropriate learning and developmental objectives, the consideration of effective methods of teaching, and the need for ongoing assessment of pupils' performance and the evaluation of and reflection on all these key processes (cf. Cameron, 1991).

The move towards curriculum-related assessment

Adding to the cognitive dissonance in the profession during the 1980s was the work which had been carried out at the University of Washington where Haring, Lovitt, Eaton and Hansen had developed their new/improved hierarchy of learning, which had been described in some detail in their pioneering text *The Fourth R: Research in the Classroom* (Haring et al., 1978). The starting point for Norris Haring and his colleagues was their conviction that 'learning' was 'the ability to carry out skills in increasingly complex situations' and their model of learning, which had emerged as a result of longitudinal, school-based research, postulated five interlocking stages of learning: acquiring a new skill, performing it fluently, maintaining it over time and finally generalising and adapting the skill to new problem situations. (See Table 1 for a summary of these steps).

Another further distinctive contribution by educational psychologist was described at the beginning of the 1990s by Boxer et al. (1991). They proposed that a comprehensive assessment framework had three parts (see Figure 1) and offered two guiding principles: assessment and record keeping should be part of the whole curriculum planning process, and any assessment must allow pupils to have the best opportunity to show what they know understand and can do.

In addition Boxer et al. (1991) detail *The Five Dimensions of Learning*, adapted from Barrs et al. (1990), see Figure 2. Certainly this framework was very influential for the second author in her approach to assessment. It was crucial at that time for the EP's approach to assessment to be thorough and systematic, particularly with the threat of judicial reviews and the power of the dyslexia lobby at the time (Denman & Lunt, 1993).

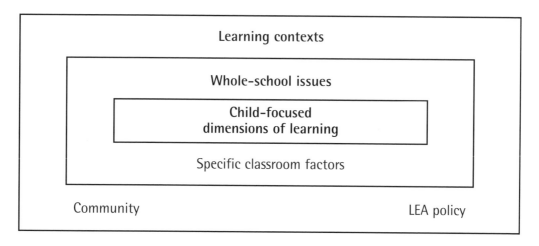

Figure 1: The framework of assessment (from Boxer et al., 1991)

Table 1: A hierarchical model of learning, adapted from White and Haring (1980)

Level of learning	General description	General teaching objectives	Suggested assessment procedures
ACQUISITION	Emphasising accuracy	To teach pupils correct new responses to avoid/ unlearn incorrect responses	Assessing levels of accuracy attained
FLUENCY	Combining speed and accuracy	To help pupils reach the required (or appropriate) level of mastery of the skill(s)	Assessing progress towards agreed levels of fluency
MAINTENANCE	Maintaining fluency	To help pupils to maintain a high level of fluency over a period of time	Assessing levels of skill retention and fluency over a period of time
GENERALISATION	Changing materials or context for required skill	To help pupils performing skill(s) fluently to achieve mastery in differing settings/contexts and with different materials	Assessing effects of (a) using different teaching materials (differentiation) (b) Using different contexts (discrimination)
APPLICATION (or ADAPTATION)	Adapting skill/ knowledge repertoire to new problem situations	To help people to discriminate key elements of new situations and provide appropriate responses	Assessing the level of adaptation, e.g. using problem-solving or simulation exercises

Emerging from the influences of the Haring et al. (1978) instructional hierarchy, together with the 'Objectives Approach' (Ainscow & Tweddle, 1979), the Direct Instruction model (Becker et al., 1981) and from the principles of Precision Teaching (Raybold & Solity, 1982) was a variety of assessment packages aimed at helping teachers to meet the needs of all children and young people in their classrooms, but especially those with learning difficulties. One well-developed example of this approach was the Hampshire Special Needs packages for Reading, Spelling (see Begley et al., 1989) and Number. These three initiatives arose from a collaboration of Hampshire EPs and advisory/specialist teachers facilitated by Southampton University, and led to extensive training across schools throughout the county, particularly on the two packages of Reading and Spelling. It may appear strange to EPs who received their professional training post-Education Reform Act and the introduction of the National Curriculum that EPs would be helping schools in their curriculum planning in literacy, but during the 1980s the consultations with schools were both on what to teach and the specifics of how to do so, especially with individuals or groups of children who were struggling to acquire literacy and numeracy skills.

In special schools for children and young people with moderate learning difficulties (MLD) and severe learning difficulties (SLD) the 'Skills Analysis Model' (Gardener, 1983) offered an approach to selecting, detailing and teaching objectives which met their particular learning needs. Later in this decade this approach was expanded through the use of the 'Education for the Developmentally Young' materials (Foxen & O'Brien, 1981) which provided training in many SLD schools throughout the country.

Figure 2: The patterns of learning (cf. Barrs et al., 1991)

Support for parents of very young children with severe developmental delay, was also an essential strand of EP work at that time. Following the introduction and evaluation of the 'Portage Early Education Project' (Smith et al., 1977), a considerable number of EPs across the UK worked closely with Portage services. The specific assessment tool used to ascertain the existing skill repertoire of each child was the 'Portage Early Education Checklist' (Bluma et al., 1976) which listed sequenced skills in six major developmental areas- infant stimulation, language, self-help, socialisation, motor and cognitive development.

The perspective of children and significant adults
According to Articles 12 and 13 of the United Nations Convention on the Rights of the Child (1989), children have the right to say what they think about anything that affects them; they have the right to express how they think and feel, so long as by doing so they do not break the law or affect other people's rights; and what they say must be listened to carefully.

Yet another important outcome of the reaction against narrow and uncritical IQ testing came in the form of a spate of questionnaires and inventories designed specifically to inform teachers and other significant adults about the child or young person's perspective. Notable here were: *All about Me: The Story of My Life So Far* (Wolfendale, 1987); *My Learning*, a series of booklets produced by Surrey Educational Psychology Service in 1994, designed to involve children more closely in recording and reviewing their achievements; *The Student Report* (Gersch, 1990), students' views about their school learning and any help they thought they needed); *Where Do I Go from Here?* (Nolan & Sigston, 1993), a booklet for students who have been excluded from school, produced by Waltham Forest Educational Psychology Service; and *Myself as Learner Scale* (Burden, 1996), assessing children's perceptions of themselves as learners and problem solvers. For an interesting perspective on how professionals can represent (and mis-represent) the views of children and young people, see Figg et al. (1996) and for an account of how young people can become more involved in the assessment, planning and evaluation processes, see Roller (1998).

Within the profession, the exhortation from Gillham (1999) not to give psychology away, but 'make it fit the special character of the setting you find yourself in' (p.221) was quickly taken up in the series of assessment portfolios which emerged in the early 1990s and have continued since then (see Dunsmuir & Frederickson, 2009; Frederickson & Cameron, 1999; Johnston et al., 1995; Milne, 1992 and Sclare, 1997). The purpose of these portfolios was to enable direct contact adults working with children and young people to have access to a variety of psychological measures which could not only offer them more information about a child's problems and strengths but also inform and generate more appropriate interventions to support the child's more effectively.

The impact of these new ideas on contemporary EP practice

While the debate over psychological within-child and interactive approaches to uncovering the needs of children and young people has continued over the years, the gap between the stated professional aspirations of many EP practitioners and their responses to the cold reality of practice has been illustrated by the surveys of Farrell and Smith (1982) and Lokke et al. (1997), who concluded that there was still extensive use of individual intelligence testing by educational psychologists, a finding that was replicated nearly 25 years later in the surveys of EPs by Woods and Farrell (2006) and by Kennedy (2006).

The survey by Lokke et al. (op. cit.) found that 65 per cent of responses from Educational Psychology Services indicated EPs use a 'high number' of psychometric cognitive assessments, with 38 per cent indicating that national policy (particularly the 1981 Education Act and the code of practice which followed this legislation) and the growing numbers of parental appeals against local authority decisions about funding support for children and young people who had special needs) had increased the use of these tests.

A questionnaire survey of 142 educational psychologists from England and Wales was employed by Woods and Farrell (2006) to ascertain their approach to the assessment of children with learning and behavioural problems. The findings indicated that 'partial' psychometric assessments of ability still figured prominently in the assessment of children with learning difficulties, though less in the assessment of children with behavioural problems.

In addition, 40 per cent of respondents indicated that their work was not influenced by any one or more theoretical orientation in psychology but could be linked to the origin of behaviour or learning difficulties or about approaches to intervention.

In Scotland, a slightly different picture emerged from the survey carried out by Kennedy (2006). She found that between 1996 and 2005 there had been a marked shift in the theoretical perspectives held by psychologists, which had moved from a cognitive/developmental and social learning theory base towards a social interactionist and ecological/systemic perspective. Paradoxically, however, there had been little change in the frequency of norm-based assessments!

Therefore an appropriate overview comment on changes in the area of psychological assessment would be the quip from French critic, journalist and novelist Jean-Baptiste Alphonse Karr: '*Plus ça change: plus c'est la même chose*' (the more things change, the more they stay the same).

So, what is distinctive about psychological assessment?

Dockrell and McShane (1993) defined assessment as 'a process by which information is collected for a specific purpose. It is a process which should guide decision making a better child by identifying a profile of strengths and needs. Assessment should be hypothesis-driven and these hypotheses should be based on an understanding of a child and the cognitive components of learning difficulties as well as an analysis of the child's current learning environment' (pp.28–9).

This is a particularly helpful definition since it reminds us that psychological assessment:
- involves checking out factors which may help to explain why a problem has occurred;
- includes data about the child and his or her living/learning environment;
- identifies strength as well as needs and difficulties; and
- provides data which should enhance future plans for the child.

The two main professional associations for educational psychologists within the UK – the Association of Educational Psychologists and the British Psychological Society Division of Educational and Child Psychology – have issued guidance on the broad principles for psychological assessment (AEP, 1998, 2004; DECP, 1999). The DECP framework highlighted the importance of hypothesis testing over time as well as collaboration on the concerns held about the child or young person within the context of psychological theory and research and viewed the key purposes of assessment as:
- addressing the concerns about a child or young person's learning or behaviour;
- meeting accountability requirements through a monitoring process; and
- generating understanding of what is happening, who is concerned, why it is a problem, and what can be done to make a difference to the situation.

However, the key characteristic of psychological assessment is that the hypotheses which influence the collection of data should be drawn from the rich knowledge base of psychological theory and research. An over-concern with one level of explanation is likely to result in the omission of key information which can lead to a deeper understanding of problems and to strong indicators the most effective ways of tackling such problems. The need for an model which encompasses both child and environmental factors and different levels of explanation was clearly summarised by the BAS revision team of Elliott, Smith and McCulloch (1997) who stated that 'the rationale for the individual assessment of a child's needs must assume that neither the cognitive, psychometric approach nor the behavioural, task analysis approach alone is adequate for designing an intervention programme, although both are usually necessary. A cognitive approach focuses on the assessment of generalised skills and abilities, whereas a behavioural approach focuses on the assessment of specific skills and abilities' (p.29).

One way of enabling psychologists to provide a logical, problem-focused approach to the often-complex problems of children and young people was offered by the 'causal model' or 'interactive factors framework' (IFF) which has been developed from the work of Morton and Firth (1995). In this framework, specific hypotheses can be considered at the biological, cognitive/affective and behavioural levels and their relationships to within-individual and environmental interactions can be unpacked. This approach is particularly helpful since it provides a way of uncovering the often-subtle links between likely factors in the problem situation which assessment data have identified, and presenting these interactions in a visual form which preserves the big picture (see Figure 3).

Figure 4 is an example of an interactive factors framework which provides an overview of the EP's assessment data relating to the reading difficulties experienced by eight-year-old Fred (or Freda). In class, this child was refusing to read and to carry out any written work, yet was delightfully articulate and often had classmates mesmerised by some of his/her story telling. While the psychologist began with a number of hypotheses about these literacy problems, the IFF provides not only a plausible explanation of how these problems arose, but also some of the low response, light touch and fun strategies which are likely to provide the support which could re-motivate and change perceptions of the written word from dread to enthusiasm.

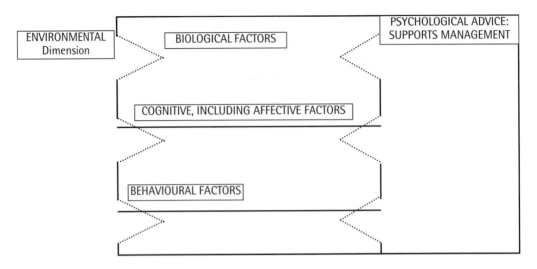

Figure 3: An outline of the Interactive Factors Framework (adapted from Morton & Frith, 1995)

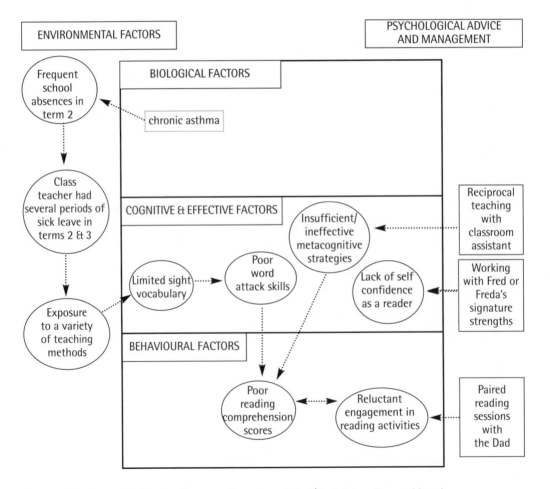

Figure 4: An Interactive Factors Framework version of Fred/Freda's 'reading problems'

Assessment and consultation

In her survey of the assessment approaches adopted by Scottish Educational Psychologists, Kennedy (op. cit.) argued that the goal of assessment should be to reduce barriers to learning, while developing a shared and comprehensive understanding of the young person's needs and that this process needed to be respectful of diversity, contextual and the least possible intrusive possible. Highlighting the important link between assessment and action, she continued, 'Assessment is not separate from intervention and is part of the ongoing cycle of planning, action and review. It should involve collaboration with those adults most closely involved with the young person, and the young person themselves' (p.519).

The emphasis on consultation and partnership approaches in educational psychology practice in schools and with families, has increased steadily. Indeed, group consultations involving EPs with teachers and parents have been highlighted as an important medium for EP service delivery for over 20 years (see Conoley & Conoley, 1990) and Gutkin and Conoley (1990) identified the paradox of school psychology, namely that 'in order to serve children effectively, school psychologists must, first and foremost, concentrate their attention and professional expertise on adults' (p.212).

Within the context of EPs embracing the consultation approach, the language and techniques from SFBT were viewed as significant (Rhodes, 1993) and although interest in these higher-order professional skills have increased in recent times, (e.g. Farouk, 2004; Monsen & Graham, 2002) the literature that influenced the dialogues associated with assessment and intervention had long been established (cf. Egan, 1975 and Schein, 1999). For a contemporary view of the initial professional training and continuing professional development issues in psychological consultation, see Kennedy et al. (2009).

It can be argued that the stimulus for the growth of this approach was the adoption of Solution-Focused Brief Therapy (SFBT) within a problem-solving model. SFBT influenced Educational Psychologists' thinking about the skills that they required when helping teachers and parents to understand problem situations, consider and adopt a different perspective of these and move to implementing ways of managing such problems more effectively. A pioneer of this approach, Steve de Shazer had even begun this work by asking the question 'What do therapists do that is useful?' (see de Shazer and Berg, 1997, p.122).

The characteristics of SFBT include:

- problem centred questioning (in the present);
- setting tasks and paying compliments (de Shazer, 1985);
- generating solutions;
- discussing goal setting;
- asking the 'Miracle' question (de Shazer, 1988);
- introducing a simple rating scale;
- providing some comments and this may include a home work task (frequently called an 'experiment'); and
- noting exceptions to the rule of the problem.

The SFBT model was developed deductively, i.e. by trying something different, seeing if it worked and then describing this intervention. Known in the USA as 'Brief Therapy' this approach, with its main focus on the observable, has been criticised for showing little interest in the 'felt' experience (the black box analogy). However, it appears to have been successful by focusing on the present and the future, rather than the causes and antecedents, with a bias towards future solutions rather than etiology (de Shazer, 1988). The analogy here is that of a skeleton key which can open many doors without finding the correct key that fits exactly.

A focus on the positive

In their seminal paper, Seligman and Csikszentmihalyi (2000) argued that the psychologists' traditional focus on assessing diagnosing and aiming to cure individuals had generally ignored the possibility of enhancing their well-being. In short, a lot of attention was given over to helping individuals to cope but psychological advice generally ignored the possibility of helping individuals to grow, develop and flourish.

One spin-off from the positive psychology movement was the recognition of the power of an individual's signature (or character) strengths: when people employ their signature strengths they are most often successful. Realise2 is an online strength assessment and development tool, developed by the Centre for Positive Applied Psychology (see www.realise2.com) It assesses 60 different attributes according to the three dimensions of energy, performance and use. The statistical and psychometric properties including reliability and discriminant validity are reported in the Realise2s tactical manual (CAPP, 2009). Realise2 combines scores for the dimensions of energy, performance and use, using a proprietary scoring formula to determine whether each attribute can be classified as a realised strength, unrealised strength, learned behaviour or weakness (see Linley, 2008 and Linley et al., 2010).

Realised strengths are those strengths that individuals recognise and use regularly; unrealised strengths are the strengths that may be lying dormant, waiting for an opportunity to arise or for the right situation to call them forth. Learned behaviours are those activities that people have to do often and at which they may be relatively good, but which are not energising for us and weakness are those activities which we perform badly and find energy draining.

The identification and sharing of signature strengths is an important source of motivation and confidence-building for all children and young people, but can have a particularly effective and re-motivating effect on those who are disaffected and/or have low levels of self-worth.

Measuring the impact of psychology-informed advice

Measuring both the extent to which change has (or has not) taken place and the importance of such change for the individual has always presented something of a challenge to applied psychology practice. Similar problems may vary considerably in the way in which they affect different people and similar outcomes may represent life-enhancing progress for some, while for others they may be perceived as a minor improvement. In educational psychology, 'goal attainment scaling' (GAS) has been used as a method of measuring the extent to which negotiated and agreed priority objectives for children and young people have been achieved as a result of psychologically informed intervention.

Using the procedure, each child or young person has their own specified outcome measures but the extent to which these are achieved is scored in a standardised way, so as to as to allow statistical analysis. Unlike traditional standardised measures, which usually include a standard set of items and normative data that allows individual outcomes to be concerned with a larger population, GAS permits the setting and measurement of idiosyncratic which have been identified to suit young person.

Although GAS was employed in the 1980s within US schools by school counsellors (see Maher & Barbrack, 1984) until recently in the UK this approach has been used extensively in health, but not education, settings. However, in the last few years it has been modified and adapted to measure the impact of evidence-based interventions that EPs have been piloting and researching. Examples here include video interaction guidance (VIG) used by teaching assistants in schools (Hayes et al., 2011) and changes resulting from cognitive behaviour therapy (Dunsmuir et al., 2009).

Assessing EP professional competence

As Kennedy et al. (op.cit.) have argued, maintaining consistency and quality assurance in EP practice are important issues. Experienced practitioners need to recognise their professional limitations, (i.e. how to continue to offer appropriate advice based on current psychological and to avoid drifting into 'practitioner folk psychology' (see Peterson, 2003 for a discussion of this issue). The problems of attrition and washout have been noted by Woolfson and colleagues (2003) who observed that practitioners were prone to drifting into techniques that were intuitive, subjective and not based on professional hunches, rather than evidence-based data.

Moore (2005) has argued for a continuing, self critical and reflective stance that examines applied psychology practice within the context of the complexities and changes of contemporary society within the UK. According to Frazer and Greenhaugh (2001) this requires the recognition that as well as competence in professional practice, an additional dynamic for professional development has emerged – capability – the latter being a characteristic which enables a practitioner to adapt to constant change. Kennedy and her colleagues offered a model which they believe will enable practitioners to achieve both the competence and capability to use the power of psychology to bring about positive change in the lives of their clients.

Final comments

Psychological assessment has remained an essential ingredient of high quality EP practice, and it also continues to be one of the most lively and contentious areas amongst practitioners.

While future developments in assessment, such as cognitive-neuropsychological assessment, are impressive (for example, see Teicher et al., 2006 for the fMRI brain scan data on the effects of psychological abuse on children and young people), such developments are likely to enhance rather than replace some of the more effective assessment procedures already in use by applied psychologists.

Of course, what is an essential element in helping significant adults (or peers) to support children and young people with the difficulties that they may experience both within and outside school, is a mediator who can link theory and research and psychology with the real-life problems faced by children and young people and children. This is a point well made by William James well over a century ago:

> *Psychology is a science and teaching is an art; and scientists will never generate arts directly out of themselves. An intermediary inventive mind must make the application, by using its originality.*

> James (1899, pp.23–4)

The key characteristic of psychological assessment is that the hypotheses which drive practitioners' thinking and problem solving are drawn from psychological theory and research. Today, consultations with significant adults, young people and/or their peers are likely to be the starting point of any assessment process. When done well, assessments can generate psychologically sound, evidence-based strategies for improvement, which are context-friendly (i.e. can be carried out by people within the child's living, learning environment) and are tailor-made for an individual/young person (i.e. adapted to his or her idiosyncratic needs and aspirations).

In other words creatively collected, collated and analysed assessment data is likely to lead to professional creativity in applied psychology practice.

Vignette 7

My last thirty years as an eductional psychology practitioner

Julia Hardy

In 1983 the context of work for educational psychologists underwent a significant change as a result of the 1981 Education Act and subsequent regulations and circulars in 1983. In this same year I started work in Hampshire with a group of new EPs, all a part of the expansion of the EPS in order to respond to the anticipated new demands. During my professional training on the Southampton four-year Masters course I recall a senior officer of the AEP predicting that the 1981 Education Act would be 'the dinner ticket for EPs for the next 50 years', whilst one of our tutors described the Act as 'the kiss of death for creative applied psychology'.

As new entrants to the profession we had been inspired by the strong ethical stance of the Warnock Report and believed that the future would improve the quality of education for children with special needs.

Core beliefs

At that time (prior to the National Curriculum) we were convinced that three crucial aspects of our work were assessment through teaching, a functional approach to changing behaviour and parental involvement. I recall in my first year working in a social services observation and assessment centre challenging the PEP's view that an IQ test score should determine whether a young girl in care would go to a special or mainstream school. I was dismayed that a differ-ence of five points alone would segregate this child from her peers and refused to complete a full IQ test. This experience convinced me to be wary of psychometric measures and to argue for the evidence of intervention over time to influence decision making.

Tools of the trade

In the early 1980s Haring and Eaton's (1978) research on instructional psychology influenced our practice. We ran training for teachers on the learning hierarchy (acquisition, fluency, maintenance, generalisation) and we took responsibility for setting up Precision Teaching interventions (Raybould & Solity, 1982) in mainstream schools for students with significant difficulties in learning. In special schools for moderate learning difficulties (MLD) and severe learning difficulties (SLD) we applied the Skills Analysis Model (Gardener, 1983). Later in this decade we expanded this approach through the use of the Education for the Developmentally Young (Farrell, Foxen & O'Brien, 1992) materials, providing training in all SLD schools in the county. I recall even today the excitement and job satisfaction of seeing one 12-year-old girl feed herself independently and an eight-year-old boy walk alone for the first time as a result of EDY interventions in that school.

Parents were an essential strand of EP work at that time too. Working in the heart of Hamp-shire where one of the first two Portage projects were evaluated (Smith, Kushlick & Glossop), EPs worked closely with Portage services and indeed I was successful in persuading administra-tors that a gap in provision (in Petersfield) should have a new Portage service! Tizard and Hughes' (1984) research also had a seminal impact: their observations contrasting the high quality conversations at home (irrespective of class) with some disappointing interactions in nursery settings had a lasting effect.

As practising EPs at this time we applied psychology in our day-to-day work, influenced for example by Brunner (1983) and Wood (1988), who were in turn quoting the most influential developmental psychologist of our time, Vygotsky. Looking back, there are concepts within psychology, such as the zone of proximal development, that last the test of time in the value offered to practicing EPs. One other significant influence on work with parents was *Behaviour Can Change* (1981). Westmacott and Cameron's accessible book helped parents and school staff alike understand functional behavioural analysis and the benefits of using observational data to evaluate interventions both in homes and schools.

Emerging movements: Systems work and inclusion

Gillham's inspiring *Reconstructing Educational Psychology* (1978) anticipated a reduced emphasis on individual work by EPs and a greater focus on preventative and indirect work with organisations and policies. Although this was an aspect of EP work in my first decade as an EP, there was still a drive to make recommendations about levels of need and resources. As Faupel and Norgate (1993) reflected: 'Perhaps the single greatest disaster for educational psychology services, as a result of the 1981 Education Act, was to be seen as providers of additional resources to schools' (p.132).

In the 1980s, as today, EPs were applying their systems knowledge (Checkland, 1986) to the process of influencing schools to change and improve. Systems work by EPs grew in the 1990s (Frederickson, 1990). Dessent's (1987) *Making the Ordinary School Special* urged us to place positive discrimination, non-segregation policies at the heart of our work. The presumption of inclusion has grown within our work (although we are no means there today), with the *Index for Inclusion* (Booth & Ainscow, 2002) and other tools helped EPs work with schools to reflect on their capacity to include. Increasingly EPs and local authorities plan for an assumption of inclusion, and one shift has been that in the early 1980s EPs would be a reason why children were segregated whereas today it is often parental choice that leads to placements in special schools.

Research and creativity

Fortunately, the prediction that the 1981 Education Act would be 'the kiss of death for creative psychology' has not been fully upheld. Effective consultations with school staff and others have led to numerous EP-led projects being commissioned, and now, with doctoral-level training the creative EP as a skilled, researcher-practitioner is the norm rather than the exception.

Chapter 8 Giving it (psychology) all away in the 1990s!

Mike Hymans

In 1992, Wolfendale et al. published a book entitled, *The Profession and Practice of Educational Psychology: Future Directions*, and rather like the wide range of practice in different services now, this publication focused on the work of educational psychologists (EPs) with individuals, organisations and the wider community. In the preface the authors write:

> *What we have tried to do in this volume is to make a coherent statement about the contemporary practice of educational psychologists in various domains and to address a number of current issues which have a bearing on educational psychologists' own work and which are relevant, too, for those other professionals who come into contact with educational psychologists.*

The authors contend that they are 'reconstructionists' whose contentions are first, 'bad' practice will fade away and become extinct as practitioners and their recipients realise and feel its limitations; second, that professional activity, at any time, provides the building blocks for future practice.

It is worth noting that educational psychology in the early 1990s was responding to the 1988 Education Reform Act (ERA). At the time the Act was widely regarded as the most important single piece of education legislation in England, Wales and Northern Ireland since the 'Butler' Education Act 1944. The ERA envisaged a scenario where schools were quasi-autonomous bodies responding to the market pressures of open enrolment. Institutions and local authorities both sought to meet these demands through applying 'business' models newly imbued at the time with public sector ethics. The main provisions of the Education Reform Act were:

■ Grant-maintained schools (GMS) were introduced. Primary and secondary schools could, under this provision, remove themselves fully from their respective local education authorities and would be completely funded by central government. Secondary schools also had limited selection powers at the age of 11.

■ Local management of schools (LMS) was introduced. This part of the Act allowed all schools to be taken out of the direct financial control of local authorities. Financial control would be handed to the head teacher and governors of a school.

■ City Technology Colleges (CTCs) were introduced. This part of the Act allowed new, more autonomous schools to be taken out of the direct financial control of local authorities. Financial control would be handed to the head teacher and governors of a school. There was also a requirement for partial private funding. Only 15 schools were eventually set up. The successor to this programme was the establishment of Academies.

■ The National Curriculum (NC) was introduced.

■ 'Key stages' (KS) were introduced in schools. At each key stage a number of educational objectives were to be achieved.

■ An element of choice was introduced, allowing parents to specify which school was their preferred choice.

■ League tables, publishing the examination results of schools, were introduced.

■ Controls on the use of the word 'degree' were introduced with respect to UK bodies.

■ Academic tenure was abolished for academics appointed on or after 20 November 1987.

The impact of local management of schools (LMS)

It had been argued (for example, in Wolfendale et al., 1992) that, at least up to the implemen-tation of ERA 1988, educational psychologists may have seriously underestimated the impact of economic forces affecting the educational goals with which they were sympathetic. Some EPs at this time often regarded their role as slightly subversive, championing the cause of vulnerable children and young people within insensitive institutions which sometimes valued examinations, academic success and compliance above everything else. Within this context, EPs' work at an organisational level was conceived of as developing expertise or helping reac-tivate schools by siphoning resources and effort towards children and young people with diffi-culties. It was argued that improved quality of education for the most needy pupils would result in beneficial changes for all. Indeed there was quite a lot of evidence to suggest that well-organ-ised organisations that promoted high expectations and emphasised achievement, rather than stressing failure and bad behaviour, demonstrated more positive pupil outcomes (e.g. Morti-more et al., 1988; Rutter et al., 1979). However, it had also been argued that in their role as arbiters of resources for individual pupils, the profession, along with others, had undermined the need for schools to make more inclusive arrangements for all pupils (e.g. Dessent, 1987; Reynolds, 1987).

So in the 1990s schools were given the remit through the local management of schools (LMS) to become self-regulating. Schools became more responsible for their own destiny, image, culture and management. The fact that schools were seen as specific organisations, following the same principles as other organisations led to an exploration culture (including a 'business culture'), leadership, management and development.

Schools were also required to become more accountable: they had to publish their exami-nation results, absentee figures, information on special needs for parents and the local community. The underlying stated government aim was to expose schools to parental choice in the hope that good schools would be popular with parents and thus would attract more pupils, while poor schools would shrink and ultimately close. LMS affected the balance of power in terms in terms of the forces for change. It was thought that if schools held the resources, local education authorities would have little power to influence change in schools and so the involvement of EPs became school-centred, focusing on process-orientated change in helping and facilitating schools undertake change.

In the 1990s there were understandable fears in some areas, emanating from the 1981 Education Act and the 1988 Education Reform Act, that EPs would come under pressure to work exclusively at the individual child level. These related to widespread anxieties concerning pressures from schools, parents and others to increase statutory assessment work. The survival of EP services was seen as being dependent upon EPs delivering a service that schools valued and desired, especially as there was a fear that the power and influence of local education authorities would decrease. In this chapter I too will reflect on my experiences of professional practice in the 1990s, in the context of working at three levels and invite readers, rather like Wolfendale et al. did, to reflect with me on the issues, ideas, practices described: did we really give our psychology away and to what effect?

Working at the individual level

Like other professional applications of psychology, educational psychology includes practi-tioners that embrace a wide range of viewpoints, for example humanistic, behaviouristic, social constructionists, phenomenological, cognitive or systemic. Yet by the 1990s a consensus appeared to have emerged, at least on pragmatic grounds, that EPs could best assist meeting the needs of individual children by indirect work, most usually through teachers and parents. This is most probably where the idea of giving psychology away first emerged. This shift from direct contact with the child or young person (client) to assisting an intermediary consultee (teacher and/or parent) mirrored changes that had taken place in other branches of professional psychology, particularly mental health consultation (Caplan, 1970). It is interesting to note how now clinical psychologists working for CAMHS prefer to be called Consultant Psychologists.

Consultation

The attractions of indirect client casework for most EPs seemed to be a mixture of pragmatism and the belief that those with the greatest contact with the child or young person (that is, teachers or parents) are best placed to effect change.

Intrinsic in this indirect approach is the assumption of dualism, starting with an assertion that there is an external, objective problem that the consultee directly senses and so it will be possible within consultation to 'get to the truth of the matter' and offer appropriate solutions. Constructionist theorists, who included psychologists as diverse as Piaget and Kelly (Kelly, 1955, 1991), argued that the consultee seeks meaning in the child's behaviour by relating it to the consultee's own knowledge (tacit or otherwise), structures or belief systems. During the consultation this is encoded and communicated to the consultant, who in turn seeks meaning in the consultee's account. The process of seeking meaning, assimilating input into current structures or accommodating through the development of new ideas becomes the basis of the consultation.

Generally the kinds of problems that consultants are asked to resolve fall into two broad categories: the first can be termed as 'technical' involvement and, to be effective in this role, the consultant will need to draw on their expert knowledge and skills to help resolve specific problems. Such an approach is dependent upon accurate and careful diagnosis with clear communication to the problem presenter. The important point about this role is that the consultant supplies the solution. The introduction of record keeping for children with special educational needs (SEN) or training teachers to use particular diagnostic reading assessments or interventions would be examples. Consultation draws upon a number of psychological theories and principles, for example:

- Solution-oriented theory
- Personal construct theory
- Systems thinking
- Narrative therapy
- Symbolic interactionism
- Social constructionism.

This means that the focus is not the child's behaviour but the consultee's interpretation of it and that the approach is eclectic in that the consultant can draw on a wide range of theoretical frameworks.

Consultation has a number of key features:
- Participants are seen as equal in status and in sharing expertise.
- Consultees should be the people most concerned and should retain ownership of the problem.
- The goals of consultation are to facilitate reflection upon potential ways forward in the current context and to develop future problem-solving skills.

The problem-solving paradigm

There is no doubt that the consultation model had, and still does have in a number of EP services, many attractive features for EPs. It was and still is argued that the beneficiaries of the model are teachers, in that the approach is aimed at working with their concerns. Within the context of this consultation approach a 'problem-solving' paradigm emerged. Figure 1 describes a number of problem-solving frameworks illustrating their fundamental similarities.

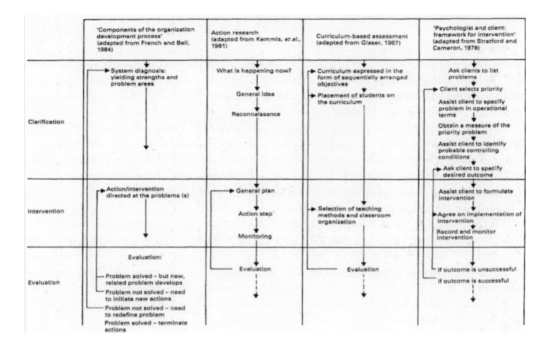

Figure 1: Problem-solving frameworks

Reprinted with kind permission of Dr Allan Sigston, Executive Director – Research at Edison Learning.

The problem-solving paradigm operationalised with teachers had an inbuilt bias for action on behalf of the child/young person that the consultation approach lacked. Perhaps the most compelling attribute of the problem-solving approach was its accountability within cases where the contributors have agreed responsibilities. Accountability was also possible across a number of cases, permitting audits of types of concerns and actions taken by EPs, schools or individuals working with the caseloads, thus allowing EPs and co-workers opportunities for reflective practice. However, the problem-solving approach could be criticised for a restrictive view of needs and problems as these were examined solely from a teacher's viewpoint without any EP input.

Some EPs, including this author, sought to deal with this criticism by dispensing with the notion of a single consultee in favour of a collective, including the person expressing a concern, with others who had a particular interest in the child or young person's well-being. This way of working combined the advantages of working with those closest to the child/young person, while also valuing the subjective experiences of participants within an accountable framework.

However, in successfully facilitating consultation the EP was faced with dilemmas regarding the appropriate choices of techniques and when to use them, with many EPs found inspiration from family therapy theory. Within the problem-solving alliance it was possible to de-emphasise pathology in favour of 'desired goals'. Nevertheless, in general the problem-solving paradigm failed to make significant inroads into EP practice in the 1990s and explicit attempts to work within a problem-solving alliance were rare. Perhaps the problems for EPs at that time were how they might have made such a contribution without subverting their casework aims. Inevitably solutions had to be placed within local conditions concerning the development of resourcing institutions as a whole in ways progressively more sensitive to children's and young people's needs and, linking the resourcing of 'exceptional' bids to problem-solving action rather to the child's/young person's psychopathology.

Popular interventions

Popular individual interventions at the time of the introduction of consultation were precision teaching approaches such as DataPac for reading, spelling, number and handwriting. DataPac stood for 'Daily Teaching and Assessment – Primary Aged Children. It provided a means of supplying individually tailored teaching programmes for primary aged children (and for some in Years 7–9 in secondary schools) with learning difficulties. It comprised a bank of teaching materials matched to individual children's needs. Each programme was designed to run for about eight to ten weeks and consisted of a series of precision teaching objectives, carefully ordered in a finely graded step-by-step way. Teachers (and sometimes their assistants or parents) were asked to use the programme for five to ten minutes each day if possible. This had to be done individually with the pupil whilst the rest of the class was occupied with other work.

The basic principles of DataPac are based on objectives that not only describe what the pupil has to be able to do but also how well the skill must be performed. Most objectives describe two levels or standards of performance: the first focuses on accuracy (that is, the maximum number of permissible errors) and the second concentrates on fluency (that is performing the same skill accurately and at speed). These two aspects of DataPac objectives represent two distinct phases of teaching. The teacher was first asked to concentrate on reducing pupil errors and to get the pupil to the point of being able to perform a skill accurately regardless of speed. This promoted over-learning.

The teacher was then asked to focus on building a pupil's speed of response. The idea of 'fluency building' was of crucial importance as it is well known (e.g. Allington, 2001) that skills which can be performed fluently are less likely to be forgotten than skills which can be performed accurately but slowly. Another important principle upon which DataPac is based is the idea of daily assessment: testing a pupil and recording their performance every day is considered an essential aspect of the programme, because the teacher needs to know at all times exactly how much progress is being made so that the teacher can decide what and when to take appropriate action.

DataPac was based on a set of well-tried principles to be particularly effective with pupils with learning difficulties in basic skills (handwriting, mathematics, reading and spelling). Field-testing carried out by teachers and EPs, predominantly in the West Midlands, showed that DataPac worked. However, this intervention did not provide a simple remedy for such children and did not replace the professional expertise of the teacher. Nevertheless there was good evidence that, combined with the commitment of the people involved with the intervention, the DataPac programme usually significantly accelerated pupil progress.

In the area of literacy, in particular, paired reading and peer tutoring are other examples where EPs gave psychology away. They are examples of co-operative learning. Topping (1989) argued that: 'co-operative pair-work has enormous potential in the classroom, given careful organisation and monitoring by a skilled teacher'. Usually it was EPs who trained teachers to develop the skills to organise and monitor such an approach. Topping (op. cit.) further argued that: 'the more powerful vehicle for effective learning is structured pair-work between children of differing ability, in the format known as peer tutoring'.

Peer tutoring occurs when 'a more able child helping a less able child in a cooperative working pair organised by the teacher'. 'Reciprocal peer tutoring', whereby tutor and tutee roles rotate, or small group peer tuition are also possible although are more complex. Research reviews on the effectiveness of peer tutoring has shown that the tutors accelerate in reading skill at least as much as, if not more than the tutees (Sharpley & Sharpley, 1981).

Where tutoring situations are structured to maximise tutor participation, gains for both parties tend to be greater. Training tutors carefully, often by EPs directly and/or via teacher training, also increases the effectiveness of the procedure for both. There has been clear evidence that children with learning and behaviour problems can benefit from acting as tutors (Topping, 1988).

The Paired Reading technique was originally devised for use by parents with their children at home (Topping, 1987). It was subsequently used by staff in schools, both teachers and learning support assistants, as well as 'peer tutors', who were trained by EPs in the use of the technique. The technique enabled tutees to be supported through texts of higher readability levels than they would be able to read independently, thereby ensuring adequate stimulation and participation for the tutor, who also had an important role in promoting understanding by discussion and questioning. On any section of text that was difficult for the tutee, the pair read aloud together. The tutor was trained to adjust to the tutee's natural reading speed so that synchrony can be established with practice. When the tutee made an error, the tutor was advised by the trainer (EP) to repeat the word correctly and asked the tutee to do likewise before proceeding. The simplicity of this universally applied error correction procedure minimised any possibility of the tutor becoming overly didactic and authoritarian. Praise for correct reading at regular intervals and for specified reading behaviours was emphasised throughout. Once the tutee became more confident with the reading material they used a non-verbal signal (e.g. knock on the table) to indicate that they wanted to 'read alone' which they were allowed to do. If they made an error, the correction was given by the tutor who then joined the tutee in 'reading together'.

Paired Reading had obvious advantages in peer tutoring. Tutorial pairs could be trained simply and easily and subsequently worked with high interest reading materials of a range of readability sufficient to focus attention and stretch the capabilities of both members. Tutoring sessions could be fitted easily into classroom routines without the need for a great deal of preparation, and could be easily alternated with other reading activities such as sustained silent reading. The use of peer-tutored Paired Reading was first reported by Winter and Low (1984). Encouraging results were found and since then the use of the approach has grown at great speed.

Working at the organisational level
BATPACK
Educational psychologists' first move from individual children into organisational work was usually via In-service Education for Teachers (INSET). Educational psychologists had generalised from the expertise built up from work with individual children and young people to run courses for school staff, teachers and support staff. The development and delivery of INSET packages was, and still is, a common method of service delivery (e.g. BATPACK, Merrett & Wheldall, 1990).

Another angle on classroom management can be seen in the Behavioural Approach to Teaching Secondary Aged Pupils (BATSACK) developed by Houghton et al. (1988). Their work aimed to induct secondary teachers into what they describe as 'positive' responses to children's behaviour through a school-based in-service training programme. The focus was on classroom management.

Teachers were taught to examine the antecedents to pupil behaviour and, by selecting appropriate behavioural responses themselves, to provide positive reinforcement or encouragement for specifically defined pupil behaviours.

An enormous amount of research on behavioural approaches to teaching had been carried out in North America, which had considerable influence in Britain. The theoretical underpinning is in learning theory, and in the assumption that the same principles govern the 'learning' of behaviour as with any other task. Thus, if children and young people enjoy receiving their teacher's attention, the teacher can use attention selectively as a way of increasing the frequency of particular behaviours. The behaviour may be working on a mathematics problem, cooperating with other pupils or sitting down except when invited to move around the classroom: the same reinforcement principles apply.

Educational psychologists often provided 'behavioural' or 'behaviour modification' programmes (a term used in the 1990s) to help teachers cope with difficult or disruptive behaviour. Typically, such programmes had six stages (see below). The evidence for the effectiveness of behavioural approaches was nevertheless contentious. On the other hand, evaluations of BATPACK, the primary version of BATSACK, have reported changes in teacher behaviour, with evidence that positive reinforcement of appropriate pupil behaviour does help teachers in managing pupils, at least in the short to medium term (Merrett & Wheldall, 1990).

The six stages included:
1. The teacher identified a behaviour or skill that they wanted the class or a particular child to acquire (or, in the case of behaviour, to modify).
2. A 'base-line' against which to measure subsequent progress was obtained by recording the frequency of the target behaviour.
3. The antecedents, or events that preceded the target behaviour, and consequences, or events that followed it were obtained. This showed what was acting as a stimulus and/or as a reinforcement for the target behaviour.
4. Using reinforcement principles, a programme to achieve the desired objective was planned.
5. The programme was put into practice, maintaining records so as to evaluate progress against the base-line measures.
6. After reviewing progress, the programme was modified or developed as necessary.

Nevertheless, two cautionary points were made about the use of behavioural approaches. First, Wheldall (1982) warned against 'behavioural overload', or the use of unnecessarily 'heavy', and perhaps primitive techniques to deal with relatively minor problems. In a similar vein, Berger (1979) warned of the danger of a 'mindless technology', and in a later article argued that 'classroom problems are influenced by a complex set of factors interacting and changing over time', and not simply by 'the behaviour of teachers or peers'. These could be regarded as essentially technical points, resulting from inappropriate use of behavioural principles. The second point is more complex and challenges one of the behaviourist most fundamental assumptions: that effective teaching depends on clear and precise specification of objectives. It is difficult to imagine teaching successfully without having clear objectives. Yet, admitting that objectives are necessary for effective teaching does not mean that they are sufficient. McNamara (1983) identified seven standard objections to an over-reliance on objectives.
1. The rationale for selecting objectives is often unclear.
2. The detail with which objectives can be specified varies unacceptably from subject to subject: what precise objective must be met on the path to producing a creative, original story?
3. Splitting a curricular task into objectives can trivialise it: 'when we move on to pupils deploying their analytical and critical skills we simply cannot talk in terms of objectives' (McNamara, 1983).

4. Specifying objectives generates either too few or too many. Unless the number is kept artificially low, children will learn far more in the course of a week than the teacher can specify as behavioural objectives.
5. The more varied and stimulating the curricular activities, the more difficult it becomes to obtain agreement on whether objectives have been achieved.
6. Whatever and however we teach, we convey attitudes through the hidden curriculum: 'The hidden curriculum which is associated with the objectives approach seems to have little to commend it.'
7. If however much detail objectives are specified, we still have to face questions about how we achieve them.

It remained true that appropriateness of reinforcement is necessary for effective classroom management. Children and young people are unlikely to respond well to teachers who appear uninterested in their efforts and unresponsive to their interests. Most teachers use reinforcement principles intuitively, but the evidence suggested that this is more frequently directed at appropriate educational tasks than at appropriate behaviour (Houghton et al., 1988).

In other words, teachers seem to have difficulty in reinforcing 'good' behaviour, and may inadvertently encourage disruptive behaviours by directing their attention to the children concerned. However, the underlying assumption behind BATPACK and BATSACK was that training teachers in a specific way would change their classroom practice and in the long run would be a whole-school effect. It was presumed that by training key members of staff changes would occur: mechanistic phrases such as the 'cascade' model of training were common.

Assertive discipline
Operating in parallel with approaches such as BATPACK and BATSACK was 'Assertive Discipline'. This was described as a behaviourist INSET package aimed to help teachers increase the amount of time pupils spend on task and reduce the teaching time lost due to disruptive and uncooperative behaviour (Canter & Canter, 1992). Assertive Discipline originated in the United States and has been available in the UK since 1991. The key difference between Assertive Discipline and other behaviourist approaches such as BATPACK is the acceptance of the need for a system of sanctions.

The results of a small-scale study in Liverpool (Swinson & Melling, 1995) were consistent with the findings of a larger study by Nicholls (1993a, 1993b), that training teachers to use Assertive Discipline techniques has at least four positive outcomes:
1. An increase in on-task pupil behaviour.
2. A decrease in the frequency of disruptive incidents.
3. A dramatic increase in the rate of teacher praise.
4. A marked decline in the rate at which pupils were 'told off'.

In general there was an increase in pupil involvement and a shift towards a more positive classroom environment. Swinson and Melling (op. cit.) therefore argued that in terms of the observed increase in positive feedback and reduced rate of punishment, Assertive Discipline could be just as effective without the inclusion of sanctions. They suggested, however, that the existence of a consistent, systematic and predictable hierarchy of sanctions is very important given that there would always be some children who needed the guarantee of a 'response cost' to compete with rewards such as peer approval which may result from rule-breaking behaviour. They argue that a decrease in the frequency of rule-breaking behaviour does not necessarily show that sanctions are superfluous and suggest that, on the contrary, it seems more likely to be a testimony to the effectiveness of making outcomes predictable and non-rewarding.

In the context of giving psychology away Swinson and Melling (op. cit.) wrote: 'It is important that as EPs we can point to empirical evidence to support innovative pupil management practices ... we are confident that the overwhelming majority of teachers, parents and children with whom we have worked would support this recommendation (of using Assertive Discipline in our schools).'

Applying a change process model
The second strategy for educational psychologists in this decade had been to provide a process for change that a school could apply to specific areas of work: for example, training schools to use a 'problem-solving model' to sort out their own problems. Stratford (1990) described how this was used to reduce 'discipline problems in schools with the underlying aim of improving a school's ethos'. Within the 'technical' or 'resource' consultation model the consultant is essentially a facilitator helping the consultee reveal hitherto unrecognised problems. However, too often consultation offered by EPs was regarded as 'narrow' in that it resulted from individual assessment and there was a view that in order to widen the EP 'brief' consultancy relating to organisational change and management would have to become part of the services to schools offered by EPs. A second category of consultancy can be termed as 'process' consultancy where the role is to help the organisation acknowledge and mobilise its own resources in order to arrive at solutions to the problem.

Here the consultee is accepted as well-intentioned and seeking to improve things. However, they lack knowledge about problem diagnosis, how to change things and the kind of help needed to achieve the change. Unless there is understanding of the problem and participation in intervention planning by the consultee, both ability and willingness to implement solutions will be lacking. The process consultant (PC) approach views the organisation as imperfect but having the potential to be more effective providing it is able to identify and manage its own strengths and weaknesses.

The PC will be unable to learn enough about the organisational culture to suggest reliable courses of action in the short time available and, in any case, such solutions are likely to fail through their inappropriateness or staff resistance. The PC will need to gather data on who communicates with whom and when and will need to be familiar with the existence of meta-communications and their implications. Therefore joint planning is essential, albeit that the final decisions for intervention must remain with the consultee: the essential function of the PC is to pass on skills of problem diagnosis, intervention planning and implementation to the consultee, thereby 'giving psychology away'.

It was evident that EPs possessed much of the knowledge necessary for operating successfully as consultants of the 'technical' or 'resource' variety, although it was debatable whether they possessed the necessary 'process consultant' skills. Most EP training courses at the time included 'systems' or 'whole-school' approaches to a greater or lesser extent, but an exercise with a group of experienced EPs carried out by Labram (1992) considered those skills that EPs had or might acquire which could be used as part of a consultancy portfolio is reported in Table 1.

In the context of 'giving psychology away' and Labram's (1992) 'straw poll' amongst experienced EPs of their skill set, the Association of Educational Psychologists' (AEP) Annual Conference in 1990, entitled *Taking an Educational Psychology Service into the 1990s,* asked participants what characteristics and features a successful service would embody, from which the following features emerged:

■ To make more explicit the skills psychologists have which could be essential in assisting the local education authority in its new role of enabling change with identified skills such as: organisational development; learning theory; staff development models; and, appraisal processes.

Table 1: Checklist of school-based educational psychology consultancy (Labram, 1992)

Areas of existing skill	Areas of skills in embryo	No existing skill
Managing meetings	Staff selection	Appraisal
Behaviour management policies	Conflict management	Staff motivation
Interpersonal skills	Decision making	Marketing school image
SEN resource deployment	Stress management	School ethos
INSET planning	Action research	Non-teaching staff
Time management	Record keeping	
Work with parents & governors	Information gathering & interpretation	
Assessment policies	Staff development	
The pastoral curriculum	The National Curriculum content & method	
Negotiating skills		
Classroom organisation		

■ To develop new areas of working by examining the current context, developing new skills and allocating time appropriately (Gersch et al., 1990).

A focus on community

Bryans et al. (1992) wrote:

> *Many educational psychologists choose to limit their field of operations to what they believe are 'manageable' dimensions of the presenting problems, so that when confronted, for example, by a partially hearing Asian child of six, living in bed-and-breakfast accommodation with a young mother, the educational psychologist and the teacher may only focus on helping the child learn to read or enjoy books in school. Yet this particular example contains almost every dimension of disadvantage associated with bias in our society – race, sexual inequality, disability, poverty, culture clashes within the family and a loss of control over life choices.*

Adding:

> *The framing of the Education Reform Act (ERA) tends to reinforce the view that it pays surface attention to equality of opportunity by using a market-force model to improve schools and therefore improve the quality of education – but probably only for those who are most likely to succeed in it anyway.*
>
> Bryans et al. (1992, p.137)

Cline and Lunt (1990) also drew attention to a number of areas of concern for educational psychologists: educational developments in a multicultural society; anti-racist education and working in multi-cultural communities; bilingualism and second language learning; equal opportunity issues; and, social, cultural and ethical aspects of assessments and factors in therapeutic interventions. Returning to the notion of 'deconstructing' the obvious assumptions about intelligence, race and gender, from whatever point of view, tended to achieve explanatory status largely because of the fit with existing constructs. Replacing these with informed and sensitive practice became a priority not only for EPs but also for others in Educational Services.

The 1989 Children Act (implemented in October 1991) introduced the notion of the role of psychologists in ascertaining the child's wishes and feelings, for example in writing their statutory psychological advice, as we were deemed the professional group best suited to establishing the emotional and educational needs of children and their likely effect of any changes in such needs. It was suggested (e.g. by Conn, 1992) that we had a potential role in looking at harm or risk of harm because of our knowledge of family dynamics and how children's needs can be met. Conn suggests that EPs, with the 'dual citizenship' in the domains of education and psychology, are in a unique position to provide a comprehensive view on child and family matters.

Furthermore, the Department of Health (1990), in *The Care of Children: Principles and Practice in Regulations and Guidance,* suggested that cooperation between organisations, departments and individuals, including EPs, was crucial in the provision of protection for vulnerable children and also in ensuring proper use of available resources. Russell (1992) suggested that the ERA (1988) meant that individuals were likely to take on new significance as virtual 'ecosystems' within their own agency. Adding that the longer-term impact of LMS would almost certainly result in the fragmentation and dismemberment of the local education authority (LEA) as the coordinator and planner of services. Russell (op. cit.) wrote:

> Parents may have greater choice in selecting an adviser with whom they feel comfortable. Indeed there is growing (albeit mainly anecdotal) evidence that many parents are turning to private assessment by educational psychologists and other professionals.

Early intervention programmes
There are of course some important lessons to learn from the positive initiatives of early intervention programmes for children with special educational needs (SEN) and their families. A major consequence of these initiatives has been the strong relationship between home background and early learning. Cameron (1989) noted the importance of acknowledging that parents have two primary educational roles when a child has SEN or a disability. First, parents need to understand how to teach a child everyday life-skills and second, they need help in managing difficult or disruptive behaviour a child may acquire. Since the mid-1970s, the Portage home-teaching model has become increasingly popular, together with the involvement of EPs. It was estimated in the early 1990s that there were over 300 schemes in the United Kingdom (Cameron, 1989; Russell, 1990). Portage is characterised by focusing upon helping parents to teach children with SEN in their own homes and by involving families in selecting their own educational goals. One of the major successes of a good Portage scheme is that it allows information transfer between parents and professionals. In addition Portage provides a 'key worker' approach to support parents through a familiar individual and it offers a model for crossing parent-professional boundaries.

Conclusion

This chapter has attempted to take a coherent view about the contemporary practice of EPs in the context of 'giving psychology away'. I have adopted a similar re-constructionist view to that taken Wolfendale et al. (1992) and considered EP practice at three (not mutually exclusive) levels. This approach is well supported by Lindsay who in 1992 wrote:

> *Educational psychologists have an important role improvising rigorous assessments of children's needs and helping with the attainment of optimal support for these children's development. This may include direct programme planning, parental support, in-service training of teachers, advice to education authorities and in some cases direct child advocacy. Psychologists may be advising on the provision of support or providing the intervention themselves.*

For me, although there may have been differences remaining between us at the level of detail, there was (and may be still is) a common purpose of giving psychology away.

Vignette 8

Setting up a special educational needs audit in the 1990s

Mike Hymans

In November 1992 I was responsible for leading a team of two local authority (LA) officers and three LA educational psychologists to design and manage a special educational needs (SEN) audit process. This audit came about as a consequence of national developments in SEN service delivery and a local Audit Commission report into SEN within the borough in which I worked as a senior educational psychologist (SEP). The draft proposals for the audit were discussed and agreed with head teachers and special needs coordinators (SENCOs) at a series of cluster meetings in early January 1993. The proposals included:

1. The development of criteria and definitions for levels of SEN to be shared across the authority.
2. Methods of identification of SEN that could be rigorously and consistently applied across all schools.
3. Procedures for delegating funds to schools that related to the level and incidence of need and, allowed maximum flexibility of deployment within the specified purpose.
4. Systems for moderating schools' own identification of SEN and for monitoring allocated provision.
5. A clarification of the respective responsibilities of schools and LA for meeting SEN and structures for accountability.
6. Programmes of in-service education and training (INSET) to further develop schools' capacity for providing for pupils for SEN.

One key 'psychological' issue in conducting the audit concerned the use of assessment: on the one hand, an effective system had to be developed that would provide information on all pupils comparable across schools, otherwise it would result in an unfair allocation of resources. On the other hand, an interactive definition of SEN implied considering children's needs in particular contexts. The working group agreed that comparability would be most easily attained through the use of normative assessment. However, we also acknowledged that context specific assessment relies heavily on the knowledge and skills of individual teachers. In an attempt to reconcile these approaches it seemed important to find ways of anchoring teachers' judgements through the use of broad criteria, hereafter referred to as 'descriptors' in order to interpret children's needs with accompanying ranges of scores that might typically describe children with these difficulties with the aim of establishing a range of interpretations in descriptor terms that teachers would give to what was termed the 'typical' performance of children within groups identified as having SEN.

In April 1993 a pilot study was carried out to identify non-statemented children with SEN in mainstream schools and a 'banding' system for the identification was used. Children in 'band 1' had 'marginal difficulties' that required in the short-term occasional specific interventions to access the National Curriculum adequately. Children in 'band 2' had 'marked difficulties' requiring longer-term regular and intensive interventions to access the National Curriculum. From a qualitative analysis the aspect of the descriptors that was most welcomed was the dialogue prompted within schools about what is meant by SEN and the interventions and strategies being used to meet these needs. The greatest difficulties in using the descriptors arose where children were bilingual and/or transient within schools. From the psychologists' viewpoint there were very few problems with the administration of the test battery. The pilot however, highlighted the need for teacher guidance for distinguishing between SEN and language needs arising out of bilingualism.

The pilot exercise also demonstrated the need for schools to demonstrate both the severity of children's difficulties as well as the implementation of plans to assist children in accessing the National Curriculum. The 'thresholds', using expectancy tables, developed for bands 1 and 2 provided a unique borough profiling system that was used to extend the descriptors to provide information about the pupils' levels of difficulty. Schools with the highest agreements between teachers' banding judgements and the borough's thresholds were generally those where a considerable amount of time had been set aside by staff for audit, training and follow-up discussions between staff. An analysis of feedback from pilot schools illustrated the need to clarify and expand the descriptors to ensure the same interpretation by each school in the borough.

In January 1994 schools carried out their audits and for the first time there was an authority-wide valid information about the numbers and difficulties of children with SEN. Every school was visited by an educational psychologist (EP) to clarify any outstanding issues about the audit and schools welcomed this opportunity for discussion and confirmed owner-ship. To ensure borough consistency a moderation of a sample of all schools banding data was planned. Training moderation teams was an important aspect of this stage of the audit proce-dure: this involved discussions about the types of acceptable evidence for moderation.

In evaluating and reflecting on the audit methodology and processes it was acknowledged that a danger with 'intense' team working is that members can find themselves in a cosy consensus where assumptions and decisions are not sufficiently challenged: this a phenom-enon called 'groupthink' (Janis, 1972). So in order to ensure that audit arrangements stood up to external scrutiny as well as seeking improvement suggestions an independent psycholo-gist was commissioned to evaluate the process.

The evaluation made a number of recommendations that were acted upon in carrying out a second SEN audit in January 1995, and then an extension of the audit into statemented pupil categories became a natural follow-on. The process of piloting and developing arrangements began in 1993 and built on the experience described. A detailed analysis of all statemented pupils' needs and the provision in place to meet these was carried out first as this gave a comprehensive overview of all the arrangements that were in place for statemented pupils at that time. The ultimate aim of the audit was to improve the quality of experiences of vulner-able and most needy children in schools. Throughout the development and implementation of the audit arrangements applied psychological knowledge and skills were at the fore in group problem-solving, promoting ownership in the change process and in conducting field research and evaluation. So much so that this author, as Principal Educational Psychologist, was asked to lead a similar process in 2010 as part of a special school formula funding exercise.

Chapter 9 The development of educational psychology in Scotland

Tommy MacKay & James Boyle

The appointment in 1923 of David Kennedy-Fraser (1888–1962) to the post of 'psychological adviser' by the education authority of the city of Glasgow after an unsuccessful approach to Cyril Burt (Blythman, 1978) heralds the beginnings of professional educational psychology in Scotland, some 10 years after the establishment of Burt's post, the first in the UK, by the London County Council. Yet psychology, and educational psychology in particular, has a longer history in Scotland. This can be dated back to the philosopher Alexander Bain (1818–1903), Professor of Logic and Rhetoric at Aberdeen University, who promoted the study of empirical, 'scientific' psychology and also the application of the 'new' science of experimental psychology, particularly the work of Wilhelm Rein (1847–1929) and Ernst Meumann (1862–1915) in Germany, to education and schools in Scotland in the early years of the 20th century (Banerjee & Probst, 1997; Boyle & MacKay, 2010; Boyle, MacKay & Lauchlan, 2008; McKnight, 1978; Tolmie & Boyle, 2011).

In this chapter, we shall consider the development of educational psychology services in Scotland, the impact of Scottish legislation upon the roles and responsibilities of educational psychologists, and the distinctive training and qualifications for educational psychologists in Scotland, concluding with a discussion of future developments for the profession in Scotland.

At the turn of the 20th century, population increases in Scotland as elsewhere in the UK, coupled with the raising of the school leaving age from 13 to 14 in 1901, fuelled a demand for teachers and courses to train them. This resulted in the growth of non-residential, day training colleges to augment existing provision run by the churches and universities. As Marker (1996) notes, in Scotland, the new colleges were funded directly by the 'Scotch' Education Department (SED), not by local authorities, and were organised around four 'Provincial Committees' set up in 1905 and centred around Glasgow, Edinburgh, St Andrews and Aberdeen. The SED regulated the curriculum for the new colleges and primary teachers were expected to follow a two-year course and secondary teachers a postgraduate course of one-year. As a result of the influence of the first professors of education in Scotland, Laurie at Edinburgh University and Meiklejohn at St Andrew's University, and other senior academics such as Rusk at Glasgow, from as early as 1906, Article 22 of the SED's regulations included compulsory classes in 'psychology, ethics and logic' as a 'professional subject' (Marker, 1996). A timetable for 1907–08 reveals that student teachers spent five hours per week on 'logic and psychology or ethics' during the winter term and some three hours per week on 'experimental psychology' in the summer term (Hutchison, 1973; Marker, 1996), a pattern which continued until 1945-46, when 'educational psychology' was introduced.

Mention should be made of Shepherd Dawson (1880–1935), the influential Principal Lecturer in Psychology at the Glasgow Provincial Teachers' Training College from 1910 until his death. Dawson was also a consultant psychologist at the Glasgow Royal Hospital for Sick Children, and worked with Henry Watt (1879–1925), the first lecturer in psychology at Glasgow University, who wrote an early book on memory for teachers (Watt, 1909).

The background to the appointment of Kennedy-Fraser was a recommendation in 1922 by

William McKechnie, HMI (later Secretary of the Scottish Education Department) to the Committee of the Education Authorities in Scotland. McKechnie advised that the 'ascertainment of mental defect' and any associated recommendations regarding provision for education should involve not only a medical officer, but also a trained school psychologist (Blythman, 1978). This had implications not only for the appointment of school psychologists *per se*, but also for the training of such psychologists.

The Central Education Committee of the National Committee for the Training of Teachers came up with a plan: a joint appointment of a 'psychological adviser' to the Glasgow Education Authority to conduct formal ascertainments and set up a child guidance clinic and a principal lecturer at the Glasgow Provincial Teachers' Training College to establish and teach on a training programme for teachers working in special schools.

Kennedy-Fraser had studied at Leipzig University and worked with G.M. Whipple at Cornell University before taking up joint lecturing posts at Moray House Training College and Edinburgh University. The salary for his joint appointment at Glasgow reflected the scale of his responsibilities. John Smith, a former Vice-Principal of Jordanhill College of Education, in a letter written in 1976 noted: 'It was the best paid post (£1,000) in the College after the Principal (£1,100) and higher than that of the Aberdeen College Principal and all other heads of department in his own college' (i.e. Jordanhill). (Extract quoted by Blythman, 1978, p.37.)

Following Kennedy-Fraser's appointment, James Drever *primus* (1873–1950) in 1925 opened what came to be the 'University Psychological Clinic' at Edinburgh University, offering advice to the parents and teachers of children and young people. William Boyd (1874–1962), Reader in Education, followed this in 1926 with an 'educational clinic' at Glasgow University, and the Notre Dame Child Guidance Clinic was founded in Glasgow in 1931, followed in turn in 1932 by a child guidance clinic at Aberdeen University. Glasgow Education Committee made further history in 1937, with the appointment of the first full-time child psychologist in Scotland.

By the outbreak of war in 1939, there were 11 child guidance clinics in Scotland (McKnight, 1978). Most of these were voluntary but practice at the Notre Dame Clinic was distinctive, as it was based upon the US child guidance approach of a multi-disciplinary team of psychiatrist, psychologist and social worker (McKnight, 1978).

The Education (Scotland) Act 1946 gave local authorities the option of setting up their own child guidance services and seven authorities did so in the years immediately following this Act. But it took a further 20 years until the Education (Scotland) Act 1969 before it became a legal requirement for each Scottish education authority to provide a child guidance service, the precursor to the expansion and development of educational psychology in Scotland in the 1970s and beyond.

Training and qualifications in educational psychology in Scotland

Training and qualifications in educational psychology in Scotland are distinctive. Indeed, Scotland can boast the first single honours degrees in psychology in the UK, BEd/EdB degrees which were qualifications in educational psychology geared towards teachers and those who wished to practice as educational psychologists (Boyle & Mackay, 2010).

As noted above, classes in psychology and experimental psychology, until 1946 offered in conjunction with logic and ethics, were mandatory for student teachers in Scotland from 1906 onwards. The early curriculum in psychology and experimental psychology dealt with assessment and teaching approaches and topics such as sensation, perception and memory. But by the 1920s, following the World War I and influenced by psychoanalysis and the US child guidance movement, concerns about the mental health of children came to the fore and these were incorporated into the psychology curriculum (Wooldridge, 1994). Later, due to Godfrey Thomson, Professor of Education at the University of Edinburgh and Director of Moray House

Training College and others, the focus of the curriculum reverted to an emphasis upon experimental psychology and mental testing (Sharp, 1980; Thomson, 1929).

The first psychology degrees established at this time were EdB degrees (at the universities of Aberdeen, Glasgow and St Andrews) and a BEd degree (at the University of Edinburgh). It should be noted that these degrees were markedly different from the BEd degrees which later followed in England and Wales, and indeed from the BEd degrees set up in Scotland following the Robbins Report (Ministry of Education, 1963). They were designed to encourage the development of enhanced conceptual understandings of teaching, learning and child development and of the implementation of new approaches into teaching practice in schools. Students would also often volunteer to help at university child guidance clinics (Hargreaves, 1985). Further, until after the World War II and the introduction of BA (Hons), MA (Hons) and BSc (Hons) degrees in psychology, they were also the only honours degrees in psychology in Scotland. As they were only open to teachers who had completed their training, they were regarded as 'higher' qualifications, despite the fact that they were Bachelor's degrees. It was not until the 1960s that the qualification was re-designated as the MEd (Hons) in educational psychology.

In the 1960s and up until the 1970s, the MEd (Hons) in educational psychology was one of the most important entry qualifications for educational psychologists in Scotland, unsurprisingly, as at this time psychologists working for local authority education departments were formally designated as 'teachers employed as psychologists' (MacKay, 2008). However, the growing demand for educational psychologists led to the introduction of the Diploma in Educational Psychology (DEP) in 1962 by Glasgow University's Psychology Department. This was a two-year integrated course in educational and child psychology incorporating teacher training for honours psychology graduates who wished to become educational psychologists. However, applicants for posts were still required to have the teacher-training qualification and two years' teaching experience or to acquire these after graduation before they would be eligible to work as educational psychologists.

The DEP and similar diploma courses in educational psychology were replaced in the 1970s by one-year Master's professional training courses for those with honours degrees in Psychology, following the growth of child guidance services in the wake of the Education (Scotland) Act 1969. Master's courses were established at this time in Aberdeen, Edinburgh, Stirling and Strathclyde Universities, and Glasgow University replaced the DEP with the Master of Applied Science (MAppSci) in Educational Psychology and Child Guidance. While teacher training was still a requirement for working as an educational psychologist in Scotland, the previously mandatory two-years' teaching experience requirement no longer applied.

The MEd (Hons) entry to the profession co-existed with the new Master's degrees until 1980, when the British Psychological Society withdrew recognition from the MEd (Hons) as a qualification to practice in Scotland. This was followed in the late 1980s by the removal of the requirement for educational psychologists to have undergone teacher training.

However, decline in the school population and budgetary constraints led to the closure of all but the training programme at Strathclyde University. By the beginning of the 1990s, a two-year Master's programme was introduced at Strathclyde, followed shortly by a new programme at the University of Dundee. With these two-year degrees a paradigm shift was complete: educational psychology in Scotland was no longer a profession for teachers who wished to become psychologists, but rather a profession of psychologists who wished to apply their skills and expertise in educational and community settings.

At the present time, although educational psychology training in the rest of the UK has moved towards pre-service doctorates, the two professional training programmes in Scotland, at the Universities of Dundee and Strathclyde, continue to offer two-year Master's degrees accredited by the British Psychological Society. However, three-year training is still required for registration with the Health Professions Council. To achieve this, the Master's degrees are 'topped up' in the probationary year by the British Psychological Society's Stage Two Award in Educational Psychology (Scotland) (BPS, 2008). This award fully meets the requirements of the Health Professions Council for registration as an educational psychologist and accordingly is held to provide an equivalent training and Level 12 qualification to the pre-service doctorates elsewhere in the UK and Ireland.

The two-year professional training programmes at the Universities of Dundee and Strathclyde follow the Core Curriculum as specified by the British Psychological Society's Scottish Division of Educational Psychology. Trainees spend two days per week during term time attending university lectures, seminars, workshops and tutorials and taking part in group activities, and two days a week in practice placements with educational psychology services under the supervision of their practice placement tutor engaged in shadowing and observation, case studies, practice-based assignments and projects. In year 2, again under supervision, trainees take on the work of an educational psychologist across the five mandatory roles for educational psychologists in Scotland and a research project. There are also block placements in psychological services and other community-based services for young people and families to help trainees further broaden their experience. Trainees also have an independent study day each week.

Entry to the programmes is extremely competitive and successful applicants require a good 2.1 honours degree in psychology and around two years of relevant professional employment with children/young people or families. A recent development is the withdrawal of grants by the Scottish Government Education Department to successful applicants from 2012–13. The impact of this upon recruitment to the profession and indeed on the possibility of introduction of pre-service doctoral degrees in Scotland is yet to be determined.

The distinctive nature of training and qualifications for educational psychology in Scotland, together with a separate legislature for education statutes, has led to the profession being the only branch of applied psychology in Scotland to be represented by a separate division of the Society, the Scottish Division of Educational Psychology, which plays a key role not only in such areas as the accreditation of training programmes but also in promoting the overall development of the profession. However, the distinctive features of Scottish educational psychology are wider than the differences in training and qualifications and in having a separate legal system. In a number of respects, the profession in Scotland may be described as being unique (Boyle & MacKay, 2010; MacKay, in press). This may be demonstrated in relation to four aspects of its history: its statutory foundation, the role and functions of psychologists, the development of nationally agreed quality standards and the establishment of post-school psychological services.

The statutory foundation

Scottish educational psychology services are built on a statutory foundation which is broader than for any other country in the world (MacKay, 1996). Their functions, with some additions and updated terminology arising from subsequent legislation, continue essentially as they were first set out in the Education (Scotland) Act 1946:

> *It shall be the duty of every education authority to provide for their area a psychological service in clinics or elsewhere, and the functions of that service shall include: (a) the study of children with additional support needs; (b) the giving of advice to parents and teachers as to appropriate methods of education for such children; (c) in suitable cases, provision for the additional support needs of such children in clinics; and (d) the giving of advice to a local authority within the meaning of the Social Work (Scotland) Act 1968 regarding the assessment of the needs of any child for the purposes of any of the provisions of that or any other enactment.*
>
> Education (Scotland) Act 1980, section 4, as amended

While these functions will be seen as having much in common with the work done by psychologists elsewhere in the UK, there are several important differences. First, while sharing many aspects of professional practice and development with services in England and Wales, Scottish services are fundamentally different in that all of the above duties are mandatory and not discretionary. While, for example, the contribution of the educational psychologist in England and Wales is generally wide ranging, the duties which must be provided by law are narrow, and are limited to the assessment of children and young people in relation to the Statement of Needs.

Second, the statutes described functions that 'include' rather than 'comprise' certain specified services. The use of the word 'include' indicated that the specific duties mentioned were not delimiting. This has provided a context for the very wide range of functions that have characterised Scottish services.

Third, the term 'additional support needs' when used to describe the functions of psychological services is intended to be of very broad interpretation. It is a direct replacement for the older term 'handicapped, backward and difficult children'. The population of children and young people embraced by this description has been defined in statutory instruments and official guidance, and includes the full range of psychological problems of childhood, whether educational, behavioural or developmental, and whether occurring in the context of school or elsewhere. Indeed, the single most important legislative statement that can be made about educational psychology in Scotland is that it is not a school psychological service, but provides such a service as part of a wider statutory remit. That remit has from the beginning encapsulated a view of educational psychology as community psychology, and as extending beyond the boundaries of school and of education (Scottish Education Department, 1952; MacKay, 1992a, 1992b, 2006a).

Fourth, the statutes governing Scottish educational psychology require services to give advice not just to the education authority but to the 'local authority', that is, to the council as a whole, in relation to areas beyond schools and education. The breadth of that function beyond education is seen in the reference to advising local authorities in relation to the Social Work (Scotland) Act 1968 or the provisions of 'any other enactment'. Much of the advice required by local authorities has been in a forensic field, as it relates to children and young people appearing before the Children's Hearings that replaced juvenile courts in Scotland in the 1960s, and indeed it has not been uncommon for educational psychologists in Scotland, on the basis of their broad remit, to transfer directly into forensic or clinical psychology.

Professional roles

Although schools, school-age pupils and the educational curriculum have always properly been at the heart of the work of the educational psychologist, any service with a statutory remit extending beyond schools and beyond education is likely to develop a wide range of roles and functions. MacKay (1989) proposed five functions for educational psychologists which were subsequently formalised in the national performance indicators for the profession (MacKay, 1999, p.2) and in the Government's review of services (Scottish Executive, 2002, p.20) as follows: 'Educational psychologists work at three main levels: the level of the individual child or family, the level of the school or establishment and the level of the local authority. In relation to each of these levels of work they have five core functions: consultation, assessment, intervention, training and research'.

It is not that these roles in themselves are unique, for the Scottish functions reflected the historical roots of educational psychology in the rest of the UK, as amply illustrated in the work of Sir Cyril Burt (see Hearnshaw, 1979). The same breadth of functions was promoted in England through the Summerfield Report (Department of Education and Science, 1968) and the later reviews of services (Department for Education and Employment, 2000a, 2000b; Farrell et al., 2006). Rather, the uniqueness of the Scottish position arises from the fact that for the past decade all of these functions and levels have been mandatory requirements of all services (Scottish Executive, 2002).

The research requirement provides an example of this. The role of the educational psychologist in research has been promoted in a UK context for many years (see, for example, Carroll, 1976; Gray, 1991; Lindsay, 1981; Thompson, 1979; Webster & Beveridge, 1997). However, research as a required core function at Government level rather than only as a professional aspiration is a distinctive feature of the Scottish position. MacKay (1982) proposed that 'research should be seen as a necessary and integral part of the work ... and not as an optional extra' (p.15), later asserting that this was a clear expectation arising from the statutes as the first statutory function was to 'study', implying not only the study of the individual child but also a commitment to systematic research (MacKay, 1996). By 1999 this position had been accepted, and research was nationally recognised as being a core requirement for every service (MacKay, 1999), and further endorsed by the Scottish Ministers following the national review of services (Scottish Executive, 2002). Research therefore has the status in Scottish services of being a core duty and one which is subject to national inspection.

The breadth of Scottish professional roles has been supported historically by very good staffing ratios in comparison with the rest of the UK. The English review in 2000 (Department for Education and Employment, 2000b) reported ratios for the 0–19 population as ranging from 1/4041 to 1/11,171, with few authorities better than 1/5000. Meanwhile in Scotland the ratios ranged from 1/2053 to 1/4231, with only one authority as poor as 1/4000 (Scottish Executive, 2002).

Quality standards

The third respect in which Scottish services are unique relates to quality standards. This has taken place in three main phases. First, the performance indicators published by the Scottish Executive (MacKay, 1999) were the first nationally endorsed quality standards in the world for educational psychology services. They were developed with the support of all interested parties including the university training programmes, the British Psychological Society, the Association of Scottish Principal Educational Psychologists, the Educational Institute of Scotland and Her Majesty's Inspectorate of Education. The exercise was further supported by a comprehensive process of consultation not only with the principal psychologists in the 32 services but through circulation to every educational psychologist in Scotland.

Second, through the BPS Scottish Division of Educational Psychology, psychologists campaigned for the establishment of a fully chartered profession, and became the only branch of UK psychology to be fully regulated in this way several years before regulation became a statutory requirement through the Health Professions Council.

Third, the profession requested that psychological services should be included in the HMIE inspections of education authority services. While the Inspectorate only have legal powers to inspect the education functions of services and not their wider statutory functions, the profession wished the inspections to be as comprehensive as possible and not to be restricted to the education functions alone. The performance indicators were further developed as a self-evaluation tool-kit in the standard format used by the Inspectorate (HMIE, 2007), and an inspection of all services was undertaken from 2006-2010 (HMIE, 2011).

Post-school psychological services

The fourth respect in which Scottish services are unique is in the requirement to make provision of post-school psychological services. In the early days of the profession the overwhelming focus of the work was with children, as implied by the original statutes. In common with the rest of the UK, an increasing emphasis on the needs of young people over the age of 16 led to the re-defining of services as making provision for children and young people in the 0–19 age range. This became statutory with the Disabled Persons (Services, Consultation and Representation) Act 1986, when services were re-named from being child guidance services to become 'regional or island authority psychological services', with a remit for the population aged 0–19 years. This new term was also soon rendered obsolete, and following the Local Government (Scotland) Act 1994 psychological services faced a period of major reorganisation under the 32 new unitary authorities established in 1996.

The Beattie Report on post-school education and training for young people with special needs (Scottish Executive, 1999) recommended that educational psychology services should be extended to provide a service to young people in the 16–24 age group who had left school. Following a period of preparatory work to develop a structure and role for such services, the Executive funded a pilot project in 12 Pathfinder authorities for the period 2004–06. On the basis of the evaluation of this initiative (MacKay, 2006b) the Government extended the provision of post-school psychological services to all 32 authorities.

Provision of post-school psychological services of this kind represents a distinctive Scottish development with no international parallel. Its uniqueness as an integral part of service provision has been argued by MacKay (2009) in a comparative review of educational psychology services throughout the world. The establishment of such services represented a significant challenge to educational psychology in terms of the structure and role of services, additional recruitment requirements, continuing professional development for staff, the curricula of university training programmes and finding field placements for trainee psychologists. It also required educational psychologists to provide a further range of services beyond education, and to work in partnership with agencies with a national rather than a local authority structure, such as Careers Scotland. More fundamentally, provision of services to adult age groups raised issues regarding the nature and scope of educational psychology itself, as a profession with a focus on children and adolescents and on models drawn from developmental psychology.

The future: the development of 'universal psychology services'

While the distinctive features of Scottish services are recognised, Scottish educational psychologists have a strong commitment to their role as an integral part of the profession in the UK. Thus, the movements that have influenced the development of the profession elsewhere in the country, such as the paradigm shifts that followed Gillham's (1978) *Reconstructing Educational Psychology*, have likewise influenced the work of Scottish services, which also face the future challenges common to UK services in general.

A major challenge for the future in Scotland will be the development of 'universal psychology services', that is, services which increasingly meet the needs of the whole population. The national review of services (Scottish Executive, 2002) envisaged a future in which the educational psychologist would provide holistic services across the contexts of home, school and community, and would contribute to the 'well-being of all children and young people, and not only to those with special educational needs' (para. 2.30). The review emphasised opportunities for psychologists in relation to all of the national priorities for education in Scotland, such as raising standards of attainment in the core skills of literacy and numeracy, enhancing school environments, promoting equality and in equipping pupils with the skills, attitudes and expectations necessary to prosper in a changing society.

It is not that the enduring centrality of working with the individual with additional support needs will be diminished, but rather that the wider role must be extended. This is reflected in the theme of the 2012 annual conference for educational psychologists in Scotland – 'Building capacity in universal services'. Two areas are highlighted here as key priorities: the mental health agenda and the physical health agenda.

As to the mental health agenda, for a number of years there has been a well-documented rise in the prevalence of mental health problems in children and young people. This includes depression, suicide rates, anorexia nervosa and other serious eating disorders, alcohol problems, drug abuse and emotional and behavioural difficulties in general. Addressing the mental health issues of children and young people has become a central political imperative to which public agencies in health, education and social services are expected to respond, and for more than a decade it has been a Scottish Government priority (Scottish Executive, 1999).

However, it has become increasingly clear that educational psychologists are a key therapeutic resource for young people, especially in educational contexts such as schools. They are the professionals most thoroughly embedded in educational systems, they have the widest training in child and adolescent psychology and they are therefore best poised to be generic child psychologists. Appropriate and evidence-based educational psychology practice can play a crucial role in bringing about positive change in the lives of children and young people, not only through expert individual therapeutic work but also through preventative programmes at whole-school and at authority level to build young people's resilience and to promote mental well-being.

As to the physical health agenda, this too reflects a central government priority. Its *Better Health, Better Care: Action Plan* (NHS Scotland, 2007) commits it to supporting good health choices and behaviours amongst children and young people. It has determined that 'health promotion will permeate every aspect of school life' (page 30). Through the *Scottish Curriculum for Excellence* children will have opportunities to take part in physical activities and learn about health and wellbeing, while an Active Schools initiative aims to promote healthy, active and well-motivated communities providing new opportunities to become involved in active pursuits.

The subject of health and educational psychology is essentially a 'greenfield site' (MacKay, 2011), but one in which educational psychologists are well positioned to play a central role, by drawing from health psychology models that focus on the links across awareness, attitudes, intentions and behaviour, and by applying these models to supporting schools in their health promotion agenda.

These areas for universal psychology initiatives reflect opportunities of relevance to all of British educational psychology, and it is expected that they will also point to significant potential developments for the profession in Scotland.

Vignette 9

David Kennedy-Fraser, MA, BSc, FBPsS, FEIS

Tommy MacKay & James Boyle

After a brief illness David Kennedy-Fraser died on 26 August 1962, at his home in Milngavie, Dunbartonshire.

He was a graduate in Arts and Science of Edinburgh University and later studied in Germany under Neumann, whose teaching influenced him greatly and gave direction to his subsequent career. His period of teaching and research in the department of Professor Whipple at Cornell University increased his interest in Experimental Psychology, and in the general problem of deficiencies in learning. His insight into the needs of the backward and the mentally handicapped, and his deep concern for their welfare, brought him to the forefront in all movements to secure amelioration of their lot.

From his lectureship in Education in Edinburgh University and in Moray House, Kennedy-Fraser transferred to Glasgow in 1923 to become the first psychologist to a local education authority with duties directly concerned with the assessment and diagnosis of mental retardation in pupils of school age. He held this post jointly with his appointment to Jordanhill Training College as Lecturer in Psychology, responsible for the training of teachers of the mentally handicapped. The course of training which he inaugurated and developed until his retiral was the first of its kind in the United Kingdom and, throughout the years of his guidance, attracted students from all parts of Scotland, from England, Ireland, South Africa, Australia and the United States. His books, *The Psychology of Education* and *The Education of the Backward Child*, were standard texts for many years.

David Kennedy-Fraser became widely known as the apostle of the handicapped, and spent himself untiringly in their service. He was an enthusiastic and stimulating lecturer, approachable at all times, helpful and encouraging. His buoyancy and cheerfulness made him a welcome visitor in the many schools for handicapped children to which he gave guidance, and won for him a secure place in the affections of his students.

His close association with the Scottish Association for Mental Health was continued after his retiral in widespread, indefatigable service to its branches throughout Scotland.

He was elected a Fellow of the Royal Society of Edinburgh in 1929. He was also a Fellow of the British Psychological Society, and of the Educational Institute of Scotland. He is survived by his wife and three daughters.

David Kennedy-Fraser was elected to the Royal Society of Edinburgh on 4 March 1929, his proposers being James Drever, George Alexander Carse, James Hartley Ashworth and Sir Edmund Taylor Whittaker. This obituary, written by 'A Former Colleague', appears in the Royal Society of Edinburgh Year Book *1963, pp.18–19.*

Chapter 10 The move to doctoral training: A study in systems change

Norah Frederickson

The vignette that follows, but which really sets the scene for this chapter, reports on a very positive professional learning process that equips educational psychologists (EPs) well to make a positive difference to the education and well-being of vulnerable children and young people in a range of contexts. However, this 'fit for purpose' training in educational psychology has only recently been achieved and it is a testament to all involved that the hoped for positive benefits have been so quickly realised, particularly in the light of the less than ideal circumstances in which three-year doctoral programmes replaced the longstanding one-year masters training route in England, Wales and Northern Ireland.

According to the first government report on psychologists in the United Kingdom (DES, 1968), the first one-year programme of professional training in educational psychology was a postgraduate diploma programme developed at UCL in 1946. This was disputed by the director of that programme who located the inauguration of the UCL diploma in the early 1930s, and reported having previously led a masters programme at the London Day Training Centre (the precursor of the Institute of Education) from 1923 (Burt, 1969). However the training in place from 1946, described by the International Bureau of Education as 'a university degree ... with honours in psychology or its equivalent, teaching experience from two to five years and a year of specialisation in child psychology' (UNESCO, 1948, p.29), would remain essentially unchanged for the following 60 years, despite influential calls for its extension from as early as 1968. Over the same period professional training in clinical psychology was extended from one, to two, to three years, with most programmes awarding a doctoral qualification from the mid 1990s (Turpin, 1995). This chapter examines the history of failed attempts to extend training from one year to two years, as well as the eventual success in introducing three-year doctoral level training in England, Wales and Northern Ireland in 2006. Lessons about the conditions necessary for achieving systemic change of this kind are drawn to inform future developments.

Reference will be made to an influential model of change in human systems, that developed by Kurt Lewin (see Lewin, 1952), which has served as the foundation for most models of change processes in the literature, across diverse disciplines (Elrod & Tippet, 2002). The model comprises two key concepts, the first of which proposes that 'force fields' determine whether social systems maintain a balanced status quo, or are unbalanced into a change process resulting in a new state. Force field analysis (see for example Figure 1 from Schein, 2002), based on this aspect of the model, is a widely used technique in organisational development whose value has been recognised in educational psychology (see for example Fox & Sigston, 1992; Jensen, Malcolm & Phelps, 2002; Smith & Reynolds, 1998).

The second of Lewin's key concepts was a three step model of change:

1. Unfreezing – involves destabilising the equilibrium that is held in place by the balance of forces in a particular situation.
2. Moving – involves engagement with a change process, iteratively identifying and evaluating possible alternatives.
3. Refreezing – involves stabilising around a new point of equilibrium where the changes are incorporated into the new modus operandi.

Although criticisms have been levelled at Lewin's model, in particular for being too linear and static, more recently it has enjoyed a resurgence (Burnes, 2004, 2009). It will be used in this chapter as a frame within which to reflect on the profession's experience of the move to three-year training.

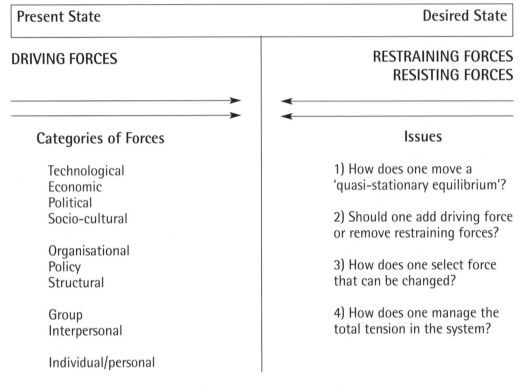

Figure 1: A sample force field analysis (adapted from Schein, 2002)

From one to two years?

There is many a slip between a clear recommendation in a government commissioned report and its implementation. It has been a cyclical pattern in the history of training in educational psychology that the professional arguments are won, the independent recommendations made, and then implementation founders on the rocks of politics and economics. The first clear example of this pattern can be seen in the fate suffered by the recommendations on training in the Summerfield Report on *Psychologists in the Education Services* (DES, 1968). In a scenario now all too familiar the then Secretary of State for Education and Science, replying to a question in parliament on 13 November 1969, pushed the responsibility for acting on the report back to the local authority employers and the training course providers.

> *The local education authorities, as employers, and the establishments responsible for providing courses in educational psychology, are I am sure carefully considering the recommendations made, including the proposal for two-year postgraduate courses following directly on graduation as an alternative to the present one-year course following on a period of experience as a teacher. The latter qualification seems likely to be the main one for some time to come, but there may well be scope for experimental 2-year 'end-on' courses as well, and if initiatives are made in this direction I shall be willing to see what, within the resources available, can be done from the point of view of student support.*

> Hansard (House of Commons debate 13 November 1969, vol 791 cc131–2W)

The Summerfield Committee, which had been established as a result of a 25 per cent shortfall in the number of educational psychologists to available posts, recommended the new two-year postgraduate courses as 'a practical and economic pattern of training' (DES, 1968, para 7.29) not only more likely to address the shortfall in supply but also to extend curriculum coverage in important ways:

...it should be possible to give more comprehensive treatment to the basic courses on normal and abnormal human development, parent-child relationships, learning problems and methods of instruction, and the psychology of social groups including schools and classes... There would also be opportunities for improving the balance and the range of skills in observing, in interviewing children, their parents and other adults, and in making investigations and assessments by tests and other means.

Department of Education and Science (1969, para 7.29)

The proposed new programme no longer required experience as a teacher, and this quickly emerged as a key issue. The Summerfield Committee had acknowledged that teaching experience might certainly be of value to candidates, but questioned why this substantial investment of time was required, and what exactly was supposed to be learnt from the experience that was essential to becoming an educational psychologist. However, levelling criticism at the weight given by Summerfield Committee to evidence from the British Psychological Society (BPS) in concluding that teaching experience was not essential, Currie (1969) noted that it was a membership requirement of the Association of Educational Psychologists (AEP), founded seven years earlier, and that many promotion opportunities for educational psychologists were restricted to qualified teachers. Teaching experience was to be a recurrent issue for debate between the BPS and the AEP over the next 50 years. While the AEP had significant influence in local authorities (LAs), it is doubtful that opposition to the loss of teaching experience was a decisive resisting force. The Secretary of State also highlighted an increase in the numbers being trained in universities between 1965 and 1969, substantially above the projections of the Summerfield Committee. It seems that workforce planning in educational psychology has long been an imprecise endeavour. The very significant weakening of the driving force that had led to the establishment of the Committee was probably of greatest importance in maintaining the status quo post-Summerfield.

The next government sponsored report to support an increase in the length of professional training in educational psychology was not followed by a period of suspense regarding implementation. On this occasion the 'in principle' support for extending training was qualified in the report itself by a recognition that 'for practical reasons of resources, supply and demand it is unrealistic to expect a general extension to two years in the immediate future' (DES, 1984, p.14). The use of the word 'general' here is relevant as two training centres (Newcastle and Sussex) had established courses of longer duration. In the light of the conclusions of this report it is not surprising that they failed to survive, as a two-year programme in the case of Newcastle, and as a provider of EP training in the case of Sussex (Maliphant, 1994).

The driver for change on this occasion came from proposals made to the Department for Education and Science in 1981 by the higher education institutions offering professional training in educational psychology. At the forefront was the increasing difficulty of covering all the relevant knowledge and skills needed to equip educational psychologists to fulfil their steadily expanding role in local authorities.

The tutors for Professional Training Courses in Educational Psychology have for some years been conscious of the fact that they have been in the business of cramming quarts into pint pots. The breadth and depth of academic and practical skills which we wish to teach to educational

> *psychologists in training will no longer conveniently fit into an academic year, nor even a calendar year. The problem is growing steadily more acute, with a fairly constant widening of the role of educational psychologists in local authorities and with a considerable increase, in recent years, in the number of assessment and intervention strategies which are available to them.*
>
> Elliott (1981a, para 1.1)

However, in the background was the serious job shortage being experienced by newly educational psychologists at the time. While the paragraph above, albeit slightly edited, opened both the proposal to the DES on 24 September 1981 and the earlier draft circulated to course tutors on 18 March 1981, the following paragraph was contained only in the earlier document:

> *A second concern of tutors, which has arisen in more recent years, has been the problem of the over production of professionally qualified educational psychologists. Our best and most recent estimate is that we are currently producing approximately twice as many psychologists as there are posts available, and this problem appears likely to get worse in the foreseeable future. Clearly something has to be done about this, but a simple 50% reduction in intake is hardly likely to be acceptable to any of our training institutions.*
>
> Elliott (1981b, p.1)

Instead the proposal submitted in September concluded with the following paragraph:

> *Funding of courses. This is to some extent a separate issue. The course tutors are keenly aware of the financial implications of these proposals. They are eager to participate with the DES and the LEAs in future manpower planning. As a first step, they would propose to reduce intakes on two-year courses to half their present levels.*
>
> Elliott (1981a, para 5)

This proposal appeared to represent a potentially neat solution to the over-production problem, which was clearly generating considerable anger among unemployed newly qualified EPs, as evidenced by the letter published in the *Bulletin of the British Psychological Society* accusing course tutors of insensitivity and smugness (Birnbaum et al., 1980). This provides a context for the consideration given in the report (DES, 1984) to fund two-year training within existing resources by reducing the numbers being trained by half. However, once again the primary driver for change, graduate unemployment, had become significantly weakened by the time the report was produced.

> *Following the passing of the 1981 Education Act a number of LEAs reassessed their demand and a number of new posts was created in 1983. The figures produced by the DES and the AEP ... suggest that this increase in the number of authorised posts has mopped up this pool of unemployment and still left some unfilled vacancies.*
>
> Department of Education and Science (1984, p.12)

The 1984 Working Group drew representation from the Association of County Councils, the Association of Metropolitan Authorities, the Society of Education Officers, Her Majesty's Inspectorate, the DES, the University Grant's Committee, the AEP and the BPS. Whether influenced by the substantial employer representation, the nature of the drivers for change, or some other factors, in this report there was no debate about teaching experience. Despite taking particular note that it was not a requirement for professional training in Scotland, the Working Group expressed conviction that teaching experience was an essential prerequisite to training as an educational psychologist. Indeed consideration was given as to whether the minimum of two years teaching experience was long enough. However, it was also noted that since the early 1970s psychology graduates had, in addition, to complete a one-year post-graduate teaching qualification, and asserted that: 'since it was now accepted that psychology, although not generally a subject taught in schools, was relevant to teaching in schools, there should be no difficulty for a suitable psychology graduate to obtain a place on a PGCE course' (DES, 1984, p.11). Over the following decade psychology graduates encountered increasing difficulty obtaining places on PGCE courses, despite the increasing popularity of psychology as a school subject. Indeed there was evidence that substantial difficulties were being experienced by psychology graduates applying for teacher training in the early 1980s (Brady, 1982; Long, 1982) despite the assertions in the report to the contrary. These difficulties were subsequently compounded by the introduction of the National Curriculum in the late 1980s and the corresponding focus on recruiting graduates able to teach national curriculum subjects.

Broader economic and social forces

In a further foreshadowing of difficulties to come, the funding arrangements for training, whereby LAs could reclaim the whole cost of seconding a teacher to train as an EP, or an EP to tutor on a training programme, were described in the 1984 report as 'somewhat exceptional'. It was noted that a reduction in the percentage was under discussion elsewhere. It took some years for this reduction to come, following the introduction of the DfE Grants for Education and Training scheme. By this time many course centres were also providing a range of post-experience training opportunities for practising educational psychologists, as had been strongly recommended by the 1984 Working Party report. Both strands of training were hit hard by the change in funding arrangements in the late 1980s/early 1990s.

At the same time a major change was introduced by the BPS in 1988 following an amendment to its Royal Charter permitting the establishment of a Register of Chartered Psychologists. Designed to offer protection to the public from inappropriately qualified persons offering psychological services, entry to the register was granted to those who had completed accredited postgraduate training in psychology. Across all branches of psychology it was specified that this postgraduate psychology training must comprise, or equate to, three years full-time study or supervised practice in psychology. BPS-approved training routes for clinical, counselling, forensic, health and occupational psychology were quickly established By 1993 the approved three-year postgraduate training in educational psychology in Scotland comprised a two-year university-based programme, followed by a year of supervised practice in an educational psychology service accredited by the BPS Scottish Division of Educational and Child Psychology for this purpose.

Exceptionally, the BPS allowed educational psychology training in England, Wales and Northern Ireland a very long lead-in time for the introduction of three-year postgraduate training in order to facilitate the re-alignment of funding streams. In the interim a year of supervised practice was needed following the one-year professional training programme. However, unlike the situation in Scotland, there was no system of service accreditation, instead it was specified that the third year should be supervised by someone eligible for Chartered educational psychologist status. The less than ideal arrangements for the third year leading to Chartered status paled into insignificance compared with the unsatisfactory nature of interim arrangements agreed in relation to the first of the three years. For this first year, two years' qualified teaching experience was accepted, even though it usually contained no formal postgraduate study of psychology and might actually take place prior even to the acquisition of an undergraduate degree in psychology.

While the anomalous position of educational psychology training programmes in relation to the criteria for chartered status was an increasing focus of concern for the BPS (Lunt, 1993), the predominant issue for training in the early 1990s was the crisis in funding. Given the diminishing percentage of the cost of a secondment available through the DfE Grants for Education and Training Scheme, the supply of educational psychologists to LEAs failed to keep up with demand due to the reduced number of secondments. Secondments were not linked to course places so each secondment advertised was applied for by almost all successful applicants to courses across the country, creating a large administrative task for services and a further disincentive to offer a secondment.

Following discussions between the BPS, the AEP, the DfE and the Local Government Association (LGA), in 1995 the DfE allocated earmarked funding for training educational psychologists via a mechanism involving a top slice from the Revenue Support Grant, to be administered centrally initially by the LGA. This created a period of relative financial stability in training, until 2007 when the top-slice mechanism was abolished and replaced with arrangements for the pooling of LA contributions. The rapid and complete failure of this approach again demonstrated, hopefully for the last time, the need for central funding of EP training (which was re-established in 2012).

The period of financial stability from 1995 and the establishment of a nationally representative steering group for EP training (the lack of which had been commented on as a barrier to change by the 1984 Working Group) facilitated the move to extend the length of training, which gathered momentum again in the mid 1990s. The national steering group comprised PEP representatives from each regional grouping of LAs in England. Chaired by a Director of Children's Services who was a former PEP, the group also had representation from the higher education institutions, the BPS, AEP, DfES and HMI. In addition to the removal of a key restraining force through the establishment of this national body with responsibility for EP training, the mid 1990s saw the emergence of new drivers for change.

New drivers for change

Europe was the source of the first of the new drivers for extension of the length of EP training in the 1990s. Lunt and Farrell (1994) described how the European Community Directive 89/84/EEC on the mutual recognition of professional qualifications led to concern that this could be used by governments to reduce qualification requirements. Consequently the European Federation of Applied Psychology Associations agreed a minimum six-year training period which, in the UK, would involve the Graduate Basis for Registration (GBR) and three years of professional psychology training. Resolving the anomalous interim arrangement in educational psychology training in England Wales and Northern Ireland had become a European as well as a national issue. Adopting the Scottish model was seen as the minimum acceptable change, and one to be urgently pursued.

The second new driver related to the level of the award increasingly being given for completion of the established three-year programmes of professional training in clinical psychology.

> ...*finally, as a matter of status, which may be less important, but does remain relevant, clinical psychologists will have doctorates, counselling psychologists will have them soon, and most other sections of the psychological profession may be moving in this direction. Clearly we do not want educational psychologists to be the 'poor relation'.*

> Gersch (1997, p.15)

At the same time the BPS was developing its own three-year qualification in educational psychology and, since the Society had become able to award its own degrees, active consideration was being given to the award of doctoral degrees (Lunt & Farrell, 1994). This meant that the BPS could establish a training route where individuals employed in trainee posts registered for the Society's qualification, which would meet chartering and European requirements, whereas one-year courses from existing EP training centres did not. However, EP training centres had not been slow to develop continuing professional development (CPD) doctorates in educational psychology, starting with the University of East London (Wolfendale et al.,

1995). Farrell (1996) reported that a further three programmes had been established within 12 months of the first, and more were to follow. This was an important development, less so as a driver than as a means of overcoming resisting forces, both in universities where there were initially some reservations about the status of professional doctorates, in relation for example to PhD programmes, and among the profession where these CPD doctorate programmes offered opportunities for existing practitioners and diminished concerns about the possible development of a 'two-tier' profession.

It should be noted that the 'status' argument quoted above was the final point raised by Gersch (1997) in his analysis of the future requirements of EP training. Writing as chair of the Division of Educational and Child Psychology (DECP) training committee, but also as a principal educational psychologist, his primary focus was on preparing new entrants to EP services for the range of roles they had to fulfil in addressing the needs of vulnerable children and their families. He drew attention to major demands on EP services from legislation enacted since the agreement in 1984 that two-year training was required (the 1989 Children Act, the 1993 Education Act and the 1994 Code of Practice), and to other expansions in the EP role, relating for example to crisis intervention, tribunals and training delivery. A review and updating of the core curriculum for EP training carried out in response to these developments by the DECP training committee had failed to identify a valid way in which the necessary competencies could be developed in one year. This led to the establishment in 1995 of a DECP Working Party on Doctoral Training in Educational Psychology. When first formed it was led by an EP course tutor and consisted of an equal number of practitioners and trainers, although it was reported that steps were being taken to co-opt PEP representatives from different regions (Farrell, 1996). The AEP was also represented, and by the time the working party's report was ready to be presented to the BPS Membership and Qualifications Board in May 1997, practitioners were in the majority on the working party and held the chair. In the mid 1990s, by contrast to the early 1980s, the move to extend training was driven by the profession, not the training institutions.

A range of consultations were carried out by the DECP working party: with educational psychology services (Portsmouth et al., 1995), Principal Educational Psychologists (Morris, 1997), and course tutors (Frederickson et al., 1996). Frederickson (1997) summarised commonalities and differences in the views of these groups. There was widespread support for the principle of extending initial training and agreement across groups on a number of potential benefits: an increase in the quality of training, for example in the breadth and depth of knowledge and the integration of theory, research and practice; more comprehensive practical experience leading to increased quality of service delivery by new EPs; improvements in image/status/self-esteem of the profession; and opportunities for developments to the research base of professional practice. However, alongside broad support for the principle, there were a number of concerns relating to the implementation of extended training in practice. Of universal concern were funding and demands for increased placement supervision from services. The likelihood of recruitment problems during the transition period and the potential loss of teacher qualification/experience were also raised in more than one of these consultations. In addition to these more formal consultations regular liaison was established with key groups, both within the BPS and outside, for example with the Department for Education and Employment (DfEE) and LGA.

The watershed

On 9 May 1997 the BPS Membership and Qualifications Board accepted the report of the DECP Working Party on Doctoral Training in Educational Psychology and endorsed the proposal the professional training course in educational psychology should be extended to three years of full time study, one-year courses ceasing to be accredited by the Society from September 2001. Despite the extensive consultations that had gone before, this decision elicited some criticism, in particular for committing to the implementation of three-year training before securing answers to questions of how the change would be implemented, and indeed funded. However the BPS took the stance that it was important to put principles first and pragmatics second, arguing that taking a stand on what needed to be done would stimulate action in working out the details of how it could be done.

Described as 'a watershed in the history of the profession' (Farrell et al., 1998, p.50), this decision can be seen in terms of Lewin's model to have had the effect of 'unfreezing' the system. LAs were legally required to obtain advice from EPs in carrying out the statutory assessments of special educational needs. It was inconceivable that EPs could be engaged for that purpose who were not considered appropriately qualified by the professional body whose royal charter conferred the authority to set appropriate standards of training and qualification. While the situation had clearly passed into the 'moving' stage of the change process, few were under any illusion that rapid change was likely, or the eventual nature of the change certain. The following cautious prediction on timescale proved remarkably accurate.

> *I think the BPS proposals are so much pie-in-the-sky. Sorry as I may be to say this, I really do not think that three-year, wholly doctorate training has got a snowflake's chance in Hades of being in place by 2001 … What the BPS has done, and I greatly welcome it, is to set us all a target … provided we are realistic we have now got something to aim for. It may be three-year training in place by, say, 2003, 2004 or 2005. Or it may be two-year training by 2001, to be extended again to three-years by, say, 2006. I am not advocating either of these time frames … I am just trying to temper the profession's enthusiasm and optimism for the start of the new century with realism and pragmatism.*

Harrison-Jennings (1998, p.52)

In response to the identification of a need for change in EP training in 1997, the DfEE took exactly the same action as on previous occasions, in 1965 and 1981, and set up a working group on the role and training of educational psychologists. The working group was established in November 1998 and the Society agreed to await publication of its report before drawing up an action plan to implement restructured training. The DfEE Working Party report on the role of the educational psychologist in July 2000 (DfEE, 2000) was followed in December by a detailed consultation document on the training and professional development of educational psychologists. It was distributed to: Chief Education Officers in England, the Local Government Association, the Local Government National Training Organisation, British Psychological Society, Educational Psychology Professional Associations, Teacher Associations, Higher Education Institutions and Special Educational Needs Organisations. In May 2001 the DfEE published a summary of the 101 responses (of which 77 were from LAs) and reported clear endorsement that the proposed new model of training (graduate basis for registration with the BPS plus three years' postgraduate professional training) that would meet the future training needs of the profession (90 per cent agreed), and would be viable from the perspective of higher education institutions and employing LAs (94 per cent agreed).

The DfES then funded two implementation studies in 2003, that brought together all interested parties in working out the details of arrangements and costs for a recommended start in September 2005, subject to the necessary funding being secured in the 2004 government spending review. The first sign that this was at risk came on 2 March 2004 when the Schools Minister, writing to the AEP, indicated that despite the agreed need for change, there could be no guarantee that Ministers would prioritise the additional funding required. Despite parliamentary questions and letters to Ministers, a lengthy period of uncertainty followed for prospective applicants, courses and the profession generally until, at the DECP conference in January 2005, a senior civil servant announced that the additional amount required to fund the agreed model of restructured training would not be forthcoming. It seemed that history had repeated itself and the move to extend training had foundered for the third time in the face of restraining economic forces.

The resolution

In a break with the past, the DfES decision not to provide additional funding in 2005 was not allowed to form an insuperable barrier to extending training. By then there was a new and powerful driver, which had not even featured in the list of arguments for extending training in the 1990s. For over 30 years the BPS had been lobbying the government to introduce statutory regulation of psychologists in order to better protect the public. The establishment of the voluntary register of chartered psychologists had been a key step towards this. In March 2003 the Minister of Health announced that statutory regulation would be introduced, although not through the establishment of a regulatory body specific to psychology as the BPS had hoped, but through the Health Professions Council (HPC). It was then expected that the Statutory Register would open in 2006 and the BPS made explicit through the curriculum guidance provided to the HPC that the standard for entry onto the statutory register would be equivalent to Chartered Psychologist/doctoral level.

The new model of EP training would meet the requirements for statutory registration of psychologists, whereas the old model would not. Educational psychology training in England, Wales and Northern Ireland was an anomaly that urgently needed to be resolved. There was also significant concern amongst the profession, and amongst service managers in particular, as the *Every Child Matters* agenda (DfES, 2004) appeared to be bringing ever closer co-located multi-agency teams under Children's Trusts, and including clinical psychologists with doctoral qualifications, that newly qualified educational psychologists needed to be eligible for HPC registration on the same basis as clinical psychologists .

In February 2005 the BPS responded to the Department's announcement by issuing a statement that re-affirmed the position that re-structured training for educational psychologists was necessary and should be pursued. The accreditation of the existing Masters courses was extended for one further year only (2005/6). A default position for the future of training was identified which involved completion of the Society three-year qualification in educational psychology while working as an assistant educational psychologist. For the second time in ten years the BPS had acted to unfreeze the situation and, as before, the disequilibrium generated created some concern, not least among the existing training providers. A working party was convened to identify other ways in which the three-year doctoral training could be implemented in the absence of additional funding from central government. The working party, which included representatives from key stakeholder groups, suggested an interim training model, to allow the implementation of three-year training within existing resources, pending resources becoming available to implement the model developed by the DfES Working Group, which was universally considered the preferred training model. The interim training model that was proposed comprised:

- Year 1 – a full time university-based programme with reduced placement experience (compared to existing MSc programmes), aspects of which may be largely supervised by university tutors.
- Years 2 and 3 – the trainee would need to secure employment as a trainee educational psychologist whilst still registered as a full-time postgraduate student on a doctoral programme. As this would be done by applying for vacant EP posts in the period 2006–8 when no EPs were qualifying, and as the trainees would be paid some £10,000 less than

qualified EPs, this would release the money needed to pay for the university fees and supervision in the service.

In April 2005 Tony Dessent, chair of the National Steering Group for Educational Psychology training, called an extraordinary meeting to discuss these proposals. The DfES representative decided not to attend, effectively washing the Department's hands of any responsibility in the matter, in terms strikingly reminiscent of the ministerial response in 1969 (see earlier):

■ Educational psychologists are not our employees, and our locus with respect to EPs is very limited.

■ The proposed new training route for EPs did not originate with us, though we sought in good faith to facilitate the development of a way forward.

■ When it became clear that there would be a financial cost to the route which was being proposed, we put this to Ministers and they indicated quite clearly that they saw the new route as too expensive. If anything the financial position has tightened even further since then, and there is no room for negotiation.

■ In this context – which has been communicated clearly by the Department – we do not understand why the BPS seem apparently intent on undermining the crucial role of EPs in improving outcomes for children with additional needs.

■ But given our extremely limited locus, we are not in any position to get involved in detailed negotiations about the way forward. We have nothing to bring to the table, and the statement from the BPS is certainly not going to change that.

Coates (2005)

However, Tony Dessent took a different view. Describing the BPS position as principled, he made it clear that compliance with its requirements was a necessity. The LGA could not provide funding to support training on a course unless it had professional body accreditation and no public service would take the risk of employing graduates of an unaccredited programme. The BPS proposals were supported by the great majority of the regional PEP representatives on the national steering group (albeit with the recognition that the details would take some working out and hard work to implement). A number of concerns were raised by the AEP, relating for example to stress on EPs from additional supervision demands and staff shortages during the first two years when there would be no supply of new EPs. There was also concern about the definition of an EP enshrined in the national pay negotiation framework and it was confirmed by the LGA that the requirements for employment as an educational psychologist in LAs would be changed to bring them in line with the new qualification route, which no longer required qualified teaching experience. Following further work by BPS, AEP, training providers and PEP representatives, in June 2005 the Children and Young Persons Board of the LGA endorsed the model proposed by the BPS working group, and provided additional funding to cover payment of university fees in years 2 and 3.

The outcomes

In September 2006 the first cohort of trainee educational psychologists commenced the new three-year doctoral programmes. Upon completion of their training in August 2009, they were eligible to apply to the HPC register, which had opened the previous June. In this respect extended training had been achieved just in time. What of the other anticipated and desired outcomes, and what of the principal concerns? Juliet Whitehead's vignette, attesting to her positive experience of extended training, paints a picture that would be widely recognised in the profession. Two aspects are worthy of particular note. The first is the challenge, but also reward, experienced in relation to the research component of the programme, probably the largest qualitative difference between masters and doctoral training. Her account of the phased sequence of opportunities to acquire a range of practice relevant research skills, and the topics investigated, puts into perspective why fears of a shift from an applied to an overly academic focus have dissipated.

The importance of research skills to engagement in evidence based practice should not be forgotten (Frederickson, 2002; Fox, 2003), and in an international context it has been argued that greater emphasis should probably be placed in research training on preparation as an informed consumer of the literature than as a contributor to it (Oakland & Jimerson, 2007). However the UK's first LA EP saw an integral role for research in all aspects of professional practice 'all my work in the Council's schools was of the nature of research. Even the individual cases .... had each to form the subject of a small intensive investigation' Burt (1964, cited in Rushton, 2002). Time will reveal the accuracy of the prediction about the move to doctoral training that 'the most important legacy will be the enormous expansion in research activity by educational psychologists' (Frederickson et al., 1998, p.14).

The other issue worth noting is the positive welcome in the vignette to the diversity of trainee background experiences, given that the loss of teacher training and experience as a prerequisite was the issue on which the profession had been most divided (Frederickson et al, 1999). One of the reasons most consistently given for the retention of teaching experience was that teachers were very conscious of the qualifications of those who set out to advise them and that successful teaching experience was necessary if EPs were to retain credibility. Maliphant (1994) noted that there was no published data to prove or disprove this often quoted assertion, although EPs in Scotland did not report any substantive differences in teacher response to those who had and had not been teachers. Finally, some relevant research was conducted in England which discovered that the majority of teachers did not even know that EPs had them-selves been teachers, and knowledge that EPs had been teachers was only associated with more positive perceptions by primary, but not by secondary or special, schools teachers (Freder-ickson et al., 2001).

Returning for the final time to Lewin's model, to what extent can the situation surrounding educational psychology training be said to have re-frozen? In many respects acceptance by the Health Professions Council in 2009 of doctoral level, or equivalent, as the threshold qualifica-tion for entry to the profession might be taken as an indication that a new status quo had been established. As such it would seem an appropriate point at which to conclude this chapter on the history of professional training in educational psychology. However, given the significant drivers that have emerged since then, for example the report on sustainable arrangements for EP training (DfE, 2011) and the Children and Families Bill, it does appear that an eventful next episode is already in full production.

Vignette 10

Memories of training in the 2000s

Juliet Whitehead

In 2006, British Psychological Society (BPS) accredited professional training for educational psychologists (EPs) in England and Wales changed. The one-year Master's degree programme was replaced by a three-year full-time programme leading to doctorate qualification. I was in the second cohort of trainee EPs studying for the doctorate qualification in Educational Psychology at Cardiff University. I welcome the opportunity to share my experiences of being a trainee EP following the revised three-year professional training route.

The extended training enables greater breadth and depth compared to the one-year Master's degree course in terms of developing understanding and experience, which provides a corresponding responsibility on trainees to reflect this knowledge in their practice. Cardiff University ensured the acquisition, consolidation and demonstration of this level of competency by delivering a comprehensive curriculum that included: assignments, group tasks (including collaborative research projects), presentations, written reflections, small-scale research projects, taught sessions, educational psychology service (EPS) placements and the writing-up of fieldwork. A key element of the programme was the submission of a thesis in the final year of training, undertaken with the support of a designated supervisor.

Trainees studying at Cardiff are placed in a different EPS each year for specified blocks of time, with periods set aside for university sessions or studying. The work I undertook during my placements illustrated the considerable difference that the application of psychology can make to children and young people. This work included assessing learning and emotional needs; developing, delivering and evaluating therapeutic and behaviour management programmes; reviewing policies; and conducting research. From my own experience, the opportunity to work as a trainee EP within a variety of EPSs provided invaluable insights into different models of practice and service delivery. It enabled me to consider the merits of various EPS structures, the roles that they play within Local Authorities, and the diverse populations that they serve.

It was especially evident during EPS placements that the EP's role is dynamic and evolving, and it was a privilege to be a trainee at a time when much emphasis was placed on collaborative working using a multi-agency team approach to deliver a comprehensive, quality service. It was my experience as a trainee that the EP's role was moving away from working with children and young people on an individual basis and towards a more consultative approach. This provided opportunities for me to seek to support children and young people through working with their families, and colleagues from various disciplines, including teaching staff, health professionals and social workers. I remember finding this multidisciplinary and multi-agency collaborative working particularly surprising; it was the first time I was aware that the professionals working with a child or young person can be so numerous and diverse. This highlighted the importance of appreciating and understanding the roles of organisations and agencies early on within the placement, the necessity for effective communication in a language common to all, and the need to consider multiple perspectives to ensure the best outcomes for the children and young people with whom we work.

University-based sessions developed my theoretical knowledge and maximised its practical application during EPS placements, not only within schools, but also in the wider community.

These sessions facilitated a safe environment to explore, debate and challenge extensive and diverse issues and practices. From my experience the increasingly eclectic mix of trainee EPs' backgrounds (a teaching qualification no longer being required for training) provided a fresh and diverse range of perspectives and skills applicable to the EP's role.

At the initial stages of the training programme, I remember feeling somewhat over-whelmed by the curriculum requirement to conduct multiple research projects. I thought that the research studies, especially those involving quantitative analyses, were somewhat daunting, having not opened my SPSS textbooks (the ones for beginners) for several years. Lectures on quantitative and qualitative research skills early on in the programme introduced and built upon my somewhat hidden, pre-existing knowledge. A collaborative research study with the support of fellow trainees allowed these skills to be applied and a subsequent small-scale research study carried out independently ensured the consolidation of these skills before the final thesis research study began. The studies were genuinely fascinating, and included an exploration of the attainment and resilience of looked after children with emotional and behavioural difficulties; the promotion of emotional health and well-being in one Welsh authority's primary and secondary schools; and factors affecting anxiety in more able adoles-cent females.

Research studies often have their own particular challenges, and those concerned with educational psychology are not exceptions to this. Collecting data from students with addi-tional learning needs; co-ordinating the return of written consent forms from parents, students and schools; participants' absences on the day of data collection; and the equipment, that had been tested and retested prior to data collection, nevertheless breaking down at the crucial moment; these were just some of the challenges encountered during my training. The experi-ences and opportunities created by trainee EPs themselves, as independent learners, also expanded on the knowledge and understanding of the profession itself.

As a trainee EP, I was privileged to represent trainee EPs at the BPS Division of Educational and Child Psychology Annual Professional Development Conference held in Manchester in 2009. The experience inspired my involvement, along with other Cardiff trainees, in hosting our own Conference for fellow trainees.

The knowledge that I acquired during my training has provided me with firm foundations from which new ideas and concepts have developed. These, in turn, have helped make a signif-icant difference to the educational success and well-being of the children and young people with whom I have worked since qualifying.

Chapter 11 Working across diverse contexts with wider populations: The developing role of the educational psychologist

Vivian Hill

This chapter will explore how the role of the Educational Psychologist (EP) has developed over the first century of the profession, following the format of Chapter Three in mapping the links between developments in psychological theory, social and political legislative contexts, and patterns of service delivery.

Norwich (2000) and Stobie (2002) reflect on the need for the profession to be responsive to changes in social systems and structures. Brofenbrenner's ecosystemic model (1979) provides a helpful framework for conceptualising the influences of the many systems and contexts within which educational psychology is operationalised, and explains the state of constant flux in the profession. To understand the development of the profession it is helpful to reflect on the interactive influences of change within these various systems and the way they are experienced and perceived within the profession. While change is an uncontrollable feature of life and the constant need to adapt is crucial to survival; it may be a consequence of the many systems within which EPs work, and the fast moving development of psychology and consequent legislation, that there seems to be a continual state of disquiet and uncertainty within the profession, prompting professional insecurity and seeking external mediation to approve professional actions, in a way rarely seen in other professions. Fallon, Woods and Rooney (2010) highlight the numerous and increasingly frequent examinations of the professional role, and observe: A consistent theme of 'reconstruction', 'reformulation and 'refocusing' for the future, which suggests to the present authors an enduring under-confidence about professional identity and direction (p.2).

Yet the historical review of the professional role highlights some striking consistencies between the models of applied practice developed by Sir Cyril Burt one hundred years ago, and those currently observed by Miller and Frederickson (2008) which typically include individual work, school-based work, family work, research activity and contributions to policy development. Whilst the profession has experienced many changes in the psychological conceptualisation of special needs and diverse social and political agendas, from segregated education to inclusion, the core strands of professional practice are still much in evidence. This raised the question of whether the systems and structures in which EPs work, or conservatism within the profession, is inhibiting change (Hill, 2005). Norwich (2000) ascribes the role confusion and ambiguity to an inability to integrate academic and applied psychologies to form a coherent framework for practice. Lunt and Majors (2000) reflect on the professional status of the EP, which is strongly influenced by the pressures of legislative duties and the local authority employment contexts, both of which limit professional autonomy and shape service delivery. They refer to the work of Barnett (1997) who proposes that in an uncertain modern world, professionals need to be critically self reflective of their own practice, and in order to survive must 'remake' themselves, claiming that the distinguishing feature of the professional is 'the duty, not the right to speak out'. All too often the small size of our profession, the state control of our professional training, and the legislative context, all toe easily distort work patterns, often in a way that is not consistent with current psychological thought or theory, thus undermining professional autonomy.

Legislative context

The 1981 Education Act introduced the statutory assessment process, and in so doing supported the expansion and secured the future of the profession. The 1996 Education Act introduced strict statutory time frames for completing assessments, and introduced both the code of practice and the SEN tribunal. Being enshrined in law, and as such protected proved to be rather a doubled edged sword. Over time the demands of the statutory process came to dominate and restrict the range of work that EPs performed, particularly as the employing local authority was accountable for meeting the statutory time frames and therefore prioritised this strand of work. In this context the role of the EP became increasingly narrow and assessment orientated, and this also meant that fewer children and families were able to access the service, and many needs went unmet.

The Labour government came to power in May 1997 and in October presented the Green Paper *Excellence for All Children*, with a number of clear objectives, firstly a commitment to the inclusion of pupils with special needs and secondly, a determination to 'challenge widespread assumptions' about achievement in the SEN population by raising standards. The political agenda had shifted to focus on developing holistic policies that cut across departmental divides to promote social inclusion. Government policy was informed by a clear understanding that complex problems require multi-faceted conceptualisations and responses. The Social Exclusion Unit (SEU) and associated task force were developed to investigate and tackle:

> *What happens when people or places suffer from a series of problems such as unemployment, discrimination, poor skills, low incomes, poor housing, high crime, ill health and family breakdown'. Recognising that: 'When such problems occur they create a vicious cycle.*

The SEU conducted research and informed policy, producing over fifty reports on issues as diverse as: rough sleeping, disability, mental health, teenage pregnancy, youth crime and children in public care. The aim was to challenge all forms of social exclusion, for the good of the individual and society more generally, and this was evident in many strands of government reform across health, education, youth justice and social care. As a consequence conceptualisations of need expanded beyond special educational needs to embrace the full range of additional needs, thereby increasing access to support and provision for an increasing number of vulnerable and socially disadvantaged children, young people and their families.

Within this context the DfEE commissioned a review of the EP profession. The report *Current Role, Good Practice and Future Directions* (2000) helped to demonstrate the wider range of skills that EPs had to support the new government agenda. EPs began to take up positions in new teams and services that had been formed to target those facing social exclusion, notably Youth Offending Teams (YOTs), and support services for looked after children. Education reform continued at a pace with the 2001 SEN Disability Discrimination Act and the radical and transforming 2004 *Every Child Matters* (ECM). The ECM agenda focused on delivering five outcomes for all children: to be healthy; stay safe; enjoy and achieve; make a positive contribution; and achieve economic well-being. This legislation aimed to change the landscape of children's services, seeking to remove false barriers between agencies and promoting a unified response to safeguarding in response to Lord Laming's report of (2003) into the death of Victoria Climbié. Within the context of unified children's services other aims included improved communication between agencies, removing child and family services from 'their professional silos' to provide community based 'wrap around' provision with the core aim of prevention and early intervention. The 2004 Children Act established procedures and structures to deliver these new services, including creating a Director of Children's Services and Lead Elected Member, integrated processes, including the common assessment framework, and integrated strategy, to target unified efforts and Extended Schools as a community-based setting in which to provide unified and accessible services from both maintained and voluntary sector providers.

The DfES commissioned a further review of the profession and the report *Functions and Contribution of Educational Psychologists in England and Wales* in the light of *Every Child Matters: Change for Children* was completed by Farrell et al. in 2006. The report highlighted the ways in which EPs could support the delivery of the every child matters five outcomes. It highlighted the broader range of skills and abilities of the profession, which has informed subsequent policy and planning from the DCSF, DFE and the coalition government. Whilst the future of EP training continues to be under review, it is heartening that in the midst of the worse financial crisis in living memory, and a double-dip recession, Children's Minister Sarah Teather, in a 2011 DfE press release, acknowledged the value of educational psychology and has pledged funds to continue EP training during the present parliament:

> *It's vital we understand how children develop – emotionally and psychologically – so we can make sure they have the opportunity to thrive and succeed at school. Educational Psychologists have a valuable role working with children and families in schools, and as part of early intervention projects. We want the most vulnerable children, and those who would benefit from extra support, to be able to access the expertise and support of Educational Psychologists.*

The DfE report *Developing Sustainable Arrangements for the Initial Training of Educational Psychologists Training* (DfE, 2011a) also concludes:

> *EPs have important roles in improving the opportunities for all children and young people, both in terms of local statutory responsibilities and more universal early intervention and preventative support offered by the public and private sectors, voluntary and community groups and social enterprises.* (p.5)

The report also adds that:

> *EPs are moving to a more varied pattern of employment – some with private sector providers of education services, and into private practice with the potential also to form social enterprises commissioned to run services.* (p.6)

The profession has demonstrated its versatility and wider range of skills and abilities to the government; the report demonstrates an understanding that early intervention by EPs is cost-effective and reduces the rate of statutory assessment. There is also formal acknowledgement that there is no clear demarcation between statutory and non-statutory work. The government included three questions in the 2011 Green Paper consultation: they focused on the role, future service structures, and training of EPs. Mechanisms for a further review of EP training are in place.

The Green Paper *Support and Aspiration: A New Approach to Special Educational Needs and Disability* (DfE, 2011b) and the subsequent publication *Support and Aspiration: A New Approach to Special Educational Needs and Disability – Progress and Next Steps* (DfE, 2012) outlines the government plans for reform. It proposes to:

■ include parents in the assessment process and introduce a legal right, by 2014, to give them control of funding for the support their child needs;

■ replace statements with a single assessment process and a combined education, health and care plan so that health and social services is included in the package of support, along with education;

■ ensure assessment and plans run from birth to 25 years old;

- replace the existing School Action and School Action Plus system with a simpler new school-based category to help teachers focus on raising attainment;
- overhaul teacher training and professional development to better help pupils with special educational needs and to raise their attainment;
- inject greater independence from local authorities in assessments by looking at how voluntary groups might coordinate the package of support; and
- give parents a greater choice of school and give parents and community groups the power to set up special free schools.

The government commitment to continue to support young people with special needs as they make the transition to adulthood provides the opportunity to develop EP services in the Further Education sector.

No doubt the future role, ways of working, and structures and systems where EPs work will be very different. To ensure the best future use of educational psychologists' skills it is important for us to lead in our own developments, to feel secure in our ability to develop and adapt our professional knowledge, skills and expertise, and be confident of our ability to respond to new challenges.

New directions in applied psychology

Psychological research is an important strand of evidence informing policy development, and as a consequence applied psychology is increasingly drawn upon to facilitate effective responses to complex issues. The constantly evolving legislative context has provided applied educational psychologists with the challenge of developing new ways of working with a more varied range of children and young people in community based settings. The following three examples provide insight into potential areas of further growth: working with young offenders, children with mental health needs, including working therapeutically in schools, and children in public care.

Young offenders

Legislative context: Reconceptualising of youth crime

Historically there have been two main perspectives in responding to youth crime, with orientations based on the principles of welfare and punishment. These reflect polar extremes in both philosophical and political orientations in the debate about youth. The welfare orientation suggests that crime reduction happens when government acts to ease the pressures of poverty and the myriad of other social risk factors associated with offending, while the punishment orientation presents the view that the use of strong deterrents reduce crime.

In 1997 the New Labour government pledged to be 'tough on crime, tough on the causes of crime' and this position acknowledged that to tackle this multi-faceted and complex problem required an integrated approach including both welfare and punishment orientations (Ryrie, 2006). The government embraced these diverse orientations in the 1998 Crime and Disorder Act to develop an integrated approach to youth crime, one that embraced a broader conceptualisation of the range of risk and resilience factors that need to be addressed when responding to such a complex phenomenon. The act also introduced a number of new court orders that included: Anti-Social Behaviour Orders (ASBOs), Parenting Orders and Curfew Orders, to reduce the impact of youth crime in stressed communities.

Population demographics

The Ministry of Justice, Home Office and Youth Justice Board publication *Youth Justice Statistics* (MoJ, 2012) provides the following figures for the period 2009/10. There were 241,737 arrests of young people aged 10–17. This reflects 17 per cent of the total arrests made during that period, from an age group that reflects just 11 per cent of the national population. In addition to the arrests there were also 49,407 reprimands and final warnings issued, 7,507 penalty notices for disorder (PCD) were given to 16–7 year olds, and 536 ASBOs. Furthermore, in the same period 2,222 young people, up to age 18, were held in custody. The re-offending rate for young people is estimated at 33.3 per cent, reflecting a 17 per cent reduction since 2000. The cost to society of youth crime is estimated at £4 billion a year. Natale (2010) reports in a recent review of data conducted for CIVITAS that the number of 15–17-year-olds in custody has doubled over that last 10 years with 70,000 school-aged children entering the youth justice system. The costs associated with this are typically £50,000 per annum for placement at a youth offenders institute and £206,000 for a secure children's home placement. Harrington and Bailey (2005) found that one-third of young offenders had an identified mental health need, including depression and self-harming.

Youth Offending Teams
The 1998 Crime and Disorder Act required each local authority to establish a Youth Offending Team (YOT) to plan preventative and proactive strategies for the management of local crime. In order to address the complex multi-faceted understanding of youth crime the teams were to include a wide range of professionals from within the local authority, including the police, probation service, social services, and health and education services. In view of the complex psychological needs profile associated young offenders many local authorities have placed an educational psychologist within their YOTs. Ryrie (2006) provides a detailed and interesting account of his work in this setting.

The teams were required to use their local knowledge to develop policy and practice tailored to the needs of the local community, and to reduce risk factors through early intervention work with children and their families, for example using Sure Start, parenting programmes, and school based interventions.

Risk and resilience factors
The evidence base for the new conceptualisation of youth crime acknowledges a complex interaction between a wide range of psychological risk factors, including learning difficulties, and social needs at the level of family, community and individual. The use of research evidence helped determine the importance of a multifaceted management approach that aimed to promote resilience and reduce risk factors, as well as offering a strong response to crime.

In 2005 the Youth Justice Board commissioned Communities that Care to review risk and protective factors associated with youth crime and effective interventions that help to prevent it. Their survey of 14,500 pupils aged 11–16 identified four key domains: the family, the school, individual and personal issues, and peer group or community related factors. Given this complex configuration of factors, their findings endorse the need for multi-model specifically tailored interventions.

Learning needs
The psychological research detailing the learning needs of young offenders is unequivocal. There is abundant evidence that young people within the youth justice system have lower than average attainment in numeracy and literacy (Farrington, 1996; Hawkins et al., 2000; Rutter et al., 1998). ECOTEC (2001) found that 51 per cent of young people in custodial settings were functioning below level 1 for literacy and 52 per cent were achieving below level 1 in numeracy. Hurry et al. (2005) found that amongst young offenders supervised within the community the underachievement was more pronounced with 57 per cent below level 1 in literacy and 63 per cent achieving below level 1 in numeracy. Data from longitudinal studies demonstrates that the

consequences of poor basic skills are greater challenges in finding employment and increased risk of social exclusion (Bynner, 2004). Whilst Hurry et al. (2010) provides evidence that enhanced numeracy and literacy skills improve a young person's chances of employment and also serve to reduce the risk of reoffending, echoing the findings of Lipsey (1995). The government has embedded this research evidence into their policy by requiring that '90 per cent of young offenders are in suitable full time education, training and employment' at the end of their sentence' (OLASS, 2004).

Truancy and exclusion

Despite the intensive focus on promoting resilience for this vulnerable group they remain extremely challenging to work with and to engage educationally (Hurry et al., 2005. Research conducted by the Youth Justice Board in 2005 found that only 35–45 per cent of young offenders supervised in the community are in full-time education, employment or training. Ryrie (2006) notes that there is a relationship between school exclusion and offending and describes research conducted by MORI in 2004 on behalf of the Youth Justice Board (YJB, 2004). They found that 51 per cent of those pupils who had been excluded from school five or more times had committed an offence in the past 12 months and that 46 per cent of those who had offended received temporary or permanent exclusions. Ryrie further notes that Berridge et al. (2001) describes a complex association between permanent exclusion and crime: the data suggests that exclusion either serves to accelerate an existing criminal path or triggers the onset of offending. Pitts (2006) notes that almost two-thirds of gang members had been excluded from school.

Summary

The evidence presented demonstrates a very clear rationale for educational psychologists working with young offenders, and those at risk of offending, both systemically within the local context by developing preventative strategies and interventions, and through direct work with individuals, their schools and families. Welsh and Farringdon (2010) reviewed crime prevention strategies and interventions, focusing on those with the most robust evidence base, and concluded that the interventions with the greatest impact were designed by those with local knowledge and were either school-based parent programmes, or teacher-led school based programmes.

Child and Adolescent Mental Health Services

There are plans within the NHS reforms to establish Health and Well-being Boards that bring together social care, public health and children's services, aimed at making provision for children with special needs and disability.

Legislative context

In recent years concerns about both raising standards of learning and improving behaviour has placed a considerable emphasis on children's social and emotional needs and development. The government's Social and Emotional Aspects of Learning (SEAL; DCSF, 2005) initiative sought to provide 'a comprehensive, whole school approach to promoting the social and emotional skills that underpin effective learning, positive behaviour, regular attendance, staff effectiveness and the emotional health and well being of all who learn and work in schools' (p.1).

Despite adding this initiative to the curriculum, it would appear that the well-being of children in the United Kingdom is well below the standard that a developed nation would aspire to. The *UNICEF Child Well-Being Report* of 2007 compared 21 developed nations on six measures of well-being: material well-being; health and safety; educational well-being; family and peer relationships; behaviours and risks; and subjective well-being. UK children scored in the lowest third on five of the six measures, and in the middle range for one (health and safety). Overall the UK was positioned at the bottom of the table. These stark findings ensured an even higher degree of political attention on developments and resources to support children's well-being. The government response was to launch the *Targeted Mental Health in Schools* (TaMH) programme (DCSF, 2008), the aim being to 'transform' the delivery of mental health support to the 5–13 population through school-based interventions. This was to be achieved by working proactively and preventatively to respond to emotional and mental health needs early, in order to prevent problems becoming established and to promote well-being. The Leicester City TaMHs project features in the 2011 Green Paper consultation (p.105) as evidence of the effective use of educational psychologists who, by working in schools, helped to build their capacity to promote well-being and intervene early in dealing with problems. The work within multi-disciplinary teams was also highlighted as evidence of sharing skills and promoting progress and achievement.

The Department of Health's (2008) *Increased Access to Psychological Therapies* (IAPT) initiative, whilst largely focused on the provision of cognitive behaviour therapy (CBT) to adults, advocates the use of CBT with children and commented that the school context was an appropriate location for this work.

Demographic profile: National population

The Office of National Statistics report on the *Mental Health of Children and Young People in Great Britain* (2004) found that one in ten children aged 5–16 had a clinical diagnosis. Of these children 4 per cent presented with an emotional disorder (3 per cent anxiety, 1 per cent depression) and 6 per cent had a conduct disorder (2 per cent hyperkinetic disorder, 1 per cent with a range of less common disorders). There were gender differences: 11 per cent of boys and 8 per cent of girls had mental health diagnoses, and within this it was found that boys were more likely to have a conduct disorder, or hyperkinetic disorder (3 per cent versus 0.4 per cent). Girls were slightly more likely to have an emotional disorder. When the researchers looked at family composition the results indicated a marked risk factor for children living in lone parent settings; 18 per cent of boys and 13 per cent of girls living in these contexts had a mental disorder, more than two thirds of these boys presented with a conduct disorder.

Access to mental health services

The Department of Health (2004) indicates that 10 per cent of 5–15 year olds have a diagnosable mental health condition but that up to 40 per cent of them are not accessing any specialist support. They also suggest that a similar number of children experiencing less serious difficulties may benefit from support. MacKay (2007) echoes these views. Furthermore, Stallard et al. (2007) reported that health agencies could not respond to the level of demand for CBT that would come from schools. This data indicates a considerable profile of need but a dearth of resources with which to respond. When considering children with special educational needs the potential demand is far greater.

Learning difficulties and mental health needs

As early as 1970 Rutter, Tizard and Whitmore reported that children with learning disabilities were three to four times more likely to have a behavioural problem than peers without a disability. The Foundation for People with Learning Disabilities (2002) and the Office of National Statistics (2004) both report an incidence of 40 per cent within the learning disabled population, with those with severe learning difficulties experiencing an incidence rate that is three to four times higher and further studies have consistently verified this finding (Cormack et al., 2000; Dykens, 2000; Einfeld & Tonge, 1996).

Evidence collected by the Mental Health Services for Children with Learning Disabilities, a National Care Pathway (2006), across a number of Health Authorities indicates that 1 in 10 of all children with referred mental health problems have a learning disability and that 50 per cent of those live in poverty.

Emerson (2006) suggests that health, including mental health is in part determined by social factors including socio-economic position. He argues that as children with learning difficulties are at increased risk of exposure to social exclusion, he feels that this may account for their increased risk of emotional and behavioural problems and speculates that 25–30 per cent of this risk relates to poverty. He feels this finding has strong implications for the service delivery of Child and Adolescent Mental Health Services (CAMHS). He makes a very strong case for preventative, context based CAMHS, able to build resilience. Building on this evidence, Hill (2006) proposes that given the strong links between poverty, learning disability and mental health needs, there is a clear rationale for making not only mental health provision, but wider parental support, including social work support, available as part of the routine provision within all special schools for children with learning disabilities.

Access to CAMHS for children with learning difficulties
The Mental Health Services for Children with Learning Disabilities, a National Care Pathway (NHS, 2006), consulted with numerous stakeholders, services users and providers nationally to consider the current state of services and future needs. They report:

> At the time of the project only 45 per cent of child mental health services were accessible to children and young people with learning disabilities, and three Strategic Health Authorities were without any specialist LD CAMHS provision.

They conclude that, apart from issues relating to their disability, learning disabled children and adolescents have similar needs to non-disabled children and respond well to similar but modified treatments: they emphasise *differentiated* rather than *different* approaches.

Summary
The evidence very clearly indicates considerable unmet demand for mental health interventions, including therapeutic work for children and families that needs to be accessible and community based. These needs exist both within the mainstream and special needs populations. EPs are ideally placed to respond to the needs of both populations. Rait et al. (2010) observe that due to the increased demand for therapeutic interventions, for example CBT, for children delivery is no longer restricted to health services. The very conceptualisation of CAMHS implies the involvement of a wide range of services providers.

EPs working therapeutically
There is considerable support for EPs engaging in therapeutic work in schools (DoH, 2008; Christner et al., 2007; Rait et al., 2010). Historically, therapeutic work was part of the EP role and MacKay (2007) welcomes the re-emergence of this strand of EP work, which he considers a key resource for children and young people. Farrell et al. (2006) commented that as statutory pressures were diminishing this was creating the opportunity for EPs to provide group and individual therapy. However, they note that as little as 2 per cent of EP time was being used in this way. Atkinson et al. (2011) report an increase in EPs undertaking training in therapeutic work, both within initial doctoral training programmes and through CPD. The authors describe a range of therapeutic work that is currently in use by EPs including: narrative, solution focused brief therapy (SFBT), personal construct psychology (PCP), and CBT. They also

report on the issues that arise from this work, which include concerns about access to specialist supervision, competence, role boundaries, time limitations and a lack of clarity about what constitutes therapy. However, they also report many positive views about this way of working, including the opportunity to work collaboratively to deliver therapy and a strong sense of this being a key future direction for the profession.

There is evidence of CBT being used by EPs to deliver both group and individual interventions (Christner et al., 2007; Squires, 2001), although it is not always delivered in the traditional format. There is substantial evidence that EPs use therapeutic approaches to guide their thinking and as an intervention tool. Pugh (2010) notes that for EPs the most widely used approaches are solution focused, PCP and CBT. Christner et al. (2007) note that in order to achieve success, mental health intervention must 'fit' within the school culture and ethos. They acknowledge that schools are complex systems which can impact on the delivery of CBT and welcome further 'real world' research in this area. Such research is very much in evidence in the doctoral theses being produced by trainee EPs and will significantly add to the knowledge and evidence base of what is undoubtedly a growth area. There can be no doubt that EPs have a very considerable role to play in responding the vast levels of unmet mental health needs observed in our child population. This is clearly being encouraged by the government and given our position within school and community settings we are extremely well placed to ensure access to some of our most needy children and young people.

Looked after children

The group within the child population that is the most vulnerable and at the greatest risk of social exclusion, are children in public care. Efforts to change the harrowingly negative outcomes for these children were given very high priority by the last government and they were the subject of numerous reforms and initiatives throughout the Labour administration.

Sonia Jackson bought a sharp focus on the poor educational outcomes of children in care observing:

> *A child who comes into care, at any age, for whatever length of time, is at risk of educational failure...the probability of falling behind at school is significantly greater than for a child from a similar socioeconomic background who does not come into care.*

Jackson (1994)

The report of the Social Services Inspectorate and Ofsted in 1995 highlighted that the educational underachievement of this group accelerates throughout their education and the children 'seldom reach standards commensurate with their ability' these findings provided the foundation for reform.

Legislative context
What follows is a brief summary of core strands of policy and legislation from a period of unprecedented and intensive political focus on improving outcomes for children in care. The Quality Protects initiative (DoH, 1998) aimed to improve the well-being of looked after children through changes in the management and delivery of children's social services, with a focus on education the initiative set targets for improved GCSE results, attendance, aiming to reduce rates of exclusion. This was followed by guidance issued by the Departments of Health and Education: *Guidance on the Education of Children and Young People in Public Care* (DfEE, 2000). The aims were to promote 'corporate parenting' by the local authority, with a focus on setting high standards and expectations for educational attainment, and recommending that schools assign a senior staff member to fulfil the role of designated teacher, with the intent that this role would provide advocacy and a resource for looked after children within their school

context. This was rapidly followed by the Leaving Care Act (2000) which aimed to delay the process of leaving care, which typically occurred mid GCSE, to support their engagement in examinations and facilitate transition to further and higher education. *Every Child Matters* (2003), and the 2004 Children Act further highlighted the notion of corporate parenting, ensuring priority in educational placements and effective planning. Section 52 of the Children Act places on statute the requirement for local authorities to promote the education and well being of children in their care. The 2007 White Paper *Care Matters: Time for Change* (DES, 2007) further highlights the importance of education, introduces the pilot of the virtual head teacher role, and allocates a personal education budget of £500 to each child. The *Children and Young People Bill* (2008) consolidated numerous strands of guidance into legislation, to ensure improved outcomes, as the evidence was that despite the huge investment in looked after children there had been few changes in their poor outcomes. The Bill required local authorities to prioritise looked after children, the designated teacher role became statutory, governing bodies were to oversee the education of looked after children, and it introduced the pledge by local authorities to ensure children in their care the same opportunities as their peers.

Demographics

The DfE *Statistical First Release* (2011) indicates that there were 65,520 looked after children in the UK, of these 2,680 were unaccompanied asylum seekers. Thirty-three per cent of care leavers were not in education, employment or employment; 54 per cent of those entering care did so because of abuse or neglect; 74 per cent of the children were living in foster homes.

Mental health and offending

The profile of needs associated with children in public care places them securely within both of the populations discussed earlier in the chapter; they are at five times more likely to suffer from a mental health concern that their peers (McAuley & Young, 2006) yet few access appropriate health care (Sempik et al., 2008). Jackson (2010) found that half of all those placed in young offenders institutions in the UK have a background in care, and a quarter of the prison population are care leavers (Social Exclusion Unit, 2003).

Educational needs

The educational attainments of this group reflect accelerating under achievement when compared to the national population. The DFE website provides data from 2010 which indicates the difference in achieving required national curriculum outcomes for looked after children and the national population (Table 1).

Looked after children are nine times more likely to have SEN than peers (Jackson & McParlin, 2006) and in 2008 28 per cent had statements of special need compared to 3 per cent of the national population and they are more likely to be placed special schools than peers living with their families. Very few of these young people progress to further or higher education (Jackson & Ajayi, 2007). Instability of school and care placements were highlighted by the Social Exclusion Unit (2003) as a significant contributor to poor academic outcomes due to the influence on curriculum access and preparation for examinations (Fletcher-Campbell et al., 2003; Blyth, 2001). Being out of school due to transitions, truancy or exclusion further affects peer relations, and self esteem (Reid, 2005. Peer relationships are known to relate to academic success for looked after children (Jackson & Martin, 1998).

Summary

These initiatives and reforms have ensured that every local authority and every school is held to account for the life and educational outcomes of the children in their care. This has led to

Table 1: The difference in achieving required national curriculum outcomes for looked after children and the national population.

Key stage	Looked After Children	All Children	Attainment Gap
KS1 (Reading)	58%	85%	27
KS2 (English)	45%	81%	36
5 A*-C (inc. English and Maths)	12%	53%	41

the establishment in many local authorities of specialist multi-disciplinary teams that aim to promote positive outcomes for children in public care. These include many EPs, and although the complexity and multiple dimensions of the needs profile of this population make it hard to bring about change, the evidence suggests that there are incremental improvements in outcomes, and that sustaining change takes time and requires a constant focus. There is evidence in government statistics that change has been bought about through the systemic and individual focus of the work conducted by multi-professional efforts and those of EPs. Sinclair et al. (2004) report that carers rated the involvement of educational psychologists as the most useful form of support. Jackson and McParlin (2006) report that looked after children are likely to have frequent contact with EPs, however, they warn that the high mobility rates of this group may influence the effectiveness of EP intervention; there is a need to sustain consistency, for example through cross borough arrangements or specialist roles within a local authority.

The Division of Educational and Child Psychology (2006) identified EPs as having a specific contribution to make through their working relationships with schools and other professionals, and their expertise in informed contextualised assessment and intervention work. Studies of interventions with looked after children form a regular feature in trainee EPs doctoral theses and DECP conference presentations, and cover diverse areas: literacy interventions, tackling bullying, building resilience, promoting social inclusion, all of which support the development of a shared evidence base to support effective intervention. Gilligan (2007 and Jackson (2010) provide evidence of the resilience enhancement that schools and teachers can provide, and the position of the EP within these systems, means that the profession is uniquely placed to support effective systemic and individual interventions.

Conclusion

The role of EPs has been thoroughly reviewed over the past two decades and the wider range of skills and expertise available has been recognised, acknowledged and embraced in recent government policies. Contemporary legislation has highlighted the most vulnerable child populations in our nation and government guidance has provided the profession with clear access to a wider range of work, across diverse settings. The professional response, evident across the country, has been the rebranding of many educational psychology services. New titles frequently include the word 'community', and the range of work on offer is set across diverse contexts and populations of children and their families. This reflects a rediscovery of the original and broader role of the EP, and shows the profession taking control of its future through the creative application of a full range of applied psychologies. This would suggest that the profession has followed Barnett's (1997) advice and is 're-making' an identity and securing its future.

Vignette 11

Memories of recent training

Reem Olivia Dean

My feelings as I come to the end of my training are mostly those of relief! It has been a long and challenging journey but one that has been incredibly rewarding. Having recently sat my *viva* examination, I am now in the position to reflect on the last three years of my training and am honoured to recount my experiences. Prior to embarking on the doctorate, I was offered a place on a PhD programme. Recently I was asked if I believed that I had made the right decision to undertake the professional doctorate instead. I can say with complete confidence that I have. It has not been easy. I have never before had so many simultaneously competing demands, and one vital skill the training enables you to develop is the ability to prioritise. I believe this is excellent preparation for the educational psychologist (EP) world of work as I have come to realise that the EP role is one that does not consist of sequential tasks, but rather requires you to manage several projects and pieces of work at the same time so multi-tasking is a crucial skill.

The educational psychology doctoral training is based on an apprenticeship model of learning and provides the opportunity to earn while you learn. Cardiff University provides a grant for its trainees; while the sum is modest, it has enabled me to be financially independent and to have the certainty of my three placements, which were collaboratively allocated between my cohort prior to beginning the course. The Cardiff course combines theory and practice and is incredibly comprehensive. It provides opportunities to learn about relevant legislation, innovative developments and best practice. In particular, it focuses on the Constructionist Model of Informed Reasoned Action (COMOIRA: Gameson et al., 2003, 2005; Gameson & Rhydderch, 2008) developed by the course directors as a model for effectively managing the change process. Great importance is placed on research, reasoned action informed by psychology and active reflection. For instance, a formalised reflective process is a component of the course which consists of the annual presentation of a process account. This consisted of an on-going, in-depth piece of fieldwork detailing how the trainee managed the change process. The process accounts highlighted the innovative and adaptable ways in which trainees work while being mindful of their personal impact on the process of change.

Lectures were provided on qualitative and quantitative research skills, and I was thankful that there was only one statistics exam to be taken. The course is designed to place incremental demands on the trainee, beginning with a collaborative research project in the first year, a small scale research project in the second year and a thesis in the third year. The research projects included exploring how EPS consultation can prevent placement breakdown for looked-after children, exploring different professionals' views when working within multi-agency Children's Action Teams (CATs) and exploring teachers' thoughts, feelings and behaviours of working with selectively mute children. Undertaking research taught me to manage the inevitable demands which present themselves when conducting research, such as the considerable and somewhat unexpected investment of time required for the transcription phase during qualitative research. However, most notably the process of gaining ethical approval for conducting research taught me the importance of ethical conduct in all aspects of work, particularly during research and the EP's role in safeguarding the participation, feelings and data of the participant. I greatly enjoy research and in a climate of increasing accountability, I believe it is important for EPs to demonstrate the impact and unique contribution of their profession. Each year of the training provided new and fresh challenges. The first year was characterised by uncertainty. I must admit that many of my anxieties originated from the unknown such as writing a process account for the first time, learning the prescribed formatting style for essay writing, and coping with the logistical challenges of finding my placement and all the local schools, thank heavens for sat navs! The first year included submitting three academic assignments and it was a relief to complete two out of these before beginning the first placement. It was also challenging to balance essay writing with placement responsibilities when meeting the third assignment deadline. However, it was also a useful exercise as it enabled me to appreciate the many demands of the EP role which is typified by many ongoing projects as opposed to a sequentialist method of working.

There is a prophetic saying 'Seek knowledge even as far as China'. I am happy to report that I did not have to travel quite so far! I did, however, relocate to England during my second year of training. The experiences during this year helped to consolidate my theoretical knowledge and further develop my interpersonal and problem-solving skills. Each year I had placements in three different local authorities which equipped me with the knowledge of a range of models of service delivery, EPS structures and highlighted the benefits of multi-agency working.

The third year consisted of my third placement and the all-consuming thesis. This explored teachers' thoughts, feelings and behaviours when working with selectively mute children. The research findings highlighted the value of EPs in providing support to parents and teaching staff through delivering interventions, training and supervision. It was an enormous undertaking and the deadlines throughout the training such as the ethics proposal and draft deadlines helped to keep me on track. Without breaking it down into small parts, it would have seemed like a near impossible undertaking.

Overall, there were many highs and lows during the training. The highs undoubtedly included the reward gained from making a positive impact on the lives of children and young people and the unsolicited positive feedback. Also, the camaraderie and support received from colleagues and during my placements, I was fortunate to be supervised by exceptional role models. The lows included sometimes feeling overwhelmed by the competing demands of research activities, placement work and university deadlines. It can also feel isolating at times when on placement, and factors which can ameliorate this are a supportive supervisor, colleagues and course mates.

I am in an extremely fortunate position to love my chosen profession and I hope to be successful in it. I recognise that a career extends over an entire lifetime and as I come to the end of my training, I realise that this is just the beginning. I am indebted to all those who have helped me on this journey; for their encouragement, for facilitating learning opportunities and the lessons I have learnt. The genesis of the profession one hundred years ago demonstrates the incredible strides undertaken and I am sure the next centenary will continue this, if not exceed it. I now look forward to making a positive and lasting impact in shaping that future as a qualified EP.

Chapter 12 The future of educational psychology

Andy Allen & Julia Hardy

Why a chapter on the future of educational psychology?
Reflecting on the past history of educational psychology and then speculating on the potential futures of the profession we must consider the interesting directions and patterns of change that we have experienced in the past and will face in the uncertain future to come. It is unusual in a history book to allow a space to imagine what the future will bring, but with so many glimmerings of changes that will face EPs and EP services, it is a responsibility of the profession to imagine and then to prepare for these possible futures.

The scope of this chapter.
Most chapters in this book have referred to the impact of legislative changes on our profession and so in a chapter looking forward we will link to current and potential future politically led movements. Irrespective of what is imposed due to legislation and budgetary pressures, there will be alterations to the structure and function of EPSs. Jonathan Solity writes about what went so wrong with the direction of educational psychology services from the 1970s onwards but gives us a glimmer of hope at the end of his chapter that, with the right values, beliefs and evidence-informed approaches, EPs can negotiate collaborative work with schools that really works. Other key developments caused by environmental and contextual influences are:
- The move to increasing EP trading.
- EPs' role in promoting the evidence-base underpinning our work.
- Child mental health as an increasing priority and EPs' distinct role in this field.
- The changes to DSM and hopefully an increased awareness of the dangers of over-labelling and it's related over medicalisation of children and young people.
- The raising of the school leaving age.
- The new cyber-age.

Finally, there are at least two areas that EPs have focused on over the decades that will not go away:
- The voice of the child.
- The impact of demographics including social deprivation.

The zeitgeist of the future and the memes that change our contexts
Many authors (such as Faupel and Hardy, see chapter four) have referred to the zeitgeist of the time, meaning the climate within our profession in that era. The concept of 'meme' (Richard Dawkins, 1976) is helpful when one thinks of ideas and practices in the EP world that are replicated by colleagues throughout the country but that also mutate and evolve. There are changes driven by new legislation (such as the *Every Child Matters* agenda and the move to multi-disciplinary working) but there are also other adaptations that occur through the influences within various EP networks. The consultation movement (Wagner, 2000) has been a bedrock of EP work and it is vital that it should not disappear. Irrespective of changes to the direction of EP work the consultation framework will be the main basis for colleagues throughout the UK over decades to come. In 1990s EPs first reflected on the benefits of taking a consultation

approach to work in schools (Leadbetter & Tee, 1991) and this has continued over three decades (Kennedy et al., 2009). We may use fashionable terms such as 'commissioning' and 'tendering', but underpinning that there will be a consultant/consultee interface.Terminology and associated legislative requirements will alter but as a framework to negotiate the EP role and the direction of travel, a consultation approach will be part, if not all of the basis of our work.

EPs functioning within increasing competitive markets

In relation to the increased commissioning of educational psychological services by stake-holders, who ultimately will be the architects of the content and forms of the psychology that will be delivered?

Here is a possible future scenario. Let's suggest that I am a senior manager in a school and the purchaser of the services of an EP. The budget that I have is fixed and as EPs' fees are time-linked, I therefore have a quantity of EP time available to be commissioned. I have already used the knowledge and support available to me within the school. I have already had meetings with pupils, parents and staff. I simply wish to commission the psychologist to assess children, in order that school staff have a greater knowledge of a child's strengths and difficulties. Whilst I may greatly value a consultational model of delivery, time is money. Instead of time taken with the EP observing the child in lessons and meeting with parents and staff, I could take a view that the finite time available could actually be spent on assessing the abilities of another child. I may simply choose to commission the services of an EP for cognitive and ability testing, for example, using EPs as they have access to specific instruments. Information obtained about the child from these assessments will be used by school staff when they meet with the pupils and parents.

Is this a service that EPs can supply, or should schools probably look elsewhere? Such scenarios raise crucial ethical dilemmas. Previous chapters have covered the history and past tensions within the profession concerning service delivery, and particularly individual casework versus consultative and systemic work.

Boyle and Lauchlan put it succinctly:

There is a need for individual casework in the education sphere, whether those in the EP profession like it or not, and, if a profession that is already uniquely placed within the field fails to deliver, then the consumer will go to another supplier.

Boyle & Lauchlan (2009)

We can each soul-search, deliberate and decide upon the type of EP we want to be and the kind of EP service we wish to provide for the future. While the profession continues to wrestle with itself over the purpose and future direction of the profession, in the absence of any agreement between ourselves, others (in the form of current and new stakeholders) outside of educational psychology will ultimately decide our future in our 'absence'.

The future is not yet written but is it healthy to rely on market logic to reform education and in turn educational psychology? Robert Kuttner, commenting upon the reliance of market logic in the US reform of health care, wrote:

The overreliance on market logic and market institutions is ruining the health-care system. Market enthusiasts fail to tabulate all the costs of relying on market forces to allocate health care - the fragmentation, opportunism, asset rearranging, overhead, underinvestment in public health, and the assault on norms of service and altruism. They assume either a degree of self-regulation that the health markets cannot generate, or far sighted public supervision that contradicts the rest of their world view.

Kuttner (1997)

This comparison between the delivery of health care in the US and the delivery of educational psychology in the UK, raises the question as to how a reliance on market forces for the present and future delivery of educational psychology would benefit children and young people.

Over four decades ago George A. Miller (1969) in his APA presidential address emphasised the need for psychologists to take responsibility for distilling and disseminating research findings, in order to educate the general public. It was a vision of giving psychology away to the public to promote human welfare.

A present and future dilemma for the profession to grapple with may be solving the conundrum of how to sell psychology whilst at the same time giving psychology away. This conundrum requires a whole new reframing in order to bring clarity: some domains are inherently beyond the reach of the market. One such domain is that of the rights of a child. Rights, which by definition, cannot be readily separated or sold!

EPs and ethical trading

One recent difference for EPs is in the ways that we are commissioned. Fortunately, most EPs are still working in teams, the majority still within educational psychology services (EPSs). There are some who have chosen or have been pushed to work separately, some setting up within clear ethical frameworks such as social enterprises (for instance the Pillars of Parenting and the National Open College Network). These include setting up as a not-for-profit organisation and ploughing all resources back into the development of existing and new products. The key change is that of EP trading. Some services have embraced this; for the second author this has led to changes in her EPS, with schools more than doubling the amount of time EPs spend in schools due to buy-back. Nevertheless the concepts of 'marketing' and 'selling services' are fraught with difficulty. At the time of going to print, the Division of Educational and Child Psychology have completed a national survey of trainee educational psychologists (TEPs) and programme directors into the impact of trading; by April 2013 the DECP will have developed guidance (in consultation with the AEP and other colleagues) on ethical trading. The guidance of the BPS *Code of Ethics and Conduct* (2009) is more important than ever. The code reminds us to apply the rational principle 'do unto others as you would be done by'. With the gradual trend in recent years to more EPs working as self-employed, there is and will inevitably be greater competition, both between EPs and between EP services and private EPs. The four ethical principles cited within the code – respect, competence, responsibility and integrity – are crucial as we move to a more complex future. Certainly, there are dangers if TEPs are offered to schools within a buy-back system. Managers need to ensure that TEPs have the appropriate range of casework and other learning opportunities and that they are not vulnerable to pressures from headteachers to deliver what is demanded or at an unreasonable pace (for their developmental needs) just because schools are buying a service. We will all need to reflect carefully on the ethics of trading, as well as to undertake our own CPD to prepare us for this more commercially driven context. However, trading does offer opportunities as well as threats. If schools and others see the evidence of successful EP work then they will (and do) request more. Services that are allowed to be flexible with their staffing may then be able to respond to the requests for more applied psychology delivered by EPs in a range of contexts and communities.

Voice of the 'consumer'

For any profession to continue to supply the quality services demanded by its consumers it will need to offer a well-tuned ear. The future challenges we face within our profession will undoubtedly mean listening simultaneously to the many different voices of our multiple consumers. This is due to the possible differing preferences, experiences and expectations of the EP role from the service users. Following research in Dumbarton, MacKay and Boyle (1994) found that head teachers felt that EPs could play a valuable role in policy development and research. This contrasts with the research findings of Ashton and Roberts (2006), who found that SENCOs did not mention these roles and valued the more 'traditional' EP role (individual assessment, advice and statutory work).

It may be that educational psychology service providers, increasingly now agree the role of the EP through service level agreements or contractual agreements and also seek consumer feedback through questionnaires, but whilst this operates at a more micro level what of the more macro level?

Gersch et al. (1990) concluded that one key change for the 1990s was to seek consumer feedback. Our language has subtly shifted over the past two decades, with calls for evidence of impact in addition to the need to listen to consumers and customers. As MacKay (2002) observes, educational psychology serves a range of others, from children and parents, school staff and local authorities, not to mention the taxpayer, the legislator and the interests of the EP service and the organisation within which they are located. As he so wisely notes: 'Is it any wonder that the profession is marked by role conflict?'

The EP role in facilitating the pupil voice

In the new era of marketing EP services, with the pressures of the market place and related commercial jargon such as customers and consumers, it is crucial that we do not underestimate the importance of putting the pupil perspective on the agenda. Many EPs have put this aspect of our work at the top of their priorities, including Raymond's (1987) research into pupil perceptions, Hardy's (2010) exploration of deaf identity and Burton, Smith and Woods' (2010) work with teachers to promote children's participation through pupil-led research. It is tempting to assume that schools, who spend much more time with their students, will protect and prioritise time to think of the students' perspectives. This may occur through student councils and other mechanisms, but often it is the EP who works collaboratively with schools, parents and others to ensure that the distinctive voice of the child/young person is heard. Although the client, not to mention the commissioner, is often an adult with power and a budget, it is imperative that EPs working in increasingly fiscally driven contexts remind those in power of the importance of hearing the views of the young.

The impact of research on the EP role

Over the decades some authors have tried to predict the future (Gersch et al., 1990; Fox,1992, Kelly & Gersch, 2000). As Norah Frederickson well illustrates in chapter 10, the change to EP training with new, doctoral-level graduates joining the profession with knowledge and confidence in research, will in many EPS have led to opportunities where the majority of EPs have negotiated their role within action research or more extensive research activities. Evidence-base is the zeitgeist of this decade, with politicians and senior managers insisting that they focus their funding on 'what works'. In the next 50 years, whether they are located within local authority EPSs or elsewhere, educational psychology will be one of the professions leading on the application of psychology through evidence-based interventions. If EPs can apply their new confidence to negotiating further opportunities for work at the systemic, organisational level, this can only auger well for our future. A decade ago Stoker warned that 'social systems often develop and change in irrational ways and that therefore change has to try to understand these irrational forces at work' (1992, p.17). As MacKay (2002) so rightly asserts, it is the EPs of the future who can influence others to see the role of psychology in supporting and researching change.

Mental health

Take, for example, the field of mental health, where many EPs are working in an increased capacity, helped in part by those insightful programme directors who chose to prioritise evidence-based interventions such as CBT to go onto the curriculum for their trainees. As employers we needed to be cognisant of the competency issues for those newly qualified EPs wanting to apply their newly acquired skills, asking whether or not we provide sufficient, high-level supervision. We should be alert to areas that were previously the sole preserve of specialist child and adolescent mental health services (CAMHS), and be thoughtful in considering ways in which EPs can directly and/or indirectly support the delivery of cognitive behaviour therapies in their work (Rait et al., 2010.) EPs are aware now that there is also a growing research base showing the effectiveness of CBT for young children (Grave & Blissett, 2004), and specifically for depression (Harrington et al., 1998), anxiety (Kendall 1994) and conduct disorders (Kazdin et al., 1992), so informed by these studies a growing group of EPs are delivering CBT in schools and other settings.

EPs have been working with colleagues in schools and other settings to measure the impact of any change, and will continue to do so in the future. EPs throughout the UK are sharing the benefits of the use of a target monitoring and evaluation (TME) system, to evaluate outcomes of a wide range of interventions (Dunsmuir et al., 2009). The area of CAMHS tier 2 interventions is a potential new area for EP intervention and research for EPs; the successes bring inherent benefits for the young people concerned, but with these we need to plan for further evaluation of such work, as well as managing the risks through commissioning ongoing supervision and training.

Dangers of an over-medicalised rather than a psycho-social perspective

The over-medicalisation of children's difficulties, rather than the application of a psycho-social perspective, is a significant and concerning area of development at present. In the past few decades there has been an evident increase in demand to diagnose, with parents seeking labels such as attention deficit and hyperactivity disorder (ADHD). Researchers at McMaster University in the US have identified five features of ADHD that contribute to its controversial nature.

- It is a clinical diagnosis for which there is no laboratory or radiological confirmatory tests or specific features.
- Diagnostic criteria have changed frequently.
- There is no curative treatment, so long term drug therapy is required.
- Therapy often includes stimulant drugs that are thought to have abuse potential.
- The rates of diagnosis and treatment substantially differ across countries.

As with the area of ethical trading, the over-medicalisation of children is a concern to EPs in the UK and the DECP is planning to issue a position paper on it in 2013. It is hoped that the next NICE guidance on ADHD, together with the planned new DSM-5 publications, will exert some influence over this concerning trend. Irrespective of future guidance, EPs must become more self-critical, reflecting on the stances they take and whether they apply a psycho-social perspective to understanding individual needs, rather than getting sucked into the current trend through accepting the over-diagnoses and related, unacceptable over-medication of the young.

The increase in focus on young adults

The future will also see a significant change to the age of students accessing educational psychology services. Whilst some EPs presently provide assessments of adults, especially EPs working privately, the vast majority of EPs have worked with children and young people aged from 0 to 19 years. In addition to this, as from 2015, the school leaving age will be increased from 16 to 18 years. Published figures from the Department of Education, Business Innovation and Skills Department (2010) indicated that in 2008/9, around 80 per cent of all 16–18-year-olds were participating in some form of education (full time, work-based and employer funded or 'other' training). The question is of the remaining 20 per cent or so, who will be required to participate in compulsory education, how many of these young adults have SEN and how will they be supported? If the EP focus does extend upward to include 19–25-year-olds EPs need to be prepared to work in a range of contexts. Clearly the recent growth in higher education enrolments (Ramsden, 2008, p.12) is a developing setting for EP consultations. We must also think broader than SEN with Higher Education (HE). There may also be a real opportunity for EPs to promote systemic change within this sector. For example Sternberg (2008), having developed his Tri-archic Theory of Intelligence, observed that some US universities would select applicants for HE courses, using traditional beliefs in intelligence (with an analytical skills bias). He proposed changes to the HE recruitment process and suggested that some of the most creative and practically intelligent (emotionally literate) students, who often did not score highly on traditional tests would not be able to access HE and therefore not get the chance to succeed. The future will witness the rise of the Eastern and South American markets and economies; it will be crucial for the success of current and future generations that we prepare for this change. Our future generation will require greater creativity and dynamism if they are to compete within the future international markets. As EPs we can use our experience and research skills to build the evidence and advise HE providers on these wider issues. Another key priority for ethical EPSs should include those not in education, employment or training (NEET) which is a significant-sized group, with the most recent figures showing at the end of 2011, 154,900 (8.1 per cent) of 16–18-year-olds were NEET (DfE, 2012). It is crucial that EPs seek out a role in applying psychology to benefit the 'non-sponsored child' or young person, particularly the most vulnerable, that include 'those with few or no qualifications and those with a health problem, disability or low aspirations' (2012, DfE). As with mental health, the young adult sector is an appropriate area for EP work so long as the discipline ensures that EPs have, in accordance with the BPS *Code of Ethics and Conduct* (2009), adequate professional training and supervision in their work with this age group.

The impacts of the cyber world

The difficulties presented by developments within information and communications technology (ICT) require EPs to be cautious. If we are aiming to cause no harm we must take care of potential risks when we mention online resources. Do we know of the risks of cyber bullying and the recent causes of suicides arising from 'sexting' (the act of sending sexually explicit messages or photographs) between mobile phones? We may aspire to be transparent but do we as professionals keep ourselves safe online? Developments in ICT may well lead to a greater inter-generational divide than ever. Parents can go to the Child Exploitation and Online Protection Centre (CEOP: www.thinkuknow.co.uk/parents) for help in the scripts they may wish to use in negotiating with their children about their online activities. Unfortunately, there are many other sources for advice on the web, such as those about self-harm or anorexia, that can in themselves do greater harm. Psychologists may be promoting new approaches, such as mindfulness-based cognitive therapy (MBCT), but we need to be wary of the plethora of courses available on the internet that are not accredited. As psychologists, we obviously need to understand the lived experience of children and young people. We will have to discuss with the young how their avatars have helped them socially. It is interesting that the APA are discussing adding internet addiction to the latest DSM. Fortunately there are eminent researchers out there exploring these issues, such as online video gaming (Griffiths, 2010); as EPs we need to keep informed of such findings so that we can apply psychology within the context of rapid change.

Research and evidence base

Any search into research by EPs today gives a rich range of sources, with links to various universities and the research published arising from doctoral research, as well as the journals produced through the Society. MacKay (1997) undertook research into the expectations of EPs held by primary and secondary school headteachers and staff and found that although schools strongly endorsed EP work focusing on individuals they also appreciated the wider roles, including EPs' contributions to research. A most significant area of research by EPs is that of inclusion for children with significant SEN, as relevant now as in 1998 when Leyden and Miller reported on the topic of mainstream inclusion and how there were many struggles and difficulties faced by many parents as they try to make sense of often conflicting professional advice and pressures. Today we are faced with potentially huge changes to the assessment procedures with the new Education Bill and still the question is how can inclusion be promoted within the new proposed frameworks?

Research for our profession should have both inward and outward facing perspectives. Imich's research into the time allocation system for EPs is also another important area. His research examined ways in which EPSs plan the deployment of their time, their systems for time allocation and their communication to service-users about their service delivery. Imich may have argued for greater consistency of practice across the profession, which is perhaps less likely today with budgetary pressures than ever before, but the need for clarity regarding any service level agreements are certainly crucial with increased trading with schools.

The profession has diverse views on the importance of evidence-base in psychological interventions. Fox (2003) notes that we don't all hold up the gold standard of randomised controlled trials as the panacea for all research. We take varied epistemological positions and accept that research has a range of purposes. We may wish to show that there is, for example, an evidence base for CBT group work in schools (Squires, 2001) but we may also aim to illuminate and communicate the perspectives a young people (Hardy, 2010; Kerfoot, 1986). Fox (2003) outlines the tensions between the different perspectives, with some EPs who want to base their professional practice on subjective experience and self-reflection, in contrast with those who seek a more objective, positivist, evidence-informed, research base. In the future we need to be clear about our areas of enquiry and then decide what is the most appropriate methodology. We may wish to influence local authority officers to hear the young person's voice (Harding & Atkinson, 2009) or indeed to help with the evaluation of children's participation in SEN procedures (Norwich & Kelly, 2006). Outward looking research is crucial for our profession's future. There is a plethora of research into the effects of the increase in multi-disciplinary working, some from an outward looking perspective and others designed to explore the lived experience (Gaskell & Leadbetter, 2009). There are diverse ways in which EPs can apply their skills as researchers: this may be through acting as the research provider, working in partnership with others to undertake joint action research or participating in a joint research ventures, or they may simply offer coaching or training in research methodology.

Funding of educational psychology services

At present there are various models for the delivery of educational psychology services across the UK. The way local authorities fund and provide their services is not at consistent. Variations include services whose budgets are entirely funded directly by the local authority; services where the budgets are part funded by the local authority and partly through commissioned traded services; and services where the budget is entirely funded through traded services. In addition to local authority educational psychology services, educational psychology is also delivered by private practitioners either operating solely or as part of a team. A very recent variant to these models is that of an educational psychology service partnership between a local authority and a private company.

There are two major driving forces to the change to service delivery: the increasing financial constraints on local authorities and findings from the Lamb report (2010). Following the Lamb inquiry local authorities were encouraged to develop alternative models for delivering educational psychology services which have the aim of 'increasing parental confidence' by having the service operate at arms-length from local authorities.

Whilst mindful of the current proposals for the future change of SEN Statementing to a single assessment process with Education, Health and Care Plans by 2014, the future is likely to witness a move away from the more traditional, fully local authority funded educational psychology services, to services which are either partly or totally operating a traded services model. In light of the Lamb Inquiry (2010) we may find that, in addition to other stakeholders and relevant government policies, it is parents as primary stakeholders who will shape the future delivery of educational psychology. This may especially be the case if the proposed changes to the statutory assessment process come to fruition and personal budgets for education are introduced and parents/carers in the future may receive direct payments for meeting their child's special educational needs. They may then choose how the budget is spent to meet the needs of their child; it is up to the EPs of the future to demonstrate the range of effective ways psychology can be applied to benefit their children.

The future could be viewed as an opportunity for the profession to be self-confident and move an 'arms length' away from the local authorities, since such a step may further increase parental confidence in educational psychology services and educational psychology itself. One alternative to the fully traded services model operating either through a local authority, or a registered company with shareholders, is the delivery of educational psychology through a social enterprise model. Social enterprises compete in the market like any other business. They pursue and make a profit; however, they are not consumed by the motive of personal gain nor forced into serving the interests of external shareholders. They continually reinvest their profits back into the business or directly into the community. They are fundamentally about doing what is right by society and the environment. Given the ethos of our profession and universal concern over the accessibility of our services to the most vulnerable, this type of service delivery (or a similar model), may be a preferred option over the notion of investors or indeed local authorities profiteering from the delivery of educational psychology.

Surviving the waves of policy changes

Few would question the notion that today education itself is going through a major and significant change; this is a change which by its very nature will not only affect the landscape of education but will also resist any simple reversal and return to previous educational models, should a future government propose this. Any discussion here of government proposals and policy will quickly become dated and will find itself in the 'past' chapters of a book covering the last 101 years of educational psychology. However, the present and proposed changes to education, and in turn to educational psychology, form part of a more complex model.

Tony Blair famously said in a speech to the Labour Party conference in Blackpool in 1996: 'Ask me my three main priorities for government, and I tell you: education, education, education.' What followed was large-scale educational reform, policy led and fuelled by substantial investment. Party politics, policy and outcomes are always a topic of debate and are best left outside this book, but what is not in dispute is the increased spending on education before 2010.

In May 2010, faced with rising national debt and an unstable economic climate on a national and international level, the Coalition Government proposed a reduction of government spending, which had grown to £87 billion in 2010–2011 (Office for National Statistics, 2011). For education, this meant reform to allow alternative providers to enter the State school system. For EPs, the main features of the Coalition's programme would also promote change due to large cuts to local authority funding, changes to the delivery of public services and to the educational landscape, including increasing numbers of academies and free schools.

Educational psychologists who are employed by local authorities are facing challenges from two sides: the move for schools to be more independent of the local authority, and the direct cuts to local authority budgets. The local authority cuts directly affecting the numbers of EPs employed and increasingly creating changes to EPs terms and conditions of employment.

There is little evidence to suggest that there will be no role for the EP within the fast changing landscape. The needs of children and families have not suddenly reduced. The demand for the services of educational psychologists remains; what will change, with the increasing market economy within education, is the way the EP will be employed and ultimately who will be the employer and stakeholder.

Embracing the future

As educational psychologists, we should all take a moment to reflect upon our profession's future and consider the proposal by Megginson (1963), paraphrasing the work of Charles Darwin (but often now incorrectly attributed to Darwin): 'It is not the most intellectual of the species that survives; it is not the strongest that survives; but the species that survives is the one that is able best to adapt and adjust to the changing environment in which it finds itself.'

The future for educational psychologists is, we believe, reliant upon adapting to this rapidly changing environment. Much like the past challenges for the profession, the proposed changes to EP service delivery are many and varied, changes to who will be employing EPs and significant changes to future EP training. This often leads to the discourse of 'surviving' the changes.

As we find ourselves within this changing environment, there is a real opportunity to be the architects of our discipline, to shape our profession, to make it fit for the next hundred years. To achieve this it will require even greater engagement with the public, a determination to be less modest about the contribution we make to society and never giving ground on the role we hold as child advocates, especially focusing on those who have the least influence and to the benefit of the most vulnerably and deprived in our society. The future for educational psychology is not simply about the profession surviving, but more about our profession thriving, driven by thoughtful and passionate beliefs and values!

References

Chapter 1

Arnold, C., Yeomans, J. & Simpson, S. (2009). *Excluded from school: Complex discourses and psychological perspectives.* Stoke on Trent: Trentham Books.

Darwin, C. (1929). *On the origin of species by means of natural selection.* London: Watts and Co. (Original work published 1859)

Descartes, R. (1972). *Treatise of man* (T.S. Hall, Trans.). Cambridge, MA: Harvard University Press. (Original work published 1650)

Ebbinghaus, H. (1964). Our knowledge concerning memory. In H.A. Ruger & C.E. Bussenious (Trans.) *Memory: A contribution to experimental psychology.* New York: Dover Publications. (Original work published 1885)

Fechner, G. (1860). Introduction. Outer psychophysics. In T. Adler, D. Howes & E. Boring (Eds.) (1966). *Elements of Psychophysics.* New York: Holt Reinhart & Winston.

Freedberg, D. (2002). *The eye of the lynx: Galileo, his friends and the beginnings of modern natural history.* Chicago: University of Chicago Press.

Helmholtz, H. (1878). The facts of perception. In D. Cahan (Ed) (1995). *Science and culture.* Chicago: University of Chicago Press.

Lloyd, G.E.R. (Ed.), Chadwick, J. & Mann, W.N. (Trans.). (1986). *Hippocratic writings.* New York: Penguin.

Locke, J. (1995). *An essay concerning human understanding.* Amherst, NY: Prometheus Books, (Original work published 1689.)

McGlashan, A.M. & Reeve, C.J. (1970). *Freud: Founder of psychoanalysis.* London: Rupert Hart-Davis Educational Publications.

McIntyre, J.L. (1904). A sixteenth century psychologist, Bernadino Telesio. *British Journal of Psychology, 1*(1), 61–77.

Morgan, M.J. (1977). *Molyneux's question.* Cambridge: Cambridge University Press.

Smith, J. (1973). *Introduction to Aristotle.* Chicago: University of Chicago Press.

Ward, J. (1904). Editorial. *British Journal of Psychology, 1*(1).

Winzer, M. (1993). *The history of special education.* Washington, DC: Gallaudet University Press.

Chapter 2

Bergen, B. (1990). *Secularising the schools in France 1870–1900: Controversy, continuity and consensus.* Harvard University web resource. Retrieved from www.people.fas.harvard.edu/~ces/publications/docs/pdfs/CES_26.pdf

Binet, A. & Simon, T. (1980). *The development of intelligence in children.* Baltimore: Williams and Williams. (Original work published 1916)

Burt, C. (1927). *The young delinquent.* London: University of London Press.

Galton, F. (1888). Co-relations and their measurement, chiefly from anthropomorphic data. *Proceedings of the Royal Society of London, 45,* 135–145.

Galton, F. (1907). *Inquiries into human faculty and its development.* New York: Dutton.

Haywood, C. (2001). *A history of childhood.* Cambridge: Polity.

James, W. (1905). *Psychology.* London: Macmillan.

Montessori, M. (1912). *The Montessori method* (A. George, Trans.). London: William Heinemann.

Richardson, J.T.E., (2011). *Howard Andrew Knox: Pioneer of intelligence testing at Ellis Island.* New York: Columbia University Press.

Terman, L.M. (1916). *The measurement of intelligence: An explanation of and a complete guide for the use of the Stanford revision and extension of the Binet-Simon Intelligence Scale.* Boston, MA: Houghton Mifflin.

Chapter 3

Binet, A. (1909). Les idées modernes sur les enfants. Paris Flammarion. In G. Stobart, G. (2008). *Testing times: The uses and abuses of assessment.* London: Routledge.

Board of Education and Board of Control (1929). *Report of the Joint Departmental Committee on Mental Deficiency (The Wood Committee).* London: HMSO.

Burt, C.L. (1912). The inheritance of mental characteristics. *Eugenics Review, 4,* 168–200.

Burt, C.L. (1921). *Mental and scholastic tests.* London: P.S. King & Son.

Burt, C.L. (1925). *The young delinquent.* London: University of London Press.

Burt, C.L. (1955). The evidence for the concept of intelligence. *British Journal of Educational Psychology, 25,* 158–177.

Burt, C.L. (1957). *The causes and treatments of backwardness* (4th edn.). London: University of London Press.

Burt, C.L. (1959). The examination at Eleven Plus. *British Journal of Educational Studies,* 7(2), 99–117.

Burt, C.L. & Moore, R.C. (1912). The mental differences between the sexes. *Journal of Experimental Pedagogy, 1,* 273–84, 355–88.

Cox, C.B. & Dyson, A.E. (Eds.) (1969). *Black paper two.* Hull: Critical Quarterly Society.

Douglas, J.W.B. (1964). *The home and the school: A study of ability and attainment in the primary school.* London: McGibbon & Kee.

Gould, S.J. (1981). *The mismeasure of man.* New York. Norton.

Hearnshaw, L.S. (1979). *Cyril Burt, psychologist.* Ithaca, NY: Cornell University Press.

Howe, M.J.A. (1997). *IQ in question. The truth about intelligence.* London: Sage Publications.

Lippmann. W. (1922). The IQ mythology. In A. Montagu (Ed.) (1999). *Race and IQ expanded edition.* New York: Oxford University Press.

Montagu, A. (Ed.) (1999). *Race and IQ expanded edition.* New York: Oxford University Press.

Quicke, J. (1982). *The cautious expert.* Milton Keynes: Open University Press.

Richardson, K. (1996). *Understanding intelligence.* Milton Keynes: Open University Press.

Richardson, K. (1999). *The making of intelligence.* London: Weidenfeld & Nicholson.

Rushton, J.P. (2002). New evidence on Sir Cyril Burt: His 1964 speech to the Association of Educational Psychologists. *Intelligence, 30,* 555–567.

Sternberg, R. (1984). A contextualist view of intelligence. In P. Fry (Ed.) *Changing conceptions of intelligence and intellectual functioning: Current theory and research.* Amsterdam: Elsevier Science.

Stobart, G. (2008). *Testing times: The uses and abuses of assessment.* London: Routledge.

Terman. L.M. (1916). *The measurement of intelligence: An explanation of and a complete guide for the use of the Stanford revision and extension of the Binet-Simon Scales.* Boston, MA: Houghton Mifflin.

White, J. (2006). *Intelligence, destiny and education: The ideological roots of intelligence testing.* London: Routledge.

Vignette 3

Rushton, J.P. (2002). New evidence on Sir Cyril Burt: His 1964 speech to the Association of Educational Psychologists. *Intelligence 30,* 555–567.

Chapter 4

Ackerman, T., Gillett, D., Kenwood, P., Leadbetter, P., Mason, E., Matthews, C., Mawer, P., Tweddle, D., Williams, H. & Winteringham, D.P. (1983). *DataPac user's guide.* Birmingham: University of Birmingham.

Ackers, M.J. (2012). Cyberbullying: Through the eyes of children and young people. *Educational Psychology in Practice,* 28(2) p141–157.

Beaver, R. (2011). *Educational psychology casework: A practice guide* (2nd edn.). London: Jessica Kingsley Publishers

Bennathan, M. & Boxall, M. (1996). *Effective intervention in primary schools: Nurture groups.* London: David Fulton.

Booth, T. & Ainscow, M. (2000). *The index for inclusion.* Bristol: Centre for Studies on Inclusive Education

Bridgeland, M. (1971). *Pioneer work with maladjusted children: A study of the development of therapeutic education.* London: Staples Press.

Cameron, R.J. & Stratford, R. J. (1987). Educational psychology: a problem centred approach to service delivery. *Educational Psychology in Practice* 2(4), 10–20.

Carson, R. (1962). *Silent spring.* Boston, MA: Houghton Mifflin.

Cattell, R.B. (1946). *The description and measurement of personality.* New York: World Book.

Chapman, A.J. & Jones, D.M. (Eds.) (1980). *Models of man.* Leicester: British Psychological Society.

Crick, N.R. & Dodge, K.A. (1996). Social information-processing mechanisms in reactive and proactive aggression. *Child Development, 67*(3), 993–1002.

de Shazer (1985). *Keys to solution in brief therapy.* New York: Norton.

Department for Education (2005). *Social and emotional aspects of learning (SEAL): Improving behaviour, improving learning.* London: Department for Education.

Department for Education (2010). *Inclusion development programme – Supporting pupils with behavioural, emotional and social difficulties.* London: HMSO.

Department of Education and Science & the Welsh Office (1989). *The Elton Report: Discipline in schools.* London: HMSO.

Egan, G. (1990). *The skilled helper* (4th edn). Pacific Grove, CA: Brooks/Cole.

Fox, M. (2003). Opening Pandora's Box: Evidence-based practice for educational psychologists. *Educational Psychology in Practice, 19*(2), p.91–102.

Fox, M. (2009). Working with systems and thinking systemically – disentangling the crossed wires. *Educational Psychology in Practice, 25*(3), p.247–258.

Fraser, B.J., Anderson, G.J. & Walberg, H.J. (1982). *Assessment of learning environments: Manual for Learning Environment Inventory (LEI) and My Class Inventory (MCI)* (3rd vers.). Perth, Australia: Western Australian Institute of Technology.

Galvin, P. & Costa, P. (1994). Building better behaved schools: effective support at the whole-school level. In P. Gray, A. Miller & J. Noakes (Eds.) *Challenging behaviour in schools.* London: Routledge

Haring, N.G., Lovitt, T.C., Eaton, M.D. & Hansen, C.L. (1978). *The fourth R: Research in the classroom.* Columbus, Ohio: Charles E. Merrill Publishing Co.

Hick, P. (2005). Supporting the development of more inclusive practices using the index for inclusion. *Educational Psychology in Practice, 21*(2), p.117–122.

Hooper, J. (2012). *What children need to be happy, confident and successful: Step by step positive psychology to help children flourish.* London: Jessica Kingsley Publishers.

Ivens, J. (2007). The development of a happiness measure for schoolchildren. *Educational Psychology in Practice, 23*(3), p.221–239.

Jackson, E., Whitehead, J. & Wigford, A. (2010). In an EBD population do looked after children have specific needs relating to resilience, self-perception and attainment? *Educational Psychology in Practice, 26*(1), p.69–77.

Jolly, M. & McNamara, E. (1991). *Towards better behaviour.* Preston: TBB.

Lake, C. (1985). Preventive approaches to disruption. *Maladjustment & Therapeutic Education, 3*(2), 47–52.

Lewin, K. (1936). *Principles of topological psychology.* New York: McGraw-Hill.

Maines, B. & Robinson, G. (1992). *The no blame approach.* Bristol: Lucky Duck.

Miller, A. (1996). *Pupil behaviour and teacher culture.* London: Cassell.

Miller, A. (2003). *Teachers, parents and classroom behaviour. A psychosocial approach.* Maidenhead: Open University Press.

Miller, A., Leyden, G., Stewart-Evans, C. & Gammage, S. (1992). Applied psychologists as problem solvers: Devising a personal model. *Educational Psychology in Practice, 7*(4), 227–236.

Monsen, J., Graham, B., Frederickson, N. & Cameron, R. J. (1998). Problem analysis and professional training in educational psychology: An accountable model of practice. *Educational Psychology in Practice, 13*(4), 234–249.

Muncey, J. & Ainscow, M. (1983). Launching SNAP in Coventry. *Special Education: Forward Trends, 10*(3), 8–12.

Myers, M., Cherry, C., Timmins, P., Brzezinska, H., Miller, P. & Willey, R. (1989). System supplied information (SSI): How to assess needs and plan effectively within schools/colleges. *Educational Psychology in Practice, 5*(2), 91–96.

Newton, C., Taylor, G. & Wilson, D. (1996). Circles of friends. *Educational Psychology in Practice, 11*(4), 41–48.

Olweus, D. (1993). *Bullying at school: What we know and what we can do.* Oxford: Blackwell.

Provis, M. (1992). *Dealing with difficulty; A systems approach to problem behaviour.* London: Hodder & Stoughton.

Rait, S., Monsen, J. & Squires, G. (2010). Cognitive behaviour therapies and their implications for applied educational psychology practice. *Educational Psychology in Practice, 26*(2), p.105–122.

Rhodes, J. (1993).The use of solution-focused brief therapy in schools. *Educational Psychology in Practice, 9*(1), 27–34.

Rutter, M., Maughan, B., Mortimore, P. & Ouston, J. (1979). *Fifteen thousand hours.* London: Open Books.

Smith, P.K., Smith C., Osborn. R. & Samara, M. (2012). A content analysis of school anti-bullying policies: Progress and limitations. *Educational Psychology in Practice, 28*(1), p.47–70.

Solity, J. & Bull, S. (1996). *Classroom management: Principles to practice.* London: Taylor & Francis.

Stratford, R.J. (2000). An analysis of the organisational constraints on educational psychologists working at whole school level: the opportunity of inclusion. *Educational and Child Psychology, 17*(1), 86–97.

Swinson, J. & Knight, R. (2007). Teacher verbal feedback directed towards secondary pupils with challenging behaviour and its relationship to their behaviour. *Educational Psychology in Practice, 23*(3), p.241–255.

Thomas, E.J. & Walter, C.L. (1973). Guidelines for behavioral practice in open community agency – procedures and evaluation. *Behaviour Research and Therapy, 11,* 193–205.

Thomas, J.D., Presland, I.E., Grant, M. D. & Glynn, T. (1978). National rates of teacher approval and disapproval in Grade 7 classrooms. *Journal of Applied Behaviour Analysis, 11*(1),91–94.

Westmacott, E.V.S. & Cameron, R.J. (1981). *Behaviour can change.* London: Macmillan Education.

Wheldall, K., Merrett, F. & Glynn, T. (Eds.) (1986). *Behaviour analysis in educational psychology.* London: Croom Helm.

ereferences*

Chapter 5

ibliography
Bowlby, J. (1952). *Maternal care and mental health.* Geneva: World Health Organization.

Bowley, A.H. (1948). *Modern child psychology.* London: Hutchinsons University Library.

Bruner, J.S. (1966). *Towards a theory of Instruction.* Cambridge, MA: Belknap Press of Harvard University Press.

Department of Education and Science (1968). *Psychologists in education services.* The Summerfield Report. London: HMSO.

Feuerstein, R. (1980). *Instrumental enrichment: an intervention programme for cognitive modifiability.* Glenview, Il: Scott Foresman and Co.

Gilham, B. (Ed.) (1978). *Reconstructing educational psychology.* London: Croon Helm.

Leyden, G. (1978). The process of reconstruction: An overview. In B. Gilham (Ed.) *Reconstructing educational psychology.* London: Croom Helm.

Ministry of Education (1945). *The nation's schools: their plan and purpose. Ministry of Education Pamphlet No.1.* London: HMSO.

Ministry of Education (1955). *Report of the Committee on Maladjusted Children.* The Underwood Report. London: HMSO.

National Association for Mental Health (1963). Proceedings of the 19th Child Guidance Inter-Clinic Conference. Clinical problems in children of primary school age. London: NAMH.

Piaget, J. (1950). *The psychology of intelligence.* London: Routledge & Kegan Paul.

Reid, R.S. (1978). Drums in the jungle. *AEP Journal, 4*(6).

Stevenson, H.W. (Ed.) (1963). The sixty-second yearbook of the National Society for the Study of Education. Child Psychology. Chicago, IL: University of Chicago Press.

Sutton, A. (1976). Child psychology and local government. *AEP Journal, 4*(1).

Vygotsky, L.S. (1962). *Thought and language.* Cambridge, MA: MIT Press.

Chapter 6

Ainscow, M. & Tweddle, D. (1979). *Preventing classroom failure: An objectives approach.* London: Wiley.

Ackerman, T., Gillett, D., Kenwood, P., Leadbetter, P., Mason, E., Matthews, C., Mawer, P., Tweddle, D., Williams, H. & Winteringham, D.P. (1983). *DataPac user's guide.* Birmingham: University of Birmingham.

Anderson, J.R. (1990). *The adaptive character of thought.* Hove: Lawrence Erlbaum Associates.

Blachford, P., Russell, A. & Webster, R. (2011). *Reassessing the impact of teaching assistants.* London: Routledge.

Booth, S. & Jewell, T. (1983) Programmes for slow learners. *Journal of the Association of Educational Psychologists, 6,*(2), 58–61.

Booth, S. (1984). Precise educational techniques for slow learners (PETSL). *DECP Newsletter, 15,* 32–33.

Bradley, L. & Bryant, P. (1978). Difficulties in auditory organisation as a possible cause of reading backwardness. *Nature, 271,* 746–747.

Bull, S.J. & Solity, J.E. (1989). *Classroom management: Principles to practice.* London: Routledge.

Carnine, D.W., Silbert, J. & Kameenui, E.J. (1997). *Direct instruction reading.* New Jersey: Prentice Hall.

Clark, C. & Poulton, L. (2011). *Book ownership and its relation to reading enjoyment, attitudes, behaviour and attainment.* London: National Literacy Trust.

Department for Education (2012). Phonic products and the self-assessment process. Retrieved 27 September 2012 from www.education.gov.uk/schools/teachingandlearning/pedagogy/phonics/b00198579/phonics-products-and-the-self-assessment-process

Department for Education and Employment (1998). T*he National Literacy Strategy: Framework for teaching.* London: DfEE.

Department for Education and Employment (1999). *The National Numeracy Strategy: Framework for teaching.* London: DfEE.

Department of Education and Science (1978). *Special educational needs.* The Warnock Report. London: HMSO.

Engelmann, S. (1992). *War against schools: Academic child abuse.* Portland, OR: Halcyon House.

Engelmann, S. & Carnine, D. (1982). *Theory of instruction: Principles and application.* New York: Irvington.

ESPO (2011). *The importance of phonics: A catalogue of systematic, synthetic phonics products and training.* Leicester: Eastern Shires Purchasing Organisation (ESPO).

Gardner, J., Murphy, J. & Crawford, N. (1983). *The skills analysis model.* Kidderminster: BIMH.

Gillham, W. (Ed.) (1978). *Reconstruction educational psychology.* London: Croom Helm.

Gladwell, M. (2008). *Outliers: The story of success.* London: Allen Lane.

Goodman, K.S. (1986). *What's the whole in whole language.* New York: Scholastic Press.

Goswami, U. & Bryant, P. (1990). *Phonological skills and learning to read.* Hove: Lawrence Erlbaum Associates.

Hammersley, M. (2002). *Educational research: Policy making and practice.* London: Paul Chapman.

Hargreaves, D. (1994). *The mosaic of learning.* London: Demos.

Hargreaves, D. (1997). In defence of research for evidence-based teaching: A rejoinder to Martyn Hammersley. *British Educational Research Journal, 23*(3), 405–19.

Hattie, J. (2009). *Visible learning: A synthesis of over 800 meta-analyses relating to achievement.* London: Routledge.

Jensen, B., Hunter, A., Sonnemann, J. & Burns, T. (2012). *Catching up: Learning from the best school systems in East Asia.* Melbourne: Grattan Institute

Johnson, R. & Watson, J. (2004). Accelerating the development of reading, spelling and phonemic awareness skills in initial readers. *Reading and Writing: An Interdisciplinary Journal, 17,* 327–357.

Johnson, R. & Watson, J. (2005). The effects of synthetic phonics teaching of reading and spelling attainment: A seven year longitudinal study. Retrieved 27 September 2012 from www.scotland.gov.uk/Resource/Doc/36496/0023582.pdf

Johnson, R. & Watson, J. (2010). *Phonics bug.* London: Pearson.

Kelly, A.V. (1982). *The curriculum: Theory and practice.* London: Paul Chapman.

Leach, D. & Raybould, E.C. (1977). *Learning and behaviour difficulties in school.* London: Open Books.

McGlashan, A.M. & Reeve, C.J. (1970). *Sigmund Freud: founder of psychoanalysis.* New York: Praeger.

Merrett, F. & Wheldall, K. (1990). *Positive teaching in the primary school.* London: Paul Chapman.

Mourshed, M., Chijioke, C. & Barber, M. (2010). *How the world's most improved school systems keep getting better.* London: McKinsey & Company.

Ofsted (1998). *The National Literacy Project: An HMI evaluation.* London: Author.

Ofsted (2004). *Reading for purpose and pleasure: An evaluation of the reading in primary schools.* London: Author.

Ofsted (2012). *Moving English forward: action to raise standards in English.* London: Author

Powell, M. & Solity, J.E. (1990). *Teachers in control: Cracking the code.* London: Routledge.

Raybould, E.C. (1984). Precision teaching and pupils with learning difficulties and perspectives, principles and practice. In D. Fontana (Ed.) Behaviourism and learning theory in education. *British Journal of Educational Psychology Monograph Series, No 1,* 43–74. Edinburgh: Scottish Academic Press.

Raybould, E.C. & Solity, J.E. (1982). Teaching with precision. *Special Education/Forward Trends, 9*(2), 9–13.

Reynolds, M. & Wheldall, K. (2007). Reading recovery 20 years down the track: Looking forward, looking back. *International Journal of Disability, Development and Education, 54*(2), 199–223.

Rhine, W.R. (Ed.) (1981). *Making schools more effective: New directions from follow through.* New York: Academic Press.

Shapiro, L. & Solity, J.E. (2008). Delivering phonological and phonics training within whole-class teaching. *British Journal of Educational Psychology, 78,* 4, 597–620.

Siegel, L. (1992). An evaluation of the discrepancy definition of dyslexia. *Journal of Learning Disabilities, 25,* 618–629.

Siegler, R.S., Duncan, G.J., Davis-Kean, P.E., Duckworth, K., Claessens, A., Engel, M., Susperreguy, M.I. & Chen, C. (2012). Early predictors of high school mathematics achievement. *Psychological Science, 23,* 691–697.

Simon, B. (1978). *Intelligence, psychology and education.* London: Lawrence & Wishart.

Simon, B. (1985). *Does education matter?* London: Lawrence & Wishart.

Skinner, B.F. (1966). *The technology of teaching.* New York: Appleton-Century Crofts.

Smith, F. (1973). *Psycholinguistics and reading.* New York: Holt, Rinehart, & Winston.

Smith, F. (1978). *Understanding reading: A psycholinguistic analysis of reading and learning to read* (2nd edn.). New York: Holt, Rinehart, & Winston.

Snowling, M.J. & Hulme, C. (2011). Evidence-based interventions for reading and language difficulties: Creating a virtuous circle. *British Journal of Educational Psychology, 81,* 1–23.

Solity, J.E. (1991). Special needs: A discriminatory concept? *Educational Psychology in Practice, 7*(1), 12–19.

Solity, J.E. (1992). *Special education.* London: Cassell.

Solity, J.E. (1993). Assessment-through-teaching: A case of mistaken identity. *Educational and Child Psychology, 10*(4), 27–47.

Solity, J.E. (1996). Reframing psychological assessment. *Educational and Child Psychology, 13*(3), 94–102.

Solity, J.E. (2008). *The learning revolution.* London: Hodder Education.

Solity, J.E. & Bull, S.J. (1987). *Special needs: Bridging the curriculum gap.* Milton Keynes: Open University Press.

Solity, J.E. & Raybould, E.C. (1988). *The 1981 Education Act: A positive response.* Buckingham: Open University Press.

Solity, J.E. & Shapiro, L.R. (2008). Developing the practice of educational psychologists through theory and research. *Educational and Child Psychology, 25*(3), 123–149.

Solity, J.E. & Vousden, J. (2009). Real books versus reading schemes: A new perspective from instructional psychology. *Educational Psychology, 29,* 469–511.

Stannard, J. & Huxford, L. (2007). *The literacy game: The story of the National Literacy Strategy.* London: Routledge.

Stanovich, K. (1991). Discrepancy definitions of reading disability: Has intelligence led us astray? *Reading Research Quarterly, 26,* 7–29.

Stanovich, K. (1994). Annotation: Does dyslexia exist? *Journal of Child Psychology and Psychiatry, 25*(4), 579–595.

Stanovich, K. & Siegel, L. (1994). Phenotypical performance profile of children with reading disabilities: A regression-based test of the phonological-core-variable-difference model. *Journal of Educational Psychology, 86,* 24–53.

Stein, M., Silbert, J. & Carnine, D. (1997). *Designing effective mathematics instruction: A direct instruction approach.* Columbus, Ohio: Prentice Hall.

Stenhouse, L. (1975). *An introduction to curriculum research and development.* London: Heinemann.

Twist, L., Sainsbury, M., Woodthorpe, A. & Whetton, C. (2003). *Reading all over the world: Progress in international reading literacy study (PIRLS). National report for England.* Slough: NFER.

Twist, L., Schagen, I. & Hodgson, C. (2007). *Readers and reading: The national report for England 2006 (PIRLS: Progress in International Reading Literacy Study).* Slough: NFER

Vousden, J.I., Ellefson, M.R., Solity, J.E. & Chater, N. (2011). Simplifying reading: Applying the simplicity principle to reading. *Cognitive Science, 35,* 34–78.

Wheldall, K. & Carter, M. (1996). Reconstructing behaviour analysis in education: A revised behavioural interactionist perspective for special education. *Educational Psychology, 16*(2), 121–140.

Wheldall, K. & Glynn, T. (1988). Contingencies in context: A behaviour interactionist perspective in education. *Educational Psychology, 8,* 5–19.

Wheldall, K. & Merrett, K. (1984). *Positive teaching: The behavioural approach.* London, Unwin Education Books.

Wolf, M. (2008). *Proust and the squid: The story and science of the reading brain.* London: Icon Books.

Wyse, D. & Styles, M. (2007). Synthetic phonics and the teaching of reading: The debate surrounding England's Rose Report. *Literacy, 41*(1), 35-42.

Chapter 7

Ainscow, M. & Tweddle, D. (1979). *Preventing classroom failure: An objectives approach.* Chichester: Wiley.

Association of Educational Psychologists (1994, revised 2004). *Guidance to educational psychologists in preparing statutory advice to the local authority.* Durham: AEP.

Barrs, M., Ellis, J., Hester, H. & Thomas, A. (1990). *Patterns of learning. The primary language record and the National Curriculum.* Centre for Language in Primary Education.

Becker, W.C., Engelman, S. & Carnine, D.W. (1981). Direct instruction model. In W.R. Rhine (Ed.) *Making schools more effective: New directions from follow-through.* New York: Academic Press.

Begley, J., Brown, M. & Cameron, R. (1989). Special needs: Spelling. *Support for Learning, 4*(1), 12–18.

Bersoff, D.N. (1973). Silk purses into sow's ears: The decline of psychological testing and a suggestion for its redemption. *American Psychologist,* October, 892–899.

Binet, A. & Simon, T.H. (1905). Application des méthodes nouvelles au diagnostic du niveau intellectuel chez des enfants, normaux et anormaux d'hospice et d'école primaire. *L'Année Psychologique, 11,* 245–336.

Bluma, S., Shearer, D., Frohman, A. & Hillard, J. (1976). *Portage guide to education: Checklist.* Windsor: NFER-Nelson.

Boxer, R., Challen, M. & McCarthy, M. (1991). Developing an assessment framework: The distinctive contribution of the educational psychologist. *Educational Psychology in Practice. 7*(1), 30–34.

Burden, R.B. (1973). If we throw the tests out roof the window, what is there left to do? *Journal of the Association of Educational Psychologists, 3*(5), 6–9.

Burden, R. (1996). Assessing children's perceptions themselves as learners and problem solvers: The construction of the 'Myself-As-Learner' Scale (MALS). *Educational and Child Psychology, 13*(3) 25–30.

Burt, C.L. (1921). *Mental and scholastic tests.* London: University of London Press.

Burt, C.L. (1925). *The young delinquent.* London: University of London Press.

Burt, C.L. (1935). *The backward child.* London: P.S. King and Sons.

Cade, B.C. & O'Hanlon, W.H. (1993). *A brief guide to brief therapy.* London: Norton.

Cameron R.J. (1991). Curriculum-related assessment: The importance of educationally relevant data. In L. Harding & J.R. Beeching (Eds.) *Educational assessment of the primary school child.* Windsor: NFER-Nelson.

Cameron R.J., Owen, A.J. & Tee, G. (1986). Curriculum management (part 3): Assessment and evaluation. *Educational Psychology in Practice, 2*(3), 3–9.

Centre for Applied Positive Psychology (2009). *Tactical manual and statistical properties for Realise2.* Coventry: CAPP.

Conoley, J.C. & Conoley, C.W. (1990). Staff consultative work in schools. In N. Jones & N. Frederickson (Eds.) *Refocusing educational psychology.* London: Falmer Press.

Cooper, C. (1995). Inside the WISC III (UK). *Educational Psychology in Practice, 10*(4), 215–219.

de Shazer, S. (1985). *Keys to solution in brief therapy.* New York: Norton.

de Shazer, S. (1988). *Clues: Investigating solutions in brief therapy.* New York: Norton.

de Shazer, S. (1991). *Putting difference to work.* New York: Norton.

Denman, R. & Lunt, I. (1993). Getting your act together. Some implications for EPs of cases of judicial review. *Educational Psychology in Practice, 9*(1), 9–16.

Deutch, R. & Mohammed, M. (2009). *The cognitive ability profile.* Canterbury: Real Group (UK).

Division of the Educational and Child Psychology (1999). *A framework for a psychological assessment and intervention.* Leicester: British Psychological Society .

Dockrell, J. & McShane, J. (1993). *Children's learning difficulties: A cognitive approach.* Oxford: Blackwell.

Dunsmuir, S., Brown, E., Iyadurai, S. & Monsen, J. (2009). Evidence-based practice and evaluation: from insight to impact. *Educational Psychology in Practice, 25*(1), 53–70.

Dunsmuir, S. & Frederickson, N. (2009) (Eds.) *Measures of children's mental health and psychological wellbeing.* London: GL Assessment.

Egan, G. (1975). *The skilled helper. A systematic approach to effective helping.* California: Wadsworth.

Elliott, C.D., Murray, D. J. & Pearson, L.C. (1979). *The British Ability Scales.* Slough: NFER.

Elliott, C.D. & Smith, C. (2011). *The British Ability Scales III.* Swindon: GL Assessment.

Elliott, C.D., Smith, P. & McCulloch, K. (1997). *British Ability Scales No. 2: Technical manual.* Windsor: NFER-Nelson.

Farrell, P., McBrien, J. & Foxen, T. (1992). *Education of the developmentally young: Teaching people with severe learning difficulties.* Manchester: Manchester University Press.

Farrell, P. & Smith, N. (1982). A survey of the methods that educational psychologists use to assess children with learning difficulties. *DECP Occasional Paper 6*(2), 31–41.

Farouk, S. (2004). Group work in schools: A process consultation approach. *Educational Psychology in Practice. 20*(3), 207–220.

Feuerstein, R. (1990). The theory of structural modifiability. In B. Presseisen (Ed.) *Learning and thinking styles: Classroom interaction.* Washington, DC: National Education Associations.

Fraser, S. & Greenhalgh, T. (2001). Coping with complexity: educating for capability. *British Medical Journal, 323,* 799–803.

Figg, J., Keeton, D., Parkes, J. & Richards, A. (1996). Are they talking about us? How EPs describes the views of children. *Educational and Child Psychology, 13*(2), 5–13.

Foxen, T. & McBrien, J. (1981). *The EDY in-service course: Training staff in behavioural methods. Two volumes: Trainee workbook and instructors handbook.* Manchester: Manchester University Press.

Frederickson, N. & Cameron, R.J. (1999). *Psychology in education portfolio.* Windsor: NFER-Nelson.

Frederickson, N. & Dunsmuir, S. (2010). *Measures of children's mental health and psychological well-being.* Swindon: GL Assessment.

Gardener, J., Murphy, J. & Crawford, N. (1983). *The skills analysis model.* Kidderminster: British Institute of Mental Handicap.

Gersch, I.S., Holgate, A. & Sexton, A. (1993). Valuing the child's perspective: A revised student report and other practical initiatives. *Educational Psychology in Practice, 9*(1), 17–26.

Ghodsian, M. (1977). Children's behaviour and the BSAG: Some theoretical and statistical considerations. *British Journal of Social and Clinical Psychology 16*(1), 22–28.

Gillham, W. (Ed.) (1975). *Reconstructing educational psychology.* London: Croom Helm.

Gillham, W. (1999). The writing of 'Reconstructing Educational Psychology'. *Educational Psychology in Practice, 14*(4), 220–2221.

Gutkin, T.B. & Conoley, J.C. (1990). Reconceptualising school psychology from a service delivery perspective: Implications for practice, training and research. *Journal of School Psychology, 28,* 203–223.

Haring, N.G., Lovitt, T.C., Eaton, M.D. & Hansen, C.L. (1978). *The 4th R: Research in the classroom.* Columbus, OH: Charles E. Merrill.

Hayes, B., Richardson, S., Hindle, S. & Grayson, K. (2011). Developing teaching assistants' skills in positive behaviour management: An application of video interactive guidance in secondary schools. *Educational Psychology in Practice, 27*(3), 255–269.

Hewstone, M., Fincham, F.D. & Foster, J. (2005). *Psychology.* Oxford: BPS Blackwell.

James, C. (2001). *Always unreliable.* London: Picador.

James, W. (1899). *Talks to teachers on psychology: And to students on some of life's ideals.* New York: Henry Holt & Co.

Johnston, M, Weinman, J. & Wright, S. (1995). *Measures in health psychology: A user's portfolio.* Windsor: NFER-Nelson.

Keir, G. (1949). The progress of matrices as applied to school children. *British Journal of Statistical Psychology, 2*(3), 140–150.

Kennedy, E.K., Cameron, R.J. & Monsen, J. (2009).Effective consultation in educational and child psychology practice: Professional training for both competence and capability. *School Psychology International. 30*(6), 603–625.

Kennedy, H. (2006). An analysis of assessment and intervention frameworks in educational psychology services in Scotland: Past, present and possible worlds. *School Psychology International, 27*(5), 515–534.

Labon, D. (1974). *Assessment of intelligence.* Chichester: West Sussex County Educational Psychology Service.

Linley, P.A. (2008). *From Average to A+: Realising strengths in yourself and others.* Coventry: Centre for Applied Positive Psychology.

Linley, P.A., Willars, J. & Biswas-Diener, R. (2010). *The strengths book: Be confident, be successful, and enjoy better relationships by realising the best of you.* Coventry: Centre for Applied Positive Psychology.

Lokke, C., Gersch, I.S., M'Gadzah, H. & Frederickson, N. (1997). The resurrection of psychometrics. *Educational Psychology in Practice, 12*(4), 222–223.

Luria, A.R. (1976). *The cognitive development: Its cultural and social foundations.* Cambridge, MA: Harvard University Press.

Mischel, W. (1977). On the future of personality measurement. *American Psychologist*, April, 246–254.

Neisser, U. (1967). *Cognitive psychology.* New York: Apple, Century and Crofts.

Maher, C.A. & Barbrack, C.R. (1984). Evaluating the individual counseling of conduct problem adolescents: The goal attainment scaling method. *Journal of School Psychology, 22*, 285–297.

Maines, B. & Robinson, G. (1988). *B/G Steem user manual and CD-ROM.* London: Sage.

Milne, D (1992). *Assessment: A mental health portfolio.* Windsor: NFER-Nelson.

Monsen, J.J. & Graham, B. (2002). Developing teacher support groups to deal with challenging behaviour: the staff sharing scheme. In P. Gray (Ed.) *Working with emotions: Responding to the challenge of difficult pupil behaviour in schools.* London: Routledge-Farmer.

Moore, J. (2005). Recognising and questioning the epistemological basis of educational psychology. *Educational Psychology in Practice, 21*(2), 103–116.

Morton, J. & Frith, U. (1995). Causal modelling: a structural approach to developmental psychopathology. In D. Cichette & D.J. Cohen (Eds.) *Manual of developmental psychopathology.* New York: Wiley.

Nolan, A. & Sigston, A. (1993). *Where do I go from here? A booklet for children who have been excluded from school.* Leyton: Waltham Forest Educational Psychology Service.

Peterson, D.R. (2003). Unintended consequences: ventures and adventures in the education of professional psychologists. *American Psychologist, 58*(10), 791–800.

Raybould, E.C. & Solity, J.E. (1982). Teaching with precision. *Special Education/Forward Trends, 9,* 9–13.

Rhodes, J. (1993). The use of solution-focused brief therapy in schools. *Educational Psychology in Practice, 9*(1), 27–34.

Roller, J. (1998). Facilitating pupil involvement in assessment, planning and review processes. *Educational Psychology in Practice, 13*(4), 266–273.

Sclare, I. (Ed.) (1997). *Child psychology portfolio.* Windsor: NFER-Nelson.

Schein, E.H. (1999). *Process consultation revisited: building the helping relationship.* Reading, MA: Addison-Wesley.

Seligman, M.E.P. & Csikszentmihalyi, M. (2000). Positive psychology: An introduction. *American Psychologist, 55*(1), 5–14.

Smith, J., Kushlick, A. & Glossop, C. (1977). *The Wessex Portage Project: a home teaching service for families with a pre-school handicapped child.* Winchester, Hants: Wessex Health Care Evaluation Research Team.

Stott, D.H. (1963). *The social adjustment of children: Manual to the Bristol social adjustment guides.* University of London Press.

Surrey Educational Psychology Service (1994). *My Learning.* Kingston upon Thames: SEPS.

Teicher, M.H., Samoon, J.A., Polcari, A. & Greenery, C.E. (2006). Sticks, stones and hurtful words: Relative effects of various forms of childhood maltreatment. *American Journal of Psychiatry, 163,* 993–1000.

Terman, L.M., Lyman, G., Ordahl, G., Ordahl, L., Galbreath, N. & Talbert, W. (1915). The Stanford revision of the Binet-Simon scale and some results from its application to 1000 non-selected children. *Journal of Educational Psychology, 6*(9), 551–562.

Terman, L.M. & Merrill, M.A. (1961). *Stanford–Binet Intelligence Scale.* New York: Harrap.

Vygotsky, L.S. (1962). *Thought and language.* Cambridge, MA: MIT Press.

Ward, J. (1975). Some comments on the current status of psychrometry. *DECP Occasional Papers, 8,* 380–387.

Wechsler, D. (1949). *Wechsler intelligence scale for children.* New York: Psychological Corporation.

Wechsler, D. (2004). *Wechsler intelligence scale for children IV* (UK edn.). Swindon: GL Assessment.

White, O.R. & Haring, N.G. (1980). *Exceptional teaching.* Columbus, Ohio: Chas E. Merrill.

Wolf, T.H. (1960). An individual who also made a difference. *American Psychologist, 16,* 245–248.

Wolfendale, S. (1987). *All about me: The story of my life so far.* London: National Children's Bureau.

Woods, K. & Farrell, P. (2006). Approaches to psychological assessment by educational psychologists in England and Wales. *School Psychology International, 27*(4), 387–404.

Woolfson, L., Whaling, R., Stewart, A. & Monsen, J. (2003). An integrated framework to guide educational psychologist practice. *Educational Psychology in Practice, 19*(4), 283–302.

Vignette 7

Brunner, J.S. (1983). *Child's talk: Learning to use language.* Oxford: Oxford University Press

Dessent, T. (1987). *Making the ordinary school special.* Lewes: Falmer Press.

Frederickson, N. (1990). Systems approaches in EP practice: A re-evaluation. In N. Jones & N. Frederickson (Eds.) *Refocusing educational psychology.* Lewes: Falmer Press.

Farrell, P., McBrien, J. & Foxen, T. (1992). *Education of the developmentally young: Teaching people with severe learning difficulties.* Manchester: Manchester University Press.

Gardener, J., Murphy, J. & Crawford, N. (1983). *The skills analysis model.* Kidderminster: British Institute of Mental Handicap.

Haring, N.G. & Eaton, M.D. (1978). Systematic instructional procedures: An instructional hierarchy. In N.G. Haring, N.G., Lovitt, T.C., Eaton, M.D. & Hansen, C.L. (Eds.) *The Fourth R: Research in the classroom* (pp.23-40). Columbus, OH: Charles E. Merrill.

Raybould, E.C. & Solity, J.E. (1982). Teaching with precision. *Special Education/Forward Trends, 9,* 9–13.

Smith, J., Kushlick, A. & Glossop, C. (1977). *The Wessex Portage project: A home teaching service for families with a pre-school handicapped child.* Winchester, Hants: Wessex Health Care Evaluation Research Team.

Tizard, B. & Hughes, M. (1984). Young children learning. Talking and thinking at home and at school. London: Fontana.

Vygotsky, L.S.(1962). *Thought and language.* Cambridge, MA: MIT Press.

Westmacott, E.V.S. & Cameron, R.J. (1981). *Behaviour can change.* London: Macmillan.

Chapter 8

Allington, R.L. (2001). *What really matters for struggling readers: Designing research-based programs.* New York: Longman.

Berger, M. (1979). Behaviour modification in education and professional practice: The dangers of a mindless technology. *International Journal of Experimental Psychology, 4*(3), pp.213–231.

Bryans, T. (1992). Educational psychologists working in a biased society. In S. Wolfendale, T. Bryans, M. Fox, A. Labram & A. Sigston, *The profession and practice of educational psychology: Future directions.* London: Cassell Educational.

Cameron, R. (1989). Teaching parents to teach children: the Portage approach to special needs. In N. Jones (Ed.) *Special Educational Review, 1.* Basingstoke: Falmer Press.

Canter, L. & Canter, M. (1992). *Assertive discipline.* Santa Monica: Lee Canter Associates.

Caplan, G. (1970). *The theory and practice of mental health consultation.* London: Tavistock Publications.

Cline, T. & Lunt, I. (1990). Meeting equal opportunities criteria: a review of progress in educational psychology training. In Training for professional practice, *DECP, 7*(3), pp.59–66.

Conn, W. (1992). Psychologists, child law and the Courts: Contexts and professional advice. In S. Wolfendale, T. Bryans, M. Fox, A. Labram & A. Sigston, *The profession and practice of educational psychology: Future directions.* London: Cassell Educational.

Dessent, T. (1987). *Making the ordinary school special.* Lewes: The Falmer Press.

Gersch, I.S., Scherer, M. & Fry, L (1990). (Eds.). *Meeting disruptive behaviour: Assessment, intervention and Partnership.* London: Macmillan.

Houghton, S., Merrett, F. & Wheldall, K. (1988). *The attitudes of British secondary school pupils to praise, rewards, punishments and reprimands: A further study. New Zealand Journal of Educational Studies, 23,* 203–214

Kelly, G. (1955, 1991). *The psychology of personal constructs.* New York: W.W. Norton.

Labram, A. (1992). The educational psychologist as a consultant. In S. Wolfendale, T. Bryans, M. Fox, A. Labram & A. Sigston, *The profession and practice of educational psychology: Future directions.* London: Cassell Educational.

Lindsay, G. (1992). Educational psychologists and Europe. In S. Wolfendale, T. Bryans, M. Fox, M., A. Labram & A. Sigston, *The profession and practice of educational psychology: Future directions.* London: Cassell Educational.

McNamara, E. (1983). *Classroom contingency management and teacher non-verbal behaviour.* Occasional papers of the Division of Educational Psychology.

Merrett, F. & Wheldall, K. (1990). Does BATPACK training of teachers lead to higher pupil productivity? *Educational and Child Psychology, 7*(1), 31–43.

Mortimore, P., Sammons, P., Stoll, L., Lewis, D. & Ecob, R. (1988). *School matters: The junior years.* Wells: Open Books.

Nicholls, D. (1993a). *The effect of Canter's assertive discipline program on teacher and student behaviour.* MEd dissertation, University of Western Australia.

Nicholls, D. (1993b). Looking into classrooms, what a research study found about assertive discipline. In D. Evans, M. Myhill & J. Izard. (Eds.) *Student behaviour problems: Positive initiatives and new frontiers.* National conference, Australian Council for Educational Research.

Reynolds, D. (1985). *Studying school effectiveness*. Lewes: Falmer Press.

Russell, P. (1990). Policy and practice for your children with special educational needs: changes and challenges, In S. Wolfendale (Ed.) *Support for learning*. Slough: NFER.

Russell, P. (1992). Boundary issues: Multidisciplinary working in new contexts – Implications for educational psychology practice. In S. Wolfendale, T. Bryans, M. Fox, M., A. Labram & A. Sigston, *The profession and practice of educational psychology: Future directions*. London: Cassell Educational.

Rutter, M., Maughan, B., Mortimore, P., Ouston, J. & Smith, A. (1979). *Fifteen Thousand hours: secondary schools and their effects on pupils*. London: Open Books.

Sharpley, A.M. & Sharpley, C.F. (1981). Peer tutoring – A review of the literature. *Collected Original Resources in Education, 5*(3), 7–11.

Sigston, A. (1992). Making a difference for children: The educational psychologist an empowerer of problem-solving alliances. In S. Wolfendale, T. Bryans, M. Fox, A. Labram & A. Sigston, *The profession and practice of educational psychology: Future directions*. London: Cassell Educational.

Sigston, A., Curran, P., Labram, A. & Wolfendale, S. (Eds.) (1996). *Psychology in practice with young people, families and schools*. London: David Fulton.

Swinson, J. & Melling, R. (1995). Assertive discipline: Four wheels on this wagon – A reply to Robinson and Maines. *Educational Psychology in Practice, 11*(3), 3–8.

Topping, K. (1987). Paired reading: A powerful technique for parent use. *The Reading Teacher, 40*. March, pp.604–614.

Topping, K. (1988). *The peer tutoring handbook: Promoting co-operative learning*. Cambridge, MA: Brookline Books; London: Croom Helm.

Topping, K. (1989). Peer tutoring and paired reading: Combining two powerful techniques. *The Reading Teacher*. March, pp.488–494.

Wheldall, K. (1982). Behavioural pedagogy or behavioural overkill. *Educational Psychology, 2*, 181–184.

Winter, S. & Low, A. (1984). The Rossmere peer tutor project. *Behavioural Approaches with Children, 8*, 62–65.

Wolfendale, S., Bryans, T., Fox, M., Labram, A. & Sigston, A. (1992). *The profession and practice of educational psychology: Future directions*. London: Cassell Educational.

Vignette 8

Audit Commission (1992). *Getting in on the Act: Provision for pupils with special educational needs*. London: HMSO

Cummins, J. (1984). *Bilingualism and special educational needs: Issues in assessment and pedagogy*. Avon: Multilingual Matters.

Department for Education (1994). *Code of practice for the identification and assessment of children with special educational needs*. London: Author.

Hymans, M., Bryans, T. & Pinks, A. (1996). In A. Sigston, P. Curran, A. Labram & S. Wolfendale (Eds.) (1996). *Psychology in practice with young people, families and schools*. London: David Fulton.

Janis, I.L. (1972). *Victims of groupthink*. Boston, MA: Houghton Mifflin.

Mason, M. (1992). *The inclusive education system*. London: The Integration Alliance.

Phillips, P. (1990). Consultative teamwork in secondary schools: A training exercise. *Educational and Child Psychology, 7*(1), 67–77.

Saunders, G. (1988). *Bilingual children: from birth to teens*. Clevedon: Multilingual Matters.

Sigston, A. (1992). Making a difference for children: The educational psychologist an empowerer of problem-solving alliances. In S. Wolfendale, T. Bryans, M. Fox, A. Labram & A. Sigston, *The profession and practice of educational psychology: Future directions*. London: Cassell Educational.

Chapter 9

Bannerjee, R., Tolmie, A. & Boyle, J. (2011). Educational psychology: History and overview. In G. Davey (Ed.) *Applied psychology*. Oxford: Wiley-Blackwell.

Blythman, M. (1978). The training of teachers for special education in Scotland. In W.B. Dockrell, W.R. Dunn & A. Milne (Eds.) *Special education in Scotland*. Edinburgh: Scottish Council for Research in Education.

Boyle, J. & MacKay, T. (2010). The distinctiveness of applied educational psychology in Scotland and early pathways into the profession. *History and Philosophy of Psychology, 12*(2), 37–48.

Boyle, J., MacKay, T. & Lauchlan, F. (2008). The legislative context and shared practice models. In B. Kelly, L. Woolfson & J. Boyle (Eds.) *Frameworks for practice in educational psychology: A textbook for trainees and practitioners.* London: Jessica Kingsley.

Carroll, H. (1976). Research and the educational psychologist. *Association of Educational Psychologists Journal, 4*(2).

Department for Education and Employment (2000a). *Educational Psychology Services (England): Current role, good practice and future directions. Report of the working group.* London: Author.

Department for Education and Employment (2000b). *Educational Psychology Services (England): Current role, good practice and future directions. The research report.* London: Author.

Department of Education and Science (1968). *Psychologists in education services.* The Summerfield Report. London: HMSO.

Farrell, P., Woods, K., Lewis, S., Rooney, S., Squires, G. & O'Connor, M. (2006). *A review of the functions and contribution of educational psychologists in England and Wales in light of Every child matters: Change for children. Research Report No. 792.* London: Department for Education and Skills.

Gillham, B. (Ed.) (1978). *Reconstructing educational psychology.* London: Croom Helm.

Gray, P. (1991). Educational psychologists as researchers: Some considerations for present and future practice. *Educational and Child Psychology, 8*(1), 36–43.

Hargreaves, J. (1985). Interviews with Professor Elizabeth D. Fraser (1920–1995), recorded on the 14 and 20 November 1985. University of Aberdeen, MS 3620/I/32, 34. Retrieved 27 July 2012 from http://calms.abdn.ac.uk/DServe/dserve.exe?dsqServer=Calms&dsqIni=Dserve.ini&dsqApp=Archive&dsqCmd =Show.tcl&dsqDb=Catalog&dsqPos=40&dsqSearch=(RefNo='3620')

Hearnshaw, L. (1979). *Cyril Burt, psychologist.* London: Hodder & Stoughton.

HM Inspectorate of Education (HMIE) (2007). *Quality management in local authority educational psychology services: Self-evaluation for quality improvement.* Livingston: Author.

HM Inspectorate of Education (HMIE) (2011). *Educational psychology in Scotland: Making a difference.* Livingston: Author.

Hutchison, H. (1973). *Scottish public educational documents 1560–1960.* Edinburgh: Scottish Council for Research in Education, Series 3(1).

Lindsay, G. (1981). Research and the educational psychologist – five years on. *Association of Education Psychologists Journal, 5*(6), 16–20.

MacKay, T. (1982). A new principal and a new principle. *Scottish Association of Local Government Educational Psychologists Quarterly, 1*(2), 13–20.

MacKay, T. (1989). Special education: The post-Warnock role for the educational psychologist. *BPS Scottish Division of Educational and Child Psychology, Newsletter 1,* 1–8.

MacKay, T. (1992a). Where now community psychology? *BPS Scottish Division of Educational and Child Psychology, Newsletter 1,* 1–6.

MacKay, T. (1992b). Where now community psychology? A Scottish perspective. *Young Minds Newsletter, 12,* 12–13.

MacKay, T. (1996). The statutory foundations of Scottish educational psychology services. *Educational Psychology in Scotland, 3,* 3–9.

MacKay, T. (1999). *Quality assurance in education authority psychological services: Self-evaluation using performance indicators.* Edinburgh: Scottish Executive Education Department.

MacKay, T. (2006a). The educational psychologist as community psychologist: Holistic child psychology across home, school and community. *Educational and Child Psychology, 23*(1), 7–13.

MacKay, T. (2006b). *The evaluation of post-school psychological services pathfinders in Scotland (2004–2006).* Edinburgh: Scottish Executive Department of Enterprise, Transport and Lifelong Learning.

MacKay, T. (2008). Psychological services and their impact. In T.G.K. Bryce & W.M. Humes (Eds.) *Scottish education* (3rd edn, pp.720–731). Edinburgh: Edinburgh University Press.

MacKay, T. (2009). Post-school educational psychology services: International perspectives on a distinctive Scottish development. *Educational and Child Psychology, 26*(1), 8–21.

MacKay, T. (2011). The place of health interventions in educational psychology. *Educational and Child Psychology, 28*(4) 7–13.

MacKay, T. (in press). Psychological services and their impact. In T.G.K. Bryce, W.M. Humes, D. Gillies & A Kennedy (Eds.) *Scottish education* (4th edn). Edinburgh: Edinburgh University Press.

Marker, W. (1996). The college under the Glasgow Provincial Committee for the Training of Teachers. In M.M. Harrison & W.B. Marker (Eds.) *Teaching the teachers: The history of Jordanhill College of Education 1828-1993.* Edinburgh: John Donald.

McKnight, R.K. (1978). The development of child guidance services. In W.B. Dockrell, W.R. Dunn & A. Milne (Eds.) *Special education in Scotland.* Edinburgh: Scottish Council for Research in Education.

NHS Scotland (2007). *Better health, better care: Action plan.* Edinburgh: Author.

Probst, P. (1997). The beginnings of educational psychology in Germany. In W.G. Bringmann, H.E. Luck, R. Miller & C. Early (Eds.) *A pictorial history of psychology.* Chicago, IL: Quintessence Publishing.

Scottish Education Department (1952). *Pupils who are maladjusted because of social handicaps. A report of the Advisory Council on Education in Scotland.* Edinburgh: HMSO.

Scottish Executive (1999). *Implementing inclusiveness – Realising potential.* The Beattie Report. Edinburgh: Author.

Scottish Executive (2002). *Review of provision of educational psychology services in Scotland.* The Currie Report. Edinburgh: Author.

Sharp, S.A. (1980). Godfrey Thomson and the concept of intelligence. In J.V. Smith & D. Hamilton (Eds.) *The meritocratic intellect: Studies in the history of educational research.* Aberdeen: Aberdeen University Press.

Thompson, D. (1979). Is research a relevant activity for educational psychologists? *DECP Occasional Papers, 3*(2), 21–26.

Thomson, G.H. (1929). *A modern philosophy of education.* London: Allen & Unwin.

Watt, H.J. (1909). *The economy and training of memory.* London: Edward Arnold.

Webster, A. & Beveridge, M. (1997). The role of educational psychologists in educational research: Some implications for professional training. *Educational Psychology in Practice, 13*(3), 155–164.

Wooldridge, A. (1994). *Measuring the mind: Education and psychology in England c1860–1990.* Cambridge: Cambridge University Press.

Chapter 10

Birnbaum, R., Blewitt, J., Gregor, A., Jensen, A., King, A., Powell, J. & Tam, P. (1980). Job hunting. (Letter to the editor.) *Bulletin of the British Psychological Society, 33,* 393–394.

Brady, S. (1982). Psychology degree and teacher training. (Letter to the editor.) *Bulletin of the British Psychological Society, 35,* 173.

Burnes, B. (2004). Kurt Lewin and the planned approach to change: A re-appraisal. *Journal of Management Studies, 41*(6), 977–1002.

Burnes, B. (2009). Reflections: Ethics and organizational change: Time for a return to Lewinian values. *Journal of Change Management, 9*(4), 359–381.

Burt, C. (1969). Psychologists in the education services. *Bulletin of the British Psychological Society, 22,* 1–11.

Coates, I. (2005, 24 March). Letter to Tony Dessent. Copy in *LGA Employers Organisation Steering Group for Educational Psychology Papers,* 15 April 2005.

Currie, J.M. (1969). Psychologists in the education services: teaching experience. *Bulletin of the British Psychological Society, 22,* 89–91.

Department for Education (DfE) (2011). Developing sustainable arrangements for the initial training of educational psychologists. Retrieved 28 June 2012 from www.education.gov.uk/schools/pupilsupport/sen/a00200017/review-of-educational-psychologist-training

Department for Education and Employment (DfEE) (2000). *Educational psychology services (England): Current role, good practice and future directions. The report of the working group.* London: HMSO.

Department of Education and Science (DES) (1968). *Psychologists in education services.* The Summerfield Report. London: HMSO.

Department of Education and Science (DES) (1984). *The training of educational psychologists. Final report of the DES Working Group.* London: HMSO.

Department for Education and Skills (DfES) (2004). *Every child matters: Change for children.* London: HMSO

Elliott, C. (1981a). Two year courses of professional training in educational psychology. Paper distributed to the Educational Psychology Tutors Group, 18 March 1981.

Elliott, C. (1981b). The case for two year courses of professional training in educational psychology. Paper submitted by the Educational Psychology Tutors Group to the Department of Education and Science, 24 September 1981.

Elrod, II, P.D. & Tippett, D.D. (2002). The 'death valley' of change. *Journal of Organizational Change Management, 15*(3), 273–291.

Farrell, P. (1996). Developments in the training of EPs: A progress report. *Division of Educational and Child Psychology Newsletter, 75*, 23–27.

Farrell, P., Gersch, I. & Morris, S. (1998). Progress towards three year professional training courses for educational psychologists. *Educational Psychology in Practice, 14*(1), 44–51.

Fox, M. (2003). Opening Pandora's Box: Evidence-based practice for educational psychologists. *Educational Psychology in Practice, 19*(2), 91–102.

Fox, M. & Sigston, A. (1992). Connecting organizational psychology, schools and educational psychologists. In S. Wolfendale, T. Bryans, M. Fox, A. Labram & A. Sigston, *The profession and practice of educational psychology: Future directions,* pp.99-117. London: Cassell Education.

Frederickson, N. (1997). Developments in training: A course director's perspective. *Division of Educational and Child Psychology Newsletter, 82*, 25–36.

Frederickson, N. (2002). Evidence based practice and educational psychology. *Educational and Child Psychology, 19*(3), 96–111.

Frederickson, N., Cameron, R.J., Dunsmuir, S., Graham, B. & Monsen J. (1998). Professional training in educational psychology: Then, now and in the New Millennium. In N. Frederickson & I. Lunt (Eds.) *Professional Training in Educational Psychology: The Next 50 Years,* pp.2–16. Leicester: British Psychological Society.

Frederickson, N., Curran, P., Gersch, I. & Portsmouth, R. (1996). Training matters: Extending and improving professional training. *Division of Educational and Child Psychology Newsletter, 73*, 10–12.

Frederickson, N., Malcolm & Osborne, L.A. (1999) Teaching or other relevant experience with children. *Educational Psychology in Practice, 15*(3) 146–156.

Frederickson, N., Osborne, L. & Reed, P. (2001) Teaching experience and educational psychologists' credibility with teachers: An empirical investigation. *Educational Psychology in Practice, 17*(2), 93–108.

Gersch, I. (1997) Training matters: the future needs of educational psychology training. *Division of Educational and Child Psychology Newsletter, 77*, 12–16.

Harrison-Jennings, B. (1998). The move to three year training: opportunities, threats and challenges. A trade unionist's perspective. In N. Frederickson & I. Lunt (Eds.) *Professional training in educational psychology: The next 50 Years,* pp.48–53. Leicester: British Psychological Society.

Jensen, A., Malcolm, L., Phelps, F. & Stoker, R. (2002). Changing patterns of thinking: Individuals and organisations. *Educational Psychology in Practice, 18*(1), 35–45.

Lewin, K. (1952). *Field theory in social science.* London: Tavistock Publications.

Long, L. (1982). PGCE places. (Letter to the editor.) *Bulletin of the British Psychological Society, 35*, 253.

Lunt, I. (1993). Training applied psychologists in education: Future trends and directions. In I. Lunt (Ed.) *Whither educational psychology? Challenges and changes for the future of our profession* (pp.37–44). Leicester: British Psychological Society.

Lunt, I. & Farrell, P. (1994). Restructuring educational psychology in the UK. *The Psychologist, 7*, 268–271.

Maliphant, R. (1994). School psychology. *The Psychologist, 7*, 263–267.

Morris, S. (1997). PEPs on extending professional training. *DECP Newsletter, 78*, 23–25.

Oakland, T.D. & Jimerson, S.R. (2007). School psychology internationally: A retrospective view and influential conditions. In S.R. Jimerson, T.D. Oakland & P.T. Farrell (Eds.) *The handbook of international school psychology,* (pp.453-474). London: Sage.

Portsmouth, R., O'Riordan, S., Morris, S. & Gersch, I.S. (1995). Training matters: doctoral training in educational psychology. *DECP Newsletter, 70*, 16–17.

Rushton, J.P. (2002). New evidence on Sir Cyril Burt: His 1964 speech to the Association of Educational Psychologists. *Intelligence, 30*(5), 55–567.

Schein, E.H. (2002). Models and tools for stability and change in human systems. *Reflections, 4*(2), 34-46.

Smith, C. & Reynolds, A. (1998). Implementing the Code of Practice pre-school. *Educational Psychology in Practice, 14*(1), 3–10.

Turpin, G. (1995). Practitioner doctorates in clinical psychology. *The Psychologist, 8*, 356–358.

United Nations Educational Scientific and Cultural Organisation (UNESCO) (1948). *School psychologists.* Paris: UNESCO.

Wolfendale, S., Curran, P., Labram, A. & Sigston, A. (1995). Doctoral level training for the new millennium. *Division of Educational and Child Psychology Newsletter, 69*, 3–5.

Chapter 11

Atkinson, C., Corban, I., Templeton, J. (2011). Educational psychologists' use of therapeutic interventions: Issues arising from two exploratory case studies. *British Journal of Learning Support, 26*(4), 161–167.

Barnett, R. (1997). *Higher education: A critical business.* Buckingham: Open University Press.

Berridge, D., Brodie, I., Pitts, J. Porteous, D. & Tarling, R. (2001). *The independent effects of permanent exclusion from school on the offending careers of young people.* RDS occasional paper 71. London: HMSO.

Blyth, E. (2001). Keeping looked after children in mainstream education. In S. Jackson (Ed.) *Nobody ever told us school mattered.* London: BAAF.

Brofenbrenner, U. (1979). *The ecology of human development: Experiments by nature and design.* Cambridge, MA: Harvard University Press.

Bynner, J. (2004). Literacy Numeracy and Employability: Evidence from the British Birth Cohort Studies. *Literacy and Numeracy Studies, 13,* 31-48.

Christner, R. W., Forrest, E., Morley, J. & Weinstein, E. (2007). Taking cognitive-behaviour therapy to school: A school-based mental health approach. *Journal of Contemporary Psychotherapy, 37,* 175–183.

Communities that Care (2005). *Findings from the Safer London Youth Survey 2004.* London: Author.

Cormack, K., Brown, A. & Hastings, P. (2000). Behavioural and emotional difficulties in students attending schools for adolescents with severe intellectual disability. *Journal of Intellectual Disability Research, 44,* 124–129.

Department of Children, Schools and Family (2005). *Social and emotional aspects of learning (SEAL): Improving behaviour, improving learning.* Nottingham: Author.

Department of Children Schools and Family (2008). *Targeted mental health in schools programme.* Nottingham: Author.

Department for Education (2011a). *Developing sustainable arrangements for the initial training of educational psychologists.* London: HMSO.

Department for Education (2011b). *Support and aspiration: A new approach to special educational needs and disability* Green Paper. London: HMSO.

Department for Education (2012). *Support and aspiration: A new approach to special educational needs and disability – Progress and next steps.* London: HMSO.

Department for Education and Employment (1997). *Excellence for all children: Meeting special educational needs.* Green Paper. London: Author.

Department for Education and Employment (2000). *Educational psychology services (England): Current role, good practice and future directions. Report of the Working Group.* London: Author.

Department of Education and Employment & Department of Health. (2000). *Guidance on the education of young people in public care.* London: DfEE.

Department for Education and Skills (2003). *Every child matters.* Green Paper. London: HMSO.

Department for Education and Skills. (2004). *Every child matters: Change for children.* White Paper. London: HMSO.

Department for Education and Skills (2007). *Care matters: Transforming the lives of children and young people in care.* London: Author.

Department of Health (1998). *Quality protects.* London: Author.

Department of Health (2008). *Children and young people in mind: The final report of the national CAMHS review.* Retrieved 4 May 2012 from www.dh.gov.uk/en/Publicationsandstatistics/Publications/PublicationsPolicyAndGuidance/DH_090399

Department of Health (2008). *Improving access to psychological therapies (IAPT) commissioning toolkit.* Norwich: Author.

Division of Educational and Child Psychology (2006). *Report of the working group on educational psychology service practice with looked after children.* Leicester: British Psychological Society.

Dykens, E.M. (2000). Psychopathology in children with intellectual disability. *Journal of Child Psychology and Psychiatry 41,* 407–417.

ECOTEC (2001). *Education, training and employment.* London. Youth Justice Board.

Einfeld, S.L. & B.L. Tonge (1996). Population prevalence of psychopathology in children and adolescents with intellectual disability, II epidemiological findings. *Journal of Intellectual Disability Research, 40,* 99–109.

Emerson, E. (2006). *The social dimension of mental health issues in learning disabilities. Conference paper.* Association of Child and Adolescent Mental Health, Royal Society of Medicine, London.

Fallon, K., Woods, K. & Rooney, S. (2010). A discussion of the developing role of educational psychologists within children's services. *Educational Psychology in Practice, 26, 1,* 1–24.

Farrell, P., Woods, K., Lewis, S., Rooney, S., Squires, G. & O'Conner, M. (2006). *Function and contribution of educational psychologists in light of the Every child matters: Change for children'agenda.* London: DfES.

Farringdon, D. (1996). *Understanding and preventing youth crime.* York: Joseph Rowntree.

Fletcher-Campbell, F., Archer, T. & Tomlinson, K. (2003). *The role of the school in supporting the education of children in public care.* Nottingham: DfES.

Frederickson, N. & Miller, A. (2008). What do educational psychologists do? In N. Frederickson, A. Miller & T. Cline (Eds.) *Educational psychology.* London: Hodder Education.

Foundation for People with Learning Disabilities (2002). *Count us in: The report of* the committee of inquiry into meeting the mental health needs of young people with learning disabilities. London: FPLD.

Gilligan, R. (2007). Adversity, resilience and the educational progress of young people in care. *Emotional and Behavioural Difficulties, 12*(2) 135–145.

Harrington, R. & Bailey, S. (2005). *Mental health needs and effectiveness of provision for young offenders in custody and the community.* London: Youth Justice Board.

Hawkins, J.D., Herrenkohl, T.I., Farringdon, D.P., Brewer, D., Catalano, R.F., Harachi, T.W. & Cothern, L. (2000). *Predictors of Youth Violence.* Washington: US Department of Justice.

Hill, V. (2005). Through the past darkly: A review of the British Ability Scales (2nd. edn). *Child and Adolescent Mental Health 10*(2), 87–98.

Hill, V. (2006). *Mental health in education or education in mental health?* Conference paper. Association of Child and Adolescent Mental Health, Royal Society of Medicine. London.

Hurry, J., Brazier, L., Moriarty, V. (2005). Improving literacy and numeracy skills of young people who offend: can it be done and what are the consequences? *Literacy and Numeracy Studies, 14*(2), 61–74.

Hurry, J., Brazier, L., Wilson, A., Emslie-Henry, R., Snapes, K. (2010). *Improving the literacy and numeracy of young people in custody and in the community.* London: National Research and Development Centre for Adult Literacy and Numeracy.

Jackson, S. (1994). Educating children in residential and foster care. *Oxford Review of Education, 20*(3), 267–279.

Jackson, S. (2010). Education for inclusion: Can we change the future for children in care? An inaugural professorial lecture. London: Institute of Education.

Jackson, S. & Ajayi (2007). Foster care and higher education. *Adoption and Fostering, 31*(1), 62–72.

Jackson, S. & Martin, P. (1998). Surviving the care system: Education and resilience. *Journal of Adolescence, 21,* 569–583.

Jackson, S. & McParlin, P. (2006). The education of children in care. *The Psychologist, 19*(2), 90–93.

Laming, H. (2003). *Report of the inquiry into the death of Victoria Climbié.* London: HMSO.

Lipsey, M. (1995). What do we learn from 400 research studies on the effectiveness of treatments with juvenile delinquents. In J. McGuire (Ed), *What works: Reducing reoffending.* Chichester: Wiley.

MacKay, T. (2007). Educational psychology: the fall and rise of therapy. *Educational and Child Psychology, 24*(1), 7–18.

McAuley, C., Young, C. (2006). The mental health of looked after children: Challenges for CAMHS provision. *Journal of Social Work Practice, 20*(1), 91–103.

Meltzer, H., Gartward, R., Goodman, R. & Ford, T. (2000). *Mental health of children and adolescents in Great Britain.* London: HMSO.

Ministry of Justice (2012). *Youth justice statistics 2010/11.* England and Wales Youth Justice Board/Ministry of Justice Statistics Bulletin. Home Office.

National Health Service (2006). Mental health services for children with learning disabilities: A national care pathway. Retrieved 6 June 2012 from www.informatics.nhs.uk/download/2806/Appendix-18-DOAS-LD-MH-Care-Pathway-Final.doc

Natale, L. (2010). *Factsheet – Youth crime in England and Wales.* CIVITAS Institute for the Study of Civil Society. Retrieved from www.civitas.org.uk/crime/factsheet-YouthOffending.pdf

Norwich, B. (2000). *Education and psychology in interaction: Working with uncertainty in interconnected fields.* London: Routledge.

Office of National Statistics (2004). *Mental health of children and young people in Great Britain.* Basingstoke: Palgrave Macmillan.

Ofsted and Social Services Inspectorate (1995). *The education of children who are looked after by local authorities.* London: Department of Health.

OLASS (2004). *The offenders learning journey: Learning and skills provision for juvenile offenders in England.* London: DfES.

Pitts, J. (2006). *An evaluation of the Lambeth X-it (gang desistance) programme.* London Borough of Lambeth.

Pugh, J. (2010). Cognitive behaviour therapy in schools: The role of educational psychology in the dissemination of empirically supported interventions. *Educational Psychology in Practice, 26*(4), 391–399.

Rait, S., Monsen, J. & Squires, G. (2010). Cognitive behaviour therapies and their implications for applied educational psychology practice. *Educational Psychology in Practice, 26*(2), 105–122.

Reid, K. (2005). The causes, views and traits of school absenteesim and truancy. *Research in Education, 74,* 59–82.

Rutter, M., Giller, H. & Hagell, A. (1998). *Antisocial behaviour by young people.* Cambridge: Cambridge University Press.

Rutter, M., Tizard, J., Whitmore, K. (1970). *Education, health behaviour: Psychological and medical study of childhood development.* New York: Wiley.

Ryrie, N. (2006). Working with a youth offending team: personal perspectives on challenges and opportunities for the practice of educational psychology. *Educational and Child Psychology, 23*(2), 6-14.

Sempik, J., Ward, H., Darker, I. (2008). emotional and behavioural difficulties of children and young people at entry into care. *Clinical Child Psychology and Psychiatry.,13*(2), 221–233.

Sinclair, I., Wilson, G. & Gibbs, I. (2004). *Foster placements: Why they succeed and why they fail.* London: Jessica Kingsley.

Social Exclusion Unit (2003). *Better education for children in care.* London. Social Exclusion Unit.

Stallard, P., Simpson, N., Anderson, S., Hibbert, S. & Osborn, C. (2007). The FRIENDS emotional health programme: Initial findings from a school-based project. *Child and Adolescent Mental Health, 12*(1), 32– 37.

Stobie, I. (2002). Processes of change and continuity in educational psychology. Part 1. *Educational Psychology in Practice, 18*(3), 203–212.

Squires, G. (2001). Using cognitive behavioural psychology with groups of pupils to improve self-control of behaviour. *Educational Psychology in Practice, 17*(4), 317–335.

Squires, G. (2010). Countering the argument that educational psychologists need specific training to use cognitive behavioural therapy. *Emotional and Behavioural Difficulties, 15*(4), 279–294.

UNICEF (2007). *Child poverty in perspective. An overview of child well-being in rich countries.* Florence: UNICEF Innocenti Research Centre.

Welsh, B.C. & Farrington, D.P. (2010). *The future of crime prevention. Developmental and situational strategies.* Prepared for the National Institute of Justice.

Youth Justice Board (2004). *MORI youth survey 2004.* London: Youth Justice Board for England and Wales.

Youth Justice Board (2005). *Risk and protective factors.* London: Youth Justice Board for England and Wales.

Vignette 11

Gameson, J. & Rhydderch, G. (2008). The constructionist model of informed and reasoned action (COMOIRA). In B. Kelly, L. Woolfson & J. Boyle (Ed.) *Frameworks for practice in educational psychology: A textbook for trainees and practitioners* (pp.94–120). London: Jessica Kingsley.

Gameson, J., Rhydderch, G., Ellis, D. & Carroll, H.C.M. (2003). Constructing a flexible model of integrated professional practice: Part 1, conceptual and theoretical issues. *Educational & Child Psychology, 20*(4), 96–115.

Gameson, J., Rhydderch, G., Ellis, D. & Carroll, H.C.M. (2005). Constructing a flexible model of integrated professional practice: Part 2, process and practice issues. *Educational & Child Psychology 22*(4), 41–55.

Chapter 12

Ashton, R. & Roberts, E. (2006). What is valuable and unique about the educational psychologist? *Educational Psychology in Practice 22*(2), 111–123.

British Psychological Society (2009). *Code of ethics and conduct.* Leicester: Author.

Burton, D., Smith, M. & Woods, K. (2010). Working with teachers to promote children's participation through pupil led research. *Educational Psychology in Action, 26*(2), 91–104.

Dawkins, R. (1976). *The selfish gene.* Oxford: Oxford University Press.

Dunsmuir, S., Brown, E., Iyadurai, S. & Monsen, J.(2009). Evidence-based practice and evaluation: from insight to impact. *Educational Psychology in Practice. 25*(1), 53–70.

Fox, M. (1992). Seeing ahead: Developing human resources in educational psychology services. *Educational Psychology in Practice 8*(1), 43–53.

Fox, M. (2003). Opening Pandora's Box: Evidence-based practice for educational psychologists. *Educational Psychology in Practice, 19*(2), 91–102.

Gaskell, S. and Leadbetter, J.(2009) Educational psychologists and multi-agency working: exploring professional identity. Educational Psychology in Practice, 25 (2), p 97-111.

Gersch, I.S., McCarthy, M., Sigston, A. & Townley, D. (1990). Taking an educational psychology service into the 1990s. *Educational Psychology in Practice 6*(3), 123–130.

Griffiths, M. (2010). Online video gaming: what should educational psychologists know? *Educational Psychology in Practice, 26*(1), 35–40.

Harding, E. & Atkinson, C. (2009). How EPs record the voice of the child. *Educational Psychology in Practice, 25*(2), 125–137.

Hardy, J. (2010). The development of a sense of identity in deaf adolescents in mainstream schools. *Educational Psychology in Practice, 27*(2), 58–67.

Imich, A. (1999). Delivering educational psychology. *Educational Psychology in Practice, 15*(1), 57–64.

Kelly, C. & Gersch, I. (2000). How newly-trained psychologists see the profession developing: A crystal ball gaze towards the year 2010. *DECP Newsletter, 94*.

Kennedy, E.K., Cameron, R.J. & Monsen, J. (2009). Effective consultation in educational and child psychology practice. Professional Training for both competence and capability. *School Psychology International 30*(6), 603–625.

Kerfoot, S. (1986). Sampling pupil opinion in the secondary school. *Educational Psychology in Practice 2*(3).

Kuttner, R. (1997). *Everything for sale: The virtues and limits of markets.* New York: Alfred A. Knopf.

Lamb, B. (2010). Improving parental confidence in the special educational needs system. Department of Children, Schools and Families Publications.

Leadbetter, J. & Tee, G. (1991). A consultancy approach to behaviour problems in school. *Educational Psychology in Practice, 6*(4), 203–209.

Leyden, G. & Miller, A. (1998). Including all our children in mainstream schools and communities. *Educational Psychology in Practice, 14*(3), 188–193.

MacKay, T. (1997). Do headteachers want research? *Educational Psychology in Practice, 13*(3), 165–169.

MacKay, T. (2002). Discussion paper. The future of educational psychology. *Educational Psychology in Practice, 18*(3), 245–253.

MacKay, T. & Boyle, J.M. (1994). Meeting the needs of pupils with learning difficulties: what do primary and secondary schools expect of the educational psychologists? *Educational Research, 36*(2), 187–196.

Megginson, L.C. (1963). Lessons from Europe for American business. *Southwestern Social Science Quarterly. 44*(1), 3–13.

Miller, G.A.(1969). The presidential address. *American Psychologist, 24*, 1063–1075.

Norwich, B. & Kelly, N. (2006). Evaluating children's participation in SEN procedures: Lessons for educational psychologists. *Educational Psychology in Practice, 22*(3), 255–271.

Rait, S., Monsen, J. & Squires, G.(2010). Cognitive behaviour therapies and their implications for applied educational psychology practice. *Educational Psychology in Practice, 26*(2), 105–122.

Ramsden, B., (2008). Patterns of higher education institutions in the UK. London: Universities UK .

Raymond, J. (1987). An educational psychologist's intervention with a class of disruptive pupils using pupil perceptions. *Educational Psychology in Practice, 3*(2), 16–22.

Stoker, R. (1992). Working at the Level of the institution and the organisation. *Educational Psychology in Practice, 8*(1), 15–24.

Squires, G. (2001). Using cognitive behavioural psychology with groups of pupils to improve self-control of behaviour. *Educational Psychology in Practice, 17*(4), 317–335.

Sternberg, R.J. (2008). Adventurous navigator of the dimensions of high ability. *Roeper Review, 30*, 75–80.

Wagner, P. (2000). Consultation: Developing a comprehensive approach to service delivery. *Educational Psychology in Practice, 16*(1), 47–52.